LIGHTNING EJECT

LIGHTNING EJECT

THE DUBIOUS SAFETY RECORD OF BRITAIN'S ONLY SUPERSONIC FIGHTER

PETER CAYGILL

Pen & Sword
AVIATION

First published in Great Britain in 2012 by
Pen & Sword Aviation
An imprint of
Pen & Sword Books Ltd
47 Church Street
Barnsley
South Yorkshire
S70 2AS

ISBN 978 1 84884 885 6

A CIP catalogue record for this book is
available from the British Library.

Typeset in 10pt Minion by Mac Style, Beverley, East Yorkshire
Printed and bound in the UK by CPI Group (UK) Ltd, Croydon,
CRO 4YY

Pen & Sword Books Ltd incorporates the Imprints of Pen & Sword
Aviation, Pen & Sword Family History, Pen & Sword Maritime, Pen
& Sword Military, Pen & Sword Discovery, Wharncliffe Local History,
Wharncliffe True Crime, Wharncliffe Transport, Pen & Sword Select, Pen
& Sword Military Classics, Leo Cooper, The Praetorian Press, Remember
When, Seaforth Publishing and Frontline Publishing.

For a complete list of Pen & Sword titles please contact
PEN & SWORD BOOKS LIMITED
47 Church Street, Barnsley, South Yorkshire S70 2AS, England
E-mail: enquiries@pen-and-sword.co.uk
Website: www.pen-and-sword.co.uk

Contents

Introduction vi

Chapter 1 The Lightning in Service 1

Chapter 2 A Golden Age 13

Chapter 3 Enter the F.6 36

Chapter 4 The Lightning Worldwide 55

Chapter 5 The Engine Fire Epidemic 69

Chapter 6 Lightning Accident Review 88

Chapter 7 Picking up the Pieces 95

Chapter 8 Still Supreme 118

Chapter 9 Wind-Down 128

Chapter 10 Lightning Lair 136

Chapter 11 Lightning Swansong 152

Chapter 12 The Final Reckoning 159

In Memoriam 167

Glossary 168

Appendix 1 *RAF Aircraft Damage Categories* 171

Appendix 2 *Lightning Write-Offs in RAF Service* 172

Appendix 3 *Lightning F.3 Selected Emergency Drills* 177

Index 182

Introduction

The Lightning is rightly regarded as one of the all-time classic fighter aircraft, its combination of power and fine handling qualities marking it out as a thoroughbred from the very beginning. During its service with RAF Fighter Command it was the dream of every aspiring fighter pilot to be posted to a Lightning squadron but the demands were such that only the very best were selected. Even then there were no guarantees, as a number of pilots were to be disappointed when they discovered they were not considered to be of the required standard during their final training course at 226 Operational Conversion Unit at Coltishall. Having been scrubbed, they were subsequently sent away to fly other less-demanding types of aircraft.

In addition to the skills needed to fly the aircraft and get the best out of its weapons system, pilots also had to spend many hours in the flight simulator. They often emerged as nervous wrecks after the examiner had bombarded them with a series of emergency situations of ever-increasing complication. This type of training was vital as the complexity of the Lightning meant that real emergencies in the air were many and varied and required prompt action if the aircraft was to be saved. However, there were to be many occasions when the appropriate drills as recorded in Pilot's Notes were not enough and the pilot was left with no alternative but to eject. By the time that the Lightning was retired from RAF service in 1988 a total of fifty-three pilots had been forced to eject as a result of in-flight emergencies and thus owed their lives to the Martin Baker Mk 4BS ejection seat. Sadly, fourteen pilots were not so lucky and were killed during their operational tours.

This book looks at the safety record of the Lightning in RAF service and catalogues the many accidents that took place over its twenty-eight year history. It also compares the Lightning with other contemporary aircraft, including the Lockheed F-104G Starfighter, which acquired a poor reputation for safety, particularly during service with the *Luftwaffe* and *Marineflieger*, to see if claims are true that the Lightning was as bad, if not worse. Much of the information has come from official accident reports, Board of Inquiry findings and RAF flight safety reviews that are held at the National Archives at Kew, although there are some first-hand accounts by pilots who were suddenly confronted with a life-or-death situation in the air. There are also appendices that include total Lightning losses and the emergency drills that were to be carried out in the event of an engine or reheat fire and hydraulic failure, which were the principal safety issues that afflicted the Lightning during its long history.

Chapter One

The Lightning in Service

Towards the end of 1959 there was an air of anticipation within RAF Fighter Command as the English Electric Lightning interceptor was nearing the end of its test schedule and was almost ready to enter squadron service. Its introduction was sorely needed as, due to political meddling in the period immediately following the Second World War, the RAF had been forced to rely on subsonic fighter types when other air forces, notably the USAF and Soviet Air Force, were introducing supersonic interceptors. The forerunner of the Lightning, the English Electric P.1, was flown for the first time on 4 August 1954 and this had been followed by the P.1B, which looked much more like the definitive Lightning. The P.1B was first flown on 4 April 1957. To facilitate the testing of the Lightning and its associated systems, twenty development batch aircraft were produced and many of these were used for trials at the Aeroplane and Armament Experimental Establishment (A&AEE) at Boscombe Down. With the trials work progressing well it was time for the first aircraft to be delivered to the Air Fighting Development Squadron (AFDS), which was part of the Central Fighter Establishment.

In respect of the Lightning, the role of the AFDS was to provide a tactical evaluation of the aircraft and the first machine to be delivered was XG334, which was flown in to Coltishall on 23 December 1959. Less than three months later this aircraft was to become the RAF's first Lightning casualty when Squadron Leader Ron Harding was forced to eject on 5 March 1960. The problem was one that would afflict the Lightning for some time to come in that there was a malfunction in the operation of the main undercarriage. In the case of XG334 the port undercarriage leg did not extend fully and, as it would have been extremely dangerous to attempt a landing in such a condition, Squadron Leader Harding was advised to eject over the sea. A large part of the port wing was recovered and taken to the English Electric facility at Warton. After a thorough investigation it was concluded that the failure of the undercarriage to operate correctly was most likely associated with an obstruction in the hydraulic pipe to the jack, which was probably caused by a collapsed inner damper tube.

Although Ron Harding's ejection should have been straightforward, it was far from so. During a normal ejection a small drogue, parachute should have deployed to slow the seat down and stabilise it as it fell, but it appeared that this did not happen. As a result the seat, and its unfortunate occupant, tumbled through the air. To make matters worse Harding realised that some of the parachute shroud lines were wrapped around his leg and the gyrations of the seat made it difficult for him to disentangle them. Eventually he was able to remove the lines and the main parachute opened almost immediately.

A similar incident occurred on 23 November 1960 when Flight Lieutenant Peter Collins of AFDS was flying XM163. Flight Lieutenant Collins successfully carried out a night interception exercise, but when selecting undercarriage – down on his return he found that only the port main leg extended (but did not lock). As his fuel state was low he flamed out No.2 engine and transferred fuel to No.1 engine before attempting several manoeuvres in the hope that the applied 'g' would assist the extension of the undercarriage. Unfortunately this had no effect so, as fuel was by now down to 500lb, Collins climbed to 10,000 feet to eject. As he levelled off, however, the port main undercarriage finally locked in position, so he decided to return to Coltishall in the hope that the starboard leg would also come down. Whilst turning during a GCA approach the starboard leg did indeed come down and Collins made a safe landing, although it was an extremely close call as only 25lb of fuel remained when the aircraft came to a halt on the runway. The subsequent investigation revealed that a hydraulic pipe had fractured and this had affected the main and emergency undercarriage lowering systems. The loss of hydraulic pressure also meant that Collins had been forced to land without the benefit of airbrakes or flaps.

Just over three weeks later AFDS was to lose another Lightning in rather different circumstances. On 16 December 1960 Flight Lieutenant Bruce Hopkins took off from Coltishall in XM138 to carry out a high altitude interception exercise. During the early part of the climb to altitude Hopkins noticed a slight heaviness of the elevator controls and at 36,000 feet he felt a heavy thump reverberate through the airframe. At the same time there was a sudden jerk on the controls. In the cockpit the attention-getter activated, although there was no associated warning light. At the same time the AI radar scope went off-line. Hopkins put his aircraft into a descent to return to base but a visual inspection by a different pilot did not reveal any outward signs of damage. He landed without further incident, although a restriction was noticed during rearward movement of the control column on the approach. During the landing roll he was informed that fuel was streaming from his aircraft. Hopkins immediately shut down No.1 engine but on reaching the end of the runway the No.2 engine fire warning light came on. Believing this to be spurious, he cancelled the warning but was informed by Air Traffic Control that his aircraft was on fire.

The remaining engine was shut down and the fire extinguisher buttons operated, at which point Hopkins noticed that the fire warning light for No.1 engine was also illuminated. As the aircraft was turned off the runway, flames could be seen emerging from the back. Shortly after Hopkins made good his escape the fire crews arrived and extinguished the fire, but not before extensive damage had been caused. It transpired that the accident had been caused by the rupture of No.1 engine exhaust cone, which had permitted a hot gas leak to come into contact with the starboard fire extinguisher bottle. This had then burst violently and had caused damage to a fuel pipe, allowing the release of free fuel into the engine bays where it had subsequently ignited. It was thought that the initial lack of a fire warning was due to the system not being sensitive enough to detect the lower temperatures of a hot gas leak. The rupture of electrical wires to the other extinguisher bottles had also prevented their discharge. Although the fire damage to the rear of XM138 was initially assessed as Category 4 (Cat. 4), it was subsequently re-assessed as Cat.5 and the aircraft had to be written off.

During the time that AFDS was carrying out its tactical trial, the Lightning entered RAF squadron service in July 1960 when the first aircraft were delivered to 74 Tiger Squadron, which had recently moved to Coltishall from Horsham St Faith and was commanded by Squadron Leader John Howe. At first serviceability was extremely poor, a situation that was not helped by the lack of a proper spares back-up. Despite this, four aircraft were able to take part in the SBAC show at Farnborough in September 1960 but it was not until January of the following year that flying for the month exceeded 100 hours. The second squadron to convert to the Lightning was No.56 at Wattisham, which received its first aircraft on 14 December 1960. This unit was led by Squadron

Leader John Rogers who was to experience the squadron's first in-flight emergency on 14 February 1961 when flying F.1A XM176.

Even though the Lightning had only been in squadron service for a matter of months, in-flight fires were a known hazard. This was not just because of the accident to XM138 but also as a result of a number of cockpit fire warnings that had occurred during early operations. In most of these cases it seemed that no damage had been caused and it therefore appeared that the warnings had been spurious. In the case of XM176, Squadron Leader Rogers took off from Wattisham but shortly after the aircraft became airborne there was a Reheat 1 fire warning. No.1 engine was shut down and a return was made to base, but as the undercarriage would not lock down with only No.2 service pump operating, No.1 engine had to be relit. With the undercarriage fully locked down a successful landing was made, No.1 engine being shut down once more when on the runway. A visual inspection was made but as there was no immediate evidence of fire Squadron Leader Rogers taxied back to dispersal. After shutting down No.2 engine, however, smoke was seen coming from the rear fuselage and the action taken to put out the fire included the operation of the fire extinguishers and the removal of the ventral tank. An investigation showed that a fire had occurred between frames 48 and 50 on the bottom of the fuselage resulting in Cat.3 damage. At the time of the accident XM176 had only flown eleven hours from new.

Further examination of the aircraft showed that the main area of damage was on the jet pipe shroud directly over the drain hole in the under section of the fuselage just forward of frame 48 and above the ventral tank. The fire appeared to have been fed by hydraulic oil and AVTAG (Aviation Turbine Gasoline). At the time of the accident there were two types of ventral tanks fitted to the Lightning but neither possessed good means of drainage to allow the inevitable build-up of fuel and oil in the lower fuselage to escape. The only way that fluid could escape from these areas above the ventral tank was for it to re-enter the fuselage through the drain holes during certain flight attitudes and by suction caused by negative pressure during flight. A test flight was carried out by English Electric with coloured fluid placed on the top surface of the ventral tank. This proved conclusively that the fluid was sucked back through the drain holes in the fuselage bottom skin and came directly into contact with the jet pipe shroud. Inspection of the bay between frames 48 and 49 where there were no drain holes showed a concentration of fluid, particularly around the tail trim actuator, which was badly burnt on XM176. Two days after this particular incident Lightning F.1A XM181 suffered fire damage during a production test flight at Warton, an accident that was virtually identical to that at Wattisham.

During the service life of the Lightning there were many occasions when cockpit canopies were lost on take off, usually as a result of the pilot failing to ensure that the canopy was securely locked. The first time this happened was on 6 March 1961 and the aircraft involved was XM163 'H' of AFDS. In such incidents the damage was usually not just confined to the cockpit area, as in most cases the canopy tended to strike the fin after it had torn free. This occurred with XM163 and considerable damage was caused to the leading edge of the fin.

A similar incident occurred on 5 May 1961. However, the outcome was rather different. Flying Officer T. Mermagen of 56 Squadron was taking off in XM183 when, shortly after raising the nose-wheel prior to lift off, he became aware that the canopy was lifting. Although his speed was approximately 170 knots IAS he immediately throttled back and streamed the braking parachute. Not long after the canopy broke free and hit the fin before falling on to the runway. Despite applying maximum braking and shutting down both engines, Flying Officer Mermagen was unable to prevent his aircraft from entering the barrier at the end of the runway. It was estimated that the speed of entry was around 40-50 knots and the aircraft came to rest in a field and caught fire. This was the first serious barrier entry for a Lightning and served to highlight the amount of damage that could be caused. The top cable in particular tended to rip open the fuselage spine which, among other items, housed the AVPIN (Isopropyl Nitrate) tank for engine starting. There was also a distinct possibility that the top cable could come into contact with the cockpit area, thus putting the pilot's life at risk, either directly, or by the cable activating the ejection seat. Runway barriers were later modified in an attempt to prevent excessive damage and lessen potential danger to the pilot. Although the level of damage to XM183 was eventually assessed as Cat.3, it would be seven months before the aircraft was returned to the squadron.

Having performed at the Farnborough display in 1960, No.74 Squadron was notified that it was required to participate in several displays during 1961 including the Paris Air Show in early June. While preparing for this event an unusual incident occurred on 16

May when the rudder and part of the fin broke away from one aircraft during a formation pass at low level and a speed of around Mach 0.97. The Lightning affected was XM141 flown by Flight Lieutenant Jim Burns, who was one of a box of four aircraft led by Flight Lieutenant Alan 'Lefty' Wright. Although the handling was sloppy in the yawing plane with undercarriage and flaps down, it was nevertheless still controllable. Fortunately there was no crosswind on the main runway at Coltishall and the aircraft was landed after a long straight approach with a threshold speed of 175 knots IAS. The Board of Inquiry found that the accident had been caused by the aircraft sustaining an aerodynamic load that was of sufficient magnitude to cause structural failure of the fin and rudder. This was most likely to have been the result of interaction between aircraft flying at high subsonic Mach number in close formation at low level. This accident led to the imposition of various flight restrictions relating to speed, spacing and 'g' loading when aircraft were flying in close formation. Aircraft were not to exceed Mach 0.87 in close formation and, when flying at speeds in the range Mach 0.70-0.87, loading was not to exceed 3g. Lateral separation was not to be less than half span or eighteen feet.

By the middle of 1961 the Lightening force had grown to include 111 Squadron at Wattisham but although the first aircraft was delivered on 30 March, the build-up was slow and only six aircraft had arrived by the end of May. This situation was not helped when Flying Officer Peter Ginger was forced to eject from XM185 on 28 June. Once again the accident was caused by failure of the undercarriage to lower. The lever for the emergency undercarriage lowering system was activated but this also failed, leaving Flying Officer Ginger with no choice but to eject at a safe height. Although the ejection was entirely straightforward, Ginger became aware of a Lightning heading towards him as he drifted down on his parachute and was somewhat alarmed to discover that it was the aircraft that he had just vacated. The aircraft appeared to be reluctant to say goodbye and flew close by before eventually falling away to crash in a field 1 mile north of Lavenham. It was later concluded that the failure of the undercarriage to operate was primarily due to a fatigue fracture of the hydraulic pressure service pipe. There were various theories as to why the emergency system had not worked but none was conclusively proved. It was thought that the locking plunger had not fully depressed when the lever was moved but subsequent investigation reve;alved that the lever might have been slightly bent at the bottom. Operation of the lever was not easy as it was in such a position that it had to be felt for. Later that day a local farm worker told everyone who would listen that he had to run for his life when the Lightning crashed. At first his rather fanciful story was treated with some suspicion. However, the hoe that he had been using at the time was later discovered amongst the wreckage.

For the remainder of 1961 the Lightning force was accident-free, although there were several potentially serious incidents including one that involved XM186 flown by Flight Lieutenant Anthony 'Bugs' Bendell of 111 Squadron on 25 August. As Wattisham's runways were being resurfaced at the time, the squadron was operating temporarily from Coltishall. Although the Lightning was usually started with an external electrical supply, it was capable of being started by the internal batteries and on this occasion it was decided to test the system. Start-up, take-off and the climb to altitude were successfully completed but shortly after commencing a series of practice intercepts with another Lightning, No.2 engine flamed out and the main (and most of the standby) flight instruments went offline. Bendell described what happened next in his autobiography *Never in Anger* (Orion, 1998):

The cockpit went deceptively quiet. There were no startling attention-getters or mind-blowing klaxons – but something was seriously amiss. The No.2 engine was rapidly unwinding. I attempted an immediate relight, but that failed. Both fuel gauges quickly ran down to below zero. I broke into a cold sweat; if lack of fuel was the problem then I would be making a Martin Baker letdown for a freezing – possibly fatal – dunking in the North Sea. Fortunately the No.1 engine kept going, but I could not maintain height above cloud on one engine alone. Instinctively I turned back towards Coltishall and rolled the wings level on a heading of 180 degrees, just as the aircraft sank into the murk.

The cockpit indications made little sense. It was fairly obvious that my aircraft had suffered a major electrical failure, but the only lights showing were the oil and hydraulic warnings associated with the flamed-out engine, and these were very dim. Both the main and standby radios appeared to be dead – although I was later informed that the emergency Mayday call I made on the international distress frequency was picked up by the GCI station. Problem was, no one could get through to me. The Lightning's main flight instruments and most of the back-up instruments depended on electrical power, whether it be for gyro-stabilisation or simply to provide heat to keep the pressure sensors clear of ice. As successive 'off-flags' flicked into view, the full implications of my predicament slowly dawned. I had to get clear of cloud before my instruments failed completely.

By 15,000 feet, still descending in cloud, my main and standby instruments had failed, and I was left with the small E2 magnetic compass and an unreliable airspeed indicator. Provided the pitot head didn't ice up I could control speed by fore-and-aft movements of the stick but, as any pilot faced with a similar situation will appreciate, the greatest hazard was the lack of roll information. Without a roll reference, the aircraft could easily overbank and enter an ever-steepening spiral dive. And if I did lose control in the prevailing weather conditions, there was not enough height for me to recover below cloud. Fortunately, it was possible to maintain roll control solely by reference to the E2 – it was a trick that I sometimes demonstrated during instrument rating tests. This time it would be put to the test. Briefly, on a heading of 180 degrees a simple magnetic compass is extraordinarily sensitive to roll and will swing away from 180 degrees – either towards east or west – immediately bank is applied. All I had to do was rock the aircraft from side–to–side, making sure the E2's mean heading remained close to 180 degrees, and in theory I would never have more than five degrees of bank applied.

I eventually broke out of cloud at 1,000 feet, in a shallow dive above a cold, inhospitable North Sea. The visibility was less than 3 miles, although there was little to be seen. Having safely made it down through the cloud I was now more concerned about fuel. Both gauges had been registering below zero since the start of the emergency. It was also possible that I was too far to the east and I might miss East Anglia altogether. If that was so, the next landfall would be the Belgian coast – although I doubted that I had sufficient fuel for that. For the second time during this emergency, ejection seemed a distinct possibility. I tightened the straps and after what seemed an age, but was probably no more than five or six minutes, I caught sight of land dead ahead. It was Norfolk right enough, and I coasted in over Cromer golf course. From there it was a simple matter to map-read back to Coltishall for a radio out circuit and landing. The flight had lasted for just fifty minutes, but it seemed like a lifetime to me.

It was subsequently discovered that a fuse between the generators and the main electrical circuits had blown during engine start, leaving only the batteries to supply electrical power. These had eventually drained to effectively leave the aircraft with a complete electrical failure.

'Bugs' Bendell was to have another fright on 18 January 1962 when flying XM191. During a tail chase exercise his No.2 called to inform him that his Lightning seemed to be venting large amounts of fuel. At the time the two aircraft were near to Wattisham, which was fortunate as it allowed Bendell to quickly position himself for an emergency approach during which he shut down No.2 engine. After landing, the Lightning was brought to a halt on a section of disused runway with fuel still pouring from drain holes on the underside of the fuselage. It transpired that the leak had been caused by a fuel transfer pipe that had split allowing fuel to pour into No.2 engine. This had obviously posed a considerable fire hazard but it was felt that the quantities of fuel involved were such that the fuel/air mix had been too rich for it to ignite. In addition the shutting down of No.2 engine had also helped by reducing temperature in the most affected areas.

The very next day 111 Squadron suffered another incident when XM189 was damaged during a night take off. The pilot was leader of a pair and as such positioned his aircraft on the left-hand side of the runway. During the early part of the take-off, however, the Lightning began to swing to port and although corrective action was undertaken, the swing continued. The aircraft eventually came to a halt after travelling 360 yards with damage to the nose-wheel leg and port main-wheel leg. It was discovered that the accident had been caused by the port wheel overlapping onto the grass as the aircraft left the Operational Readiness Platform (ORP) extension at the beginning of the take–off run.

The next squadron to fly the Lightning was No.19, which was the first to be equipped with the F.2 variant. There were severe delays in the arrival of the new aircraft and it was not until 17 December 1962 that the first F.2 was delivered to the squadron's base at Leconfield. In the meantime pilots had been getting acquainted with the Lightning at Middleton St George, which was home to the Lightning Conversion Squadron (LCS). This unit had been formed in August 1961 and although the first Lightning (T.4 XM970) had been delivered on 2 November of that year it soon had to be returned to the manufacturers due to problems with its hydraulic systems. This work took just over six months to complete and was indicative of serious problems with the Lightning's hydraulics.

The subject of hydraulics had caused much debate, and a certain amount of mud–slinging, between the Air Ministry, the Ministry of Aviation and English Electric. By the end of 1961 two aircraft had been lost as a result of faults in the hydraulic system and in addition there had been a number of emergency landings. Serious questions were being asked of the design of hydraulic pipe runs and the fact that chafing of the pipes was almost inevitably leading to leaks that resulted in inoperative systems and the possibility of in-flight fires. The speed with which the Lightning had been rushed into service was undoubtedly a factor, although accusations of bad design and poor workmanship made for an uncomfortable period for the manufacturers. The obvious effect on air safety was only half the story as aircraft already in service had to undergo considerable rectification work that seriously affected aircraft availability on the squadrons.

The second delivery flight of XM970 to LCS was on 27 June 1962, and more T.4s (the two-seater training version of the Lightning) arrived at Middleton St George over the next few months. Lightning availability at LCS took a turn for the worse however on 21 August 1962 when XM969 suffered a compressor failure in flight, which led to a fire. The sortie was to include a reheat take off followed by formation flying and a fast run. On the second fast run, reheat was selected when flying at 500 knots IAS at a height of 750 feet above ground level in level flight. Around ten-to-fifteen seconds later a triple bang was heard and this was followed by severe airframe vibration. A smell of burning was evident and the No.2 engine fire warning light illuminated. Speed was immediately reduced and the emergency fire drill was carried out, the warning light going out approximately four seconds after the fire extinguisher button was pressed. The pilot was able to return to Middleton St George and he touched down without further incident. When the engine was examined it was seen that two holes had been burnt through the No.2 engine compressor outlet casing and flames from these had severely damaged fuel and hydraulic pipes, cables and fuselage structure. As a result of the damage that had been caused XM969 was out of action for nearly four months.

Back at Wattisham XM183 of 56 Squadron was involved in another barrier engagement on 9 October when the braking parachute failed to deploy on landing. The aircraft was last in a stream landing of four Lightnings and made a normal approach, crossing the threshold at 165 knots IAS. The landing conditions were good with a dry runway and a crosswind from starboard of only 8 knots. Touch-down was rather heavy and there were two bounces before the aircraft settled on all three wheels. When the brake parachute was released it failed almost immediately but there still should have been ample distance available to come to a standstill, although braking action was not as effective as it should have been and the aircraft went into the barrier still travelling at a speed of around 50 knots. It turned out that the starboard tyre had burst during the landing roll and in the process the wheel had been damaged, although the pilot was not aware of this and had no difficulty keeping straight. The reliability of the braking parachute was particularly poor in the early days of Lightning operations, to the point where pilots had to anticipate that it would fail to deploy on every landing.

Problems with the undercarriage on the Lightning took on a different dimension on 18 December 1962 when T.4 XM993 of LCS crashed on landing at Middleton St George. The aircraft was being flown by Flight Lieutenant Al Turley and Wing Commander Charles Gibbs on a dual instructional sortie that had included a number of circuits and landings. On the last scheduled landing the nose-wheel was lowered onto the runway and the braking parachute deployed but almost immediately the port wing began to lower and the aircraft started to swing to the left. Assuming that the port tyre had burst, the pilot applied full starboard rudder and brake in an attempt to keep the aircraft straight, but it soon became apparent that the port undercarriage leg had collapsed. The Lightning then slewed 90 degrees to port before rolling to starboard, breaking the fuselage. Although the aircraft caught fire, both pilots managed to escape unhurt. The damage sustained by XM993 was enough for it to be written off, having flown a total of just forty-two hours. The post-crash investigation showed that the accident was caused by a defect in the casting of the undercarriage leg, a situation that would lead to further problems in the coming months.

The last Lightning accident of 1962 occurred on 18 December when F.2 XN777 ended up in the barrier at Binbrook. The pilot was Air Commodore E.G.L. Millington, who was the commander of the Central Fighter Establishment, and the sortie was his first flight in an F.2. After the aircraft settled on the runway following a normal approach and touch-down, Millington applied the brakes for a functional check before streaming the braking parachute. At the time the runway was wet and there was a crosswind component of 12 to 15 knots. The braking parachute deployed satisfactorily, the impact being felt in the cockpit, but unbeknown to the pilot, it failed almost immediately. When it became apparent that the level of deceleration was not as it should be, maximum braking was applied but it was not possible to slow the aircraft down sufficiently and a barrier engagement was made at considerable speed. The barrier was extended by nearly 600 feet and the aircraft went through the boundary fence and finally came to a halt with the nose-wheel and nose strut buried in ploughed earth. The upper barrier cable had cut into the fuselage spine, just forward of the No.2 engine hatch, and the lower cable had caught around both main undercarriage legs.

During an instrument approach the pilot's workload was reduced to a considerable extent by employing the autopilot and an auto-throttle system to position the aircraft at a height of 200 feet above the runway and at the correct approach speed. At this height the autopilot and auto-throttle would normally be disengaged for the pilot to carry out the landing manually. It appeared that in the case of the accident to XN777, the throttle was still in 'auto-throttle' mode when the aircraft touched down on the runway so that the system attempted to maintain speed at the correct setting of 170 knots. Not surprisingly Air Commodore Millington was somewhat shaken by the experience but was completely unhurt. Aircraft damage was assessed at Cat.3 and repairs took just under two months to complete.

Chapter 2

A Golden Age

The period 1963 to 1965 might be termed the Lightning's golden age as it saw a return to ever more elaborate squadron markings and dramatic colour schemes not seen since the 1930s. This trend was epitomised by 56 Squadron, which formed the Firebirds aerobatic team of nine Lightnings in 1963 and two years later introduced a scheme in which the entire fin and rudder were painted in red and white checks. Sadly this proved to be a step too far for some of those in the upper echelons of the Air Ministry who decreed that a return to more conservative markings be made. During this period the Lightning force was strengthened with the addition of two more squadrons. No.92 Squadron undertook its conversion to the F.2 during the first half of 1963 to join 19 Squadron at Leconfield, and the following year 23 Squadron swapped its Javelins for Lightning F.3s at Leuchars.

The first Lightning mishap of 1963 occurred at Binbrook and involved T.4 XM973 of AFDS. The crew comprised Les Hargreaves and John Mitchell, who were taxying out to the runway on 22 January when the starboard undercarriage leg collapsed in similar fashion to XM993 at Middleton St George the previous year. Thankfully on this occasion the failure occurred at low speed and the pilots were able to vacate their stricken aircraft safely. Once again the collapse was due to a faulty casting in the undercarriage leg. The damage was repaired by the end of May, when the aircraft was returned to service.

No.74 Squadron was still flying the Lightning F.1 from Coltishall and on 3 April one of its aircraft (XM140) suffered an engine fire shortly after take–off. The fire warning was for No.1 engine and was noticed as the aircraft was climbing through 1,400 feet, the pilot immediately throttled back but the warning light stayed on. He then descended below cloud and carried out his fire drill at the same time as turning onto the downwind leg. The ventral tank was jettisoned over a clear area so that the fuel (or vapour) did not catch fire and by the end of the downwind leg the fire warning light had gone out. A safe landing was made, at the end of which the pilot manoeuvred his aircraft onto the ORP before shutting down No.2 engine. The fire was found to have been caused by a fuel leak into the rear of the No.1 engine bay, where it had been ignited by heat from the exhaust unit. It was thought that the leak may have been caused by foreign matter trapped between a fuel pipe and its mating union, allowing fuel to seep through, even though the union was correctly tightened and locked.

Up to now 74 Squadron had not lost an aircraft but this all changed on 26 April when Flight Lieutenant Jim Burns was forced to eject from XM142. Burns, who was now known as 'Finless Jim' after his previous incident on the Lightning, was carrying out an air test after an engine and tailplane change but No.2 re-heat failed to light at an altitude of 36,000 feet despite four attempts. He therefore decided not to attempt the acceleration and zoom climb tests but continued with the other elements of the air test, which included ten seconds of inverted flight that was carried out at 10,000 feet. As he rolled out and turned to starboard, however, the No.2 hydraulic light illuminated, the IAS at this point being 400 knots with 90 per cent RPM set on both engines. The turn was continued towards base and as Burns was about to inform Air Traffic Control of the failure, the Standard Warning Panel operated. The aircraft was brought to wings level and the audio warning cancelled. The hydraulic warning light remained on and although the services pressure was normal, as were the controls, Burns decided to eject. He did so safely and was soon picked up by a rescue helicopter, his aircraft crashing into the sea off Cromer.

By early June the Firebirds aerobatic team from 56 Squadron had already performed two displays at Waterbeach and North Weald and were preparing for participation in the Paris Air Show. However on 6 June two aircraft collided whilst the team were performing a practice display over Wattisham. The aircraft flown by Flight Lieutenant Mike Cooke (XM179) came into contact with the underside of XM181 piloted by Flight Lieutenant Malcolm Moore. Although Moore's aircraft only received minor damage, XM179 lost its wing tip and Cooke ejected at a height of 800 feet. Although he survived, Cooke suffered severe injuries as a result of the ejection and was to be wheelchair-bound for the rest of his life. Although previous accounts have stated that the collision happened during a horizontal bomb burst manoeuvre, Tom Taylor, who was an armourer on 56 Squadron and witness to the crash, has since stated that the accident took place during the final pass along the runway in a vic of five as the aircraft broke for landing. The aircraft were supposed to have turned onto the downwind leg in sequence but it appears that Moore and Cooke broke almost at the same time, which positioned Cooke's aircraft behind and slightly below that flown by Moore. Cooke realised his error and attempted to turn away but before he could do so Moore straightened up, making a collision inevitable.

There was to be further drama at Wattisham later the same day when XM190 of 111 Squadron was involved in an accident during a night landing. Having taken off to carry out practice interceptions with another Lightning, concern over the prospect of fog forming in the area around the airfield led to an early return and a ground–controlled approach. As the aircraft was still relatively heavy with fuel (2,200lb per side), the pilot decided to touch–down at 160 knots IAS. The landing was firm, although not considered to be heavy, and the braking parachute was streamed but no deceleration was felt. The landing was completed under normal braking but after taxying back to dispersal it was discovered that the rear of the fuselage had come into contact with the runway. As a result the brake parachute doors had been damaged, thus preventing deployment of the parachute. The level of damage was sufficient for XM190 to spend the next two months in the hangar under repair. A similar accident occurred on 28 June involving XN730 of 19 Squadron, although in this case the tail hit the runway during take off resulting in the severing of the brake parachute cables.

The Lightning force suffered its first fatal accident on 18 July 1963 when Flying Officer Alan Garside of 111 Squadron was killed during an aerobatic display at Wittering. A former Hunter pilot with 66 Squadron, Garside was authorised for a low level display down to a minimum height of 500 feet above ground level, but the weather conditions at the time included variable amounts of cloud from 900 feet up to the main cloud base of 4,500 feet and because of this it was decided to do a flat display. As Flying Officer Garside was waiting for his take–off clearance a weak cold front was passing over the airfield and the clouds at the end of the runway appeared to be clearing. After take–off he pulled into a steep climb, rolling to the inverted position below the cloud base at 4,500 feet. This was the normal routine for a fair weather display, though various witnesses considered that the half roll was made at an altitude of between 3,500 and 4,000 feet which was a little lower than normal. Even at this slightly reduced height it was considered that Garside had sufficient height to execute a pull-through manoeuvre.

The Lightning was seen descending vertically before it entered cloud at between 1,600 and 2,000 feet. It eventually emerged from cloud at around 900 feet in a horizontal attitude, but still descending, before entering a spin in which it completed two complete turns prior to hitting the ground a mile north of the airfield. Garside ejected at a height estimated at 150-200 feet but there was insufficient time for his parachute to deploy and he was killed instantly when his seat impacted the ground. The most likely cause of the accident was that a 'g' stall occurred during the attempted recovery to level flight.

Another engine fire occurred at Leconfield on 14 August, although on this occasion it followed an inspection and servicing error. XN778 of 19 Squadron was being taxied from dispersal when the attention-getter flashed and audio warning sounded. The standard warning panel indicated a fire in the No.2 engine and the pilot informed Air Traffic before switching off the HP and LP cocks and the fuel pump. As the fire indication persisted, the fire extinguishers were activated. The pilot then switched off the electrics before abandoning the aircraft as the crash crews arrived. It was later discovered that the fire was caused by fuel that had been spilled when an unserviceable float switch had been replaced in the port main-plane inboard fuel tank. Although most of the fuel had been mopped up by the tradesmen, some fuel had found its way into the No.2 engine bay in the region of frames 43 and 44. When the engine was started the fuel had been ignited by the hot starter exhaust pipe which passed through the engine bay at this point.

On 19 August there was another Lightning barrier engagement, this time at Coltishall. After carrying out a training detail, Flight Lieutenant P. Stanning of 74 Squadron was landing in XM145 when the braking parachute collapsed immediately after deployment. He decided to jettison the failed 'chute and took off again before making a precautionary landing with a threshold speed of 165 knots IAS. Weather conditions were good with a wind of 14 knots in line with the runway which was dry (fuel state was 600/700lb). Although the brakes appeared to work normally at first, there appeared to be little deceleration in the last 1,000 yards of the landing run and the aircraft went into the barrier. Once again the top cable cut into the fuselage spine and a fire broke out in the region of the AVPIN tank which severely damaged electrical equipment. Examination of the brake parachute showed that twelve of the rigging lines had been severed resulting in collapse of the canopy. No fault could be found with the brakes, although excessive brake-pad wear was noted which was indicative of a previous 'hot stop' landing. Repairs were carried out on site but XM145 was not returned to service until the end of January the following year.

Although most undercarriage problems thus far had affected the main gear, it was also possible for the nose-wheel leg to remain up when the undercarriage was selected down before landing. In such a situation, assuming that the main gear had lowered satisfactorily, it was possible to attempt a landing, albeit with great care. Flight Lieutenant Dave Jones of 19 Squadron was faced with such a situation on 15 October 1963 when flying XN774 from Leconfield. He recalls the sequence of events:

I was briefed and authorised for a routine radar training sortie and took off as No.2 thirty seconds after my leader. The take–off was normal, however at 200 feet the main wheels locked up but the nose–wheel remained red. I climbed at 200 knots to 3,000 feet and selected undercarriage down, obtaining two mainwheel greens and a nose–wheel red. I then turned downwind, called for a GCA as the cloud base was about 900 feet and flew past the tower. They informed me that the nose–wheel was up but that the doors appeared to be open.

I then climbed back up to 3,000 feet and selected undercarriage up, the main wheels retracted normally, but again the nose–wheel remained red. During and after all the selections the services HYD pressure remained normal and the situation did not change even after the application of positive and negative 'g'. When the fuel was 1800/1800 lbs I selected emergency undercarriage down with negative 'g' and then maintained positive 'g' (3½) at 320 knots without effect. I continued to pull and push 'g' at speeds between 180 and 320 knots and carried out a roller landing, but still there was no change.

I flew out to sea and jettisoned the ventral tank at 3,500 feet – this left the aircraft cleanly at 250 knots with little change of trim. I then returned to the airfield and jettisoned the canopy at 220 knots at 200 feet with flaps up. It appeared to leave the aircraft very cleanly with a loud pop, and I was later told that the canopy missed the fin by about 6 feet. There was little disturbance in the cockpit without the hood and it was very similar to driving an open-top sports car. I was able to raise the seat for landing without any problems. The landing was carried out with 600lbs fuel and I held the nose in the air and lowered it gently onto the runway at about 75 knots. Pitch control was positive down to this speed. The aircraft came to rest in the middle of the pre-prepared foam strip and stopped in about 1,200 yards.

Flight Lieutenant Jones was commended for his calm and professional handling of this particular emergency and was recommended for a Green Endorsement for his logbook (an accolade given for having shown exceptional flying skill). The accident was caused by the starboard pip-pin that retained the nose-wheel rear door strut becoming detached. The strut then penetrated the inner surface of the rear door and formed a lock across the shimmy damper. which prevented either an up or down selection being carried out. It was noted that there had been one case earlier in the year of this particular pin becoming detached, but on this occasion the nose-wheel leg had not jammed. A snap check on all Lightnings in Fighter Command found a total of four aircraft with the pin partially removed.

The month of November proved to be a difficult one for 111 Squadron. On the 8th, Flying Officer Jack O'Dowd, a New Zealander who had previously flown Javelin night-fighters, was flying the squadron's T.4 XM992 when he received a No.1 engine fire warning having just carried out a practice overshoot at Honington. He jettisoned the ventral tank and landed safely although the warning proved to be spurious, which had become a regular and somewhat unfortunate feature of Lightning operations. Much worse was to follow and on the 19th XM187 was seriously damaged in a landing accident at night. After completing a practice night interception, the pilot (Flight Lieutenant M. R. Smith) returned to Wattisham and made a radar approach. The wind was virtually straight down the runway at 20 knots (with occasional gusts to 30 knots) and the main cloud base was 3,500 feet with 4/8 cloud at 1,400 feet. Visibility was 6 miles with light rain. Although the aircraft touched down at the correct GCA position, it landed heavily and bounced. About 460 feet from the initial touch-down point, the aircraft left the runway again, rising to a height of 15-20 feet. Unfortunately Flight Lieutenant Smith did not realise that the aircraft had taken off again and proceeded to lower the nose and stream the braking parachute. This led to the Lightning striking the runway in a nose-down attitude and the nose-wheel broke off and both main tyres burst. The port wheel assembly then broke away and the aircraft slid off the runway, breaking the starboard undercarriage before coming to rest. On hitting the ground the aircraft was subject to a positive 'g' loading in excess of +10, which resulted in Flight Lieutenant Smith suffering a compression fracture to his spine. Although initially assessed as Cat.4, XM187 was eventually written off as Cat.5 and delivered to No.9 School of Technical Training at RAF Newton as a ground instructional airframe.

Six days later Flight Lieutenant Brian Mason was airborne on a training flight in XM215 when an instrument failure prompted him to cut the sortie short and return to base. To use up fuel he elected to make a GCA-monitored TACAN-ILS approach (an instrument landing system approach also using the aircraft's TACAN navigation system), and this was followed by another ILS and two practice GCAs, all of which were flown in clear conditions. He decided to land after the second GCA and touched down normally at 160 knots IAS. The brake parachute was released but Mason suspected that it had failed to deploy and this was confirmed by Air Traffic. He elected to stay down and having already shut down No.1 engine, he then reduced power on No.2 engine to idle and requested that the barrier be raised. Although at first he was confident that he would be able to stop before the end of the runway, braking action in the final quarter of the landing run was less than expected and the aircraft entered the barrier at a speed of around 15 knots. As he began to unstrap the Tower informed him that his aircraft was on fire and a few seconds later the No.1 engine fire warning light illuminated. He immediately activated the fire extinguisher before making good his escape. Although the barrier engagement had been at a relatively slow speed, the top cable had still caused severe damage to the Lightning's spine and the fire had been the result of a ruptured AVPIN tank. XM215 was to be out of action for just over four months and was finally returned to 111 Squadron on 30 March 1964.

Sadly, another Lightning pilot lost his life on 27 April 1964 when XN785 flown by Flying Officer George Davie of 92 Squadron crashed on returning to Leconfield. Davie had been carrying out an in-flight re–fuelling exercise with a Valiant tanker but towards the end of the sortie he had experienced difficulty taking on any more fuel. He then reported that the engines were not giving full power and, on descending to 10,000 feet, his cockpit also misted up, prompting him to request a 'quickie GCA'. Whilst in a left-hand turn to come onto the extended runway centreline at 1,200 feet he informed Air Traffic that he had an AC failure.

Almost immediately he called again to say that he was unable to retain control of his aircraft and that he was ejecting, but there was insufficient time for the firing sequence to be completed before the aircraft hit the ground in a dive of around 35 to 45 degrees. The crash site was at the former airfield of Hutton Cranswick, which was approximately 5 miles north of Leconfield.

Although the subsequent investigation was of the opinion that there was little fuel remaining in the aircraft at the time of impact, others were not so sure. At no time did Davie give any concern over his fuel state and it was felt that certain other factors were ignored by the Inquiry. Chief among these was the AC failure that Davie had experienced as fuel transfer would then have been taken over by DC-powered pumps in the wing tanks. These were prone to icing, especially if subjected to a prolonged cold-soak at altitude, and by the time of the crash Davie had been airborne in excess of ninety minutes. In such a situation the engines would have been starved of fuel and would have flamed out. Flying Officer Davie had been with 92 Squadron for almost exactly a year having joined from 85 Squadron in April 1963. In fact this was the second fatality of the month for 92 Squadron as Flight Lieutenant C. M. Cameron was killed on 16 April during a practice aerobatic display in Hunter T.7 XL594, which dived into the ground near Carnaby.

Unfortunately for 111 Squadron, the unit lost another aircraft on 9 June when Flight Lieutenant Mike Smith was flying XM191. Having departed Wattisham for a practice diversion sortie, he was in a climbing turn after take off when the rpm on No.1 engine dropped to 85 per cent. Flight Lieutenant Smith was instructed to burn off fuel in the local area before landing back at base and as his aircraft appeared to be handling normally, he decided to carry out an ILS approach. Half a mile from the runway he began an overshoot and applied 90 per cent power to both engines, but there was a surge-like noise from No.1 and it rapidly wound down. In response to this the HP cock was closed, but shortly afterwards the No.1 engine fire warning light came on. Standard procedure was followed, i.e. activation of the fire extinguisher and jettisoning of the ventral fuel tank, and Smith positioned his aircraft on the downwind leg of the circuit. The fire warning light went out after some thirty seconds but came on again as the Lightning was turning onto finals. A safe landing was made, Smith turning onto the ORP at the end of the runway before making a hasty exit from the cockpit. It was later discovered that No.1 engine had suffered a compressor blade failure, probably as a result of ingesting some foreign object during taxying prior to take off. There was extensive fire damage to the No.1 engine hatch and rear fuselage structure, together with extensive damage to the wiring in the fuselage and the port mainplane. Overall, the level of damage was sufficient as to cause a Cat.5 write off.

Although the Lightning was occasionally prone to losing its canopy on take off, one departed in rather unusual circumstances at Wattisham on 23 June. A number of Lightnings from 56 and 111 Squadrons were taking part in an exercise and were required to scramble from the ORP. Unfortunately the pilot of 111 Squadron's T.4 (XM992) had difficulty starting his No.2 engine and was forced to make a second attempt. By this time the other aircraft were all on the move and some were taking off in close proximity. As a result of its delayed start the T.4 still had its canopy open and this was ripped off by jet blast from one or more of the other Lightnings. The canopy could not be repaired and the fuselage structure was damaged at the starboard hinge point. The canopy jack was also strained and the release unit damaged. As the aircraft was needed back in service as quickly as possible it was decided to fly it without a canopy to 60 Maintenance Unit (MU) at Leconfield. This task was undertaken by 111 Squadron's C.O. Squadron Leader George Black who flew the aircraft there at low level and with a speed restriction of 300 knots.

During the service life of the Lightning there were a number of in-flight rudder failures and one of the first instances of this particular problem occurred on 25 July. A pair of Lightnings, flown by Squadron Leader Paddy Hine and Flying Officer Jeff Denny of 92 Squadron, flew to Culdrose for an aerobatic display. On arrival they carried out a high-speed pass along the runway before breaking into the circuit, but after landing it was noticed that the aircraft of Flying Officer Denny (XN789) had nearly all of its rudder missing. A lack of balance at high speed and low level had resulted in excessive vibration, which was sufficient to cause the rudder to fail. Of the three control surfaces, the rudder was the least used so although it looked dramatic, the effect on aircraft handling was not as great as might be imagined.

Another Lightning was lost during an aerobatic routine on 28 August and once again it proved to be fatal for the pilot. The accident took place at Leuchars and involved F.3 XP704 of 74 Squadron flown by thirty-one-year-old Flight Lieutenant Glyn Owen who had been cleared for a practice display ahead of the station's Battle of Britain Open Day in

September. The clearance allowed for the sequence to be flown in two parts, the first with a minimum height of 1,500 feet and the second down to 500 feet. The cloud base was estimated to be 4,500 feet and the first part of the display was carried out satisfactorily, although the loop was omitted as Flight Lieutenant Owen was unsure as to whether the manoeuvre could be completed without entering cloud. The second part of the sequence was then flown and this included a loop that was carried out successfully. After his final manoeuvre Flight Lieutenant Owen informed the Tower that he would like to do another loop, but his aircraft was seen to stall at the top and enter a spin. He attempted to eject but did so at too low a height and was killed when his aircraft struck the ground. Early in his RAF career Glyn Owen had twice ejected safely from F-86 Sabre aircraft. He was buried in St Michael's Cemetery in Leuchars.

The hazards that Lightning pilots had to contend with were many and varied. Not long after take-off on 9 September the pilot of XM175 from 56 Squadron was flying straight and level at 15,000 feet when his senses were assailed by various klaxons, attention-getters and warning lights in the cockpit. The first indication of trouble was when the AC warning light came on and this was quickly followed by the turbine and generator lights. The pilot immediately switched off all non-essential electrics and AC instruments and made a rapid return to Wattisham using his stand-by radio. After landing an investigation revealed major internal damage to air supply trunking and air cooling pipes that had been caused by vibration as a result of overspeeding of both the alternator and generator.

Two days later undercarriage problems reappeared when XM134 of 226 OCU was being flown on an air test by Flight Lieutenant Terry Bond (226 OCU had been formed from LCS on 1 June 1963 and had moved to Coltishall in April 1964). On its previous sortie the pilot had reported a malfunction of the undercarriage indicator lights and rectification work had comprised replacement of the undercarriage micro-switches. Having reached a safe altitude, Flight Lieutenant Bond cycled the undercarriage successfully three times but on the fourth selection the starboard leg jammed in a half-extended position. Not long afterwards the HYD 1 warning light came on, which indicated that one of the hydraulic systems powering the flying controls had failed. This system also provided power to lower the undercarriage in an emergency. Bond manoeuvred his aircraft to set up positive 'g' and also worked the rudder to apply yaw in an attempt to lower the leg, but it was all to no avail and a visual check confirmed that the starboard leg had not moved. As his fuel was beginning to run low he climbed to 10,000 feet before ejecting over the coast and was picked up by a rescue helicopter, his aircraft crashing in the sea 30 miles east of Happisburgh. As the wreckage was never recovered the precise cause of the accident remained a mystery.

On 24 September there was a further case of finger trouble when another canopy departed on take off. The offender this time was Pilot Officer Doug Aylward of 92 Squadron who was on his first solo flight in an F.2. Before take off in XN793 he had experienced radio problems and it was postulated that he may have been distracted by this and failed to lock the canopy properly. By now the sequence of events was becoming depressingly familiar as the top rear fuselage behind the cockpit was damaged, as was the fin when it was hit by the canopy. The aircraft became airborne but was landed safely despite having sustained Cat.3 damage, which was enough to keep it in the hangar for the next seven weeks. This incident did not cause too much harm to Doug Aylward's RAF career as by 1979 he had attained the rank of Wing Commander.

Another Lightning ended up on its nose on 29 September when the nose-wheel leg failed to extend on XM144. The unfortunate pilot on this occasion was Flying Officer Ian Macfadyen who was one of six pilots taking No.15 Lightning Conversion Course with 226 OCU at Coltishall. The incident was similar to that of Flight Lieutenant Dave Jones the previous year as Macfadyen was confronted with two mainwheel greens and a nose-wheel red. Repeated undercarriage selections made no difference and the Tower confirmed that the nose-wheel was up, but that the doors were open. Having jettisoned his canopy and ventral tank over the sea, Macfadyen made a perfect landing and gently lowered the nose onto the runway at a speed of around 80 knots so that damage to his aircraft was minimal. The failure was put down to a broken grub screw, which allowed the shock absorber to extend and foul the nose leg axle nut in the nose-wheel bay, thus preventing extension.

If there had been a competition to find the unluckiest Lightning, XM183 of 56 Squadron would have been a strong candidate. Having ended up in the barrier on two occasions, it suffered major damage once again on 14 October when fire broke out during an engine run at Wattisham. As a result of its previous mishaps it had spent a total of twelve months under repair and the damage on this occasion (initially Cat.4 but subsequently re-assessed as Cat.3) took just over seven months to put right.

By now the Lightning had been in service for four-and-a-half years and its accident record for 1964 had shown a significant improvement over previous years. In the first year of Lightning operations (1960) there were two major accidents and as total flying time was 727 hours, this represented an accident rate of 27.5 per 10,000 hours. The following year flying time had risen to 5,346 hours, so with five major accidents the rate per 10,000 hours was 9.4. The figures for 1962 and 1963 were broadly similar at 10.4 and 9.9 (5,750 hours – six majors and 13,110 hours – thirteen majors respectively); however, the accident rate per 10,000 hours fell to 4.9 in 1964 when 16,319 hours were flown with a total of eight major accidents. By contrast, accident rates for the Javelin had shown a steady increase over the same period. In 1960 the Javelin force had flown a total of 54,054 hours with twenty-two major accidents resulting in a rate of 4.1 per 10,000 hours. By 1964, however, although total hours had been reduced to 22,037, there were still fourteen majors resulting in an increased rate of 6.4. As a further comparison, rates for the Hunter, which by now was being used mainly for ground attack, varied from 6.6 to a high of 11.3 during the period 1960–64.

Although it appeared as though the Lightning's safety record was improving, another was lost on 11 January 1965 when Squadron Leader Andy Whittaker ejected from XG335. This was one of the development batch aircraft and was being used by A&AEE for trials with the Red Top missile programme. On the day of the accident the Lightning was to have fired a Red Top against a Jindivik drone over the Aberporth range but failure to acquire the target led to the sortie being aborted. On returning to base there was another case of undercarriage malfunction as the starboard leg did not fully extend. The usual manoeuvres were flown in an attempt to persuade the recalcitrant leg to come down, but these were unsuccessful and Whittaker was eventually forced to eject over the Larkhill ranges. It was later concluded that the starboard undercarriage leg had not extended fully due to failure of the side-stay bracket; this was an identical failure to one that had occurred on XG311, which crashed on 31 July 1963 during trials conducted by the manufacturers. Don Knight, one of the company's test pilots, ejected safely.

The first Lightning incident to affect 23 Squadron took place on 16 February and involved XP760, which was being flown by Commanding Officer Squadron Leader John McLeod. Once again the snag was to do with the undercarriage, although in this case it was caused by failure of the hydraulic system. The emergency lowering system was operated but still the undercarriage refused to come down fully. McLeod went through the regular repertoire of high 'g' turns and eventually, after about fifteen minutes, the gear reluctantly swung into position and locked, after which a safe landing was made. It appeared that the emergency system had not worked due to insufficient travel of the selector and as a result the system had not been activated.

Over the next two months it was the turn of 56 Squadron to be in the spotlight as far as Lightning incidents were concerned. On 5 March Flight Lieutenant Mike Wraight had warning of a fire in No.2 engine when flying XM171, although this was successfully extinguished and a safe landing was made. The following month there were two separate incidents where pilots had to contend with control restrictions, the first occurring on 23 April when Flight Lieutenant P. Wild was flying XR719. Despite limited lateral control he was able to return to Wattisham where a successful landing was carried out. When the aircraft was examined a loose bolt was found in the wing, which had fouled the aileron control rod resulting in limited travel. Five days later Flight Lieutenant Pete Clee had a similar problem in the unit's T.4 XM989. On return to Wattisham it was found that a spanner had been left in the wing during servicing and this had eventually jammed the ailerons to the extent that Clee was unable to turn to port.

At Coltishall 226 OCU lost one of its F.1As for a considerable period when it was badly damaged in an explosion on start-up on 26 April. The pilot of XM216 was able to start both engines but before the ground electrical supplies could be removed an explosion was heard and a cloud of smoke emerged from the No.2 engine jet pipe. Despite prompt action in shutting the engines down and switching off all the electrics, the aircraft had already suffered serious internal damage that took over a year to rectify. The explosion was caused by a defective starter exhaust pipe that had allowed flames or hot gases to ignite residual vapours in the engine bay.

By June 1964 the air display season was in full swing with Flight Lieutenant Tony Doyle of 111 Squadron a regular participant. On the 26th, Flight Lieutenant Doyle flew to St Mawgan in XR712 as this was to be his base prior to being one of the highlights of the Exeter Air Show. As was now customary, the completion of his display was a high-speed run in reheat, but as this was being completed spectators were horrified to see black smoke and flames emerge from the back of the Lightning. As he put his aircraft into a climb Doyle was aware of a number of loud bangs from the rear end and at the same time there was also considerable airframe buffeting. As the jet pipe temperature for No.1 engine had gone off the scale, he shut down this engine and was just completing this particular task when the Fire 1 warning light came on. As No.2 engine was still giving 94 per cent power, however, he decided to head back towards St Mawgan. Although his attempt to transfer fuel from the port wing tank to that in the starboard wing was unsuccessful, there was sufficient fuel for a straight-in approach.

Prior to landing the undercarriage was lowered, but when it was selected down Doyle noticed that there was a control restriction and he could not move the stick further aft than the central position. Also when the flaps were lowered it became apparent that the nose tended to drop uncontrollably below speeds of about 230 knots IAS. Despite his best attempts to free the control column, it refused to move so he was left with no alternative but to head out to sea and eject. This was accomplished safely once the coast had been crossed and a favourable on-shore breeze drifted his parachute back towards the land where he eventually came down.

Tony Doyle gave a personal view of this accident in his autobiography *Flying at the Edge* (Pen and Sword 2010):

As the nose came up above the horizon I felt a dull tremor shake the airframe. Because of my tight-fitting bone-dome, with its sealed earpieces, I didn't hear anything, but it was obvious that something had just happened at the back. There were no other signs of trouble. No warning lights or bells. As I came back out of reheat I glanced down at the engine instruments. It took several staring seconds to absorb the full impact of their message. The jet pipe temperature of the top engine was over 800 degrees, well above its limit. The lower engine appeared to have gone out, as the temperature was on zero. Something was happening and I hadn't yet worked out what. I pulled both throttle levers back to the idle position, trying to decide what to do next. If the No.1 was out, was it damaged? Should I try to relight it or rely on the No.2, even though it had gone way over the temperature limit? I was saved the trouble of making up my mind when the emergency warning bell suddenly filled my earphones with its clangor. The reheat and engine fire warning lights were on, and to my astonishment the needle on the No.1 temperature gauge was slowly moving anti-clockwise back down towards the upper limit. It had been so far round the dial that I had misread it as zero. In view of this, the No.2 would have to take its chances, and I wasted no time shutting down the No.1.

At the time the procedure was to get rid of the ventral tank if there was a persistent fire in the lower engine. It was thought that the tank, lying along the bottom of the fuselage, would prevent the skin cooling, and being full of fuel vapour it might even explode. Having throttled back I had to check the rocket climb and level out much lower than I had originally planned. I took a look over the side and saw that my trajectory had taken me right over the northern environs of Exeter. Eventually, after what seemed an age, I reckoned I was clear of the built-up area and pulled the jettison handle, causing the aircraft to take a terrible lurch. The ventral was gone, but the No.1 fire lights had not gone out so it was time to jump for it. I levelled the wings and prepared to eject. It seemed unreal, even ludicrous, for the only proof that I had of a serious malfunction were those silly little lights. No smoke. No flames. Not even odd noises. Nothing to urge me to leave the familiar comfort of the cockpit. I was reaching for the handle when, at last, the fire lights went out.

The Lightning fuselage is a dense structure, and the rear ends of the engines are a long way behind you, so there could be a roaring inferno down at the back and you would never realise it. If the fire lights go out it means either that the fire has gone out or that the wiring has burnt through. However, I had a bit of height in hand and we still seemed to be flying so I busied myself about getting back to St Mawgan, which was still ten minutes flying time away. As I climbed gently to the west over Dartmoor I realised that I had another big problem on my hands – fuel. The explosion must have damaged the transfer system because I could not get any of the fuel from the No.1 engine across to the live engine. As I crossed Dartmoor I found that the No.2 engine was running rather more economically than the book suggested and by the time St Mawgan was in sight some 10 miles away, I had just about enough to make a second attempt at landing should it become necessary. The fuel situation was tight, but not the worst I had experienced.

My main worry was that the remaining engine might also have been damaged and would fail somewhere near the ground during the approach to land. I kept remembering the jet pipe temperature sitting up there, well above the limit. And then there was the explosion. What else had it damaged apart from the fuel transfer system? As if in reply, the aircraft suddenly slewed sideways, staggered for a second and then resumed normal flight. What the heck was THAT? Everything seemed to have gone back to where it was before, and the aircraft was flying normally again, but my mind pondered darkly on what might be going on down at the back to cause that lurch. Bodmin Moor passed by to the north. Luckily there was a strong wind blowing from the sea, which would enable me to make a straight-in approach to St Mawgan's north-westerly runway. If it had been blowing the other way I would have been faced with the decision of whether to land downwind or going right round to the far side and risk running out of fuel.

With 4 miles to go and plenty of height in hand, I reduced speed and selected the wheels down. As they came out into the airstream the nose dipped gently and I checked back on the stick. It moved a fraction of an inch and then came up against a solid restriction. The nose continued to drop. I grasped the stick with both hands and tried to smash it through the blockage, but it would not budge. As I dropped the flap the nose rose gently, and slowly we resumed level flight. Normally under these circumstances one would climb to a safe height and check out the handling at landing speed, but I did not have the fuel for that. Gently I reduced the speed, but immediately the nose began to drop again uncontrollably. The shoulder wing position on the Lightning, together with the exaggerated sweep back, made a belly-landing a very dangerous prospect, and the procedure in the event of no wheels was to bale out. Anyway, it was not just that I couldn't fly any slower than 230 knots, but with the stick stuck I had no way of checking the descent for the touch-down.

By this time I had got too close to the airfield for a straight-in approach. I looked with misgivings at my dwindling fuel supply, called the tower to let them know what had happened and began a turn into the circuit, hoping against hope that the restriction would free itself. It didn't, and every time I turned I couldn't prevent the aircraft from losing height. I tried every combination of autopilot, artificial feel and autostabilisers I could think of, but it made no difference. I raised the undercarriage and flaps, increased the speed and climbed towards the sea, telling the Tower that I intended to eject. I had decided long ago that if I had to eject, and I had time, I would get rid of the hood first. On some aircraft you can eject through the hood if it fails to go, indeed on some that is the normal way.

The Lightning hood was so massive that there was no question of going through it, so there was a device that prevented the seat from firing if the hood was still in place. Pulling either ejector-seat handle fired the hood off first, and then, as it went, it automatically unlocked the seat-firing sequence, which paused a moment to allow the hood to get clear and then fired. There had been a number of incidents where debris had jammed the hood-release mechanism, trapping the pilot in the cockpit at the end of a sortie. I knew because it had happened to me. If, for some reason, the hood failed to fire after the handle had been pulled, then there were a couple of other things you could do to get rid of it. I did not like the idea of having to do this with the seat all primed and ready to fire pretty well as soon as the hood had gone, because you needed to be in a really exact posture to take the force of the seat gun. I had also decided that in a deliberate ejection at moderate speed I would use the bottom handle rather than the face-blind, because experience had shown that you could adopt a much better posture with the former and so reduce the likelihood of spinal damage. I pulled the jettison lever, and away went the hood in fine style. I suppose I must have been at about 5,000 feet and a mile from the shore when I drew my shoulders back against the seat and pulled the firing-handle.

Many people who have ejected have described remembering seeing the seat lift up out of the aircraft, but I have absolutely no recollection of the first few seconds. I remember everything as going black and thinking that it felt as though I had been put into a large tin and shaken violently. Later the medics worked out that my chin strap had failed, allowing the airstream to wrench off my helmet. As it went it stretched the oxygen pipe till the fastenings holding the mask to the helmet parted and the mask came rushing back and hit me in the face. The fibreglass frame of the mask was quite hefty, and presumably the blow knocked me momentarily unconscious. I recovered full consciousness in time to see the seat falling away towards the sea. I couldn't see the aircraft anywhere, but a few moments later I heard the engine stop, and then quite a bit later there was a dull thump and looking down between my feet I saw a great circular patch of foam spreading on the surface of the sea.

Now that there was nothing for me to do, I felt much more frightened than before. I remembered a friend who had also baled out, telling me that he had been afraid of falling out of the parachute harness and had come down all the way with his fingers hooked into the two metal rings at the top of his straps. As soon as I thought of this my own hands flew up to the rings above my head. The 'chute began to swing sickeningly and I had an irrational fear that I was in danger of falling down into the canopy. I could see that the wind was so strong that it was beginning to blow me back towards the shore. However the fear of drowning out at sea was replaced with a new threat; my trajectory was taking me along a line of hideously high cliffs and sea stacks, against which the great Atlantic rollers were hurling themselves. Looking straight down between my feet I could see the faces of people on the cliff path staring up at me. In agonising slow motion I gradually drifted clear of the cliffs, only to see a whole mass of power cables approaching. I pulled down vigorously on one side of the shroud lines to increase my rate of descent in an attempt to land before I reached them.

As I fell towards the fields, the last few hundred feet rushed by in a flash. My 'chute was swinging so far over that the last thing I saw before hitting the ground was the lip of the 'chute hitting the ground while I was still in the air. Then down I came onto my back with a crash. I can remember thinking that this must be what it is like to fall off the roof of a two-storey building and, appreciating the sudden calm, I lay there for a while to get my breath back. When I sat up I saw that my flying boots were actually touching the lowest strands of a barbed wire fence that ran across the field in which I had landed. A few feet either side of where I lay were the sharp angle-iron posts that held it up. Drowning or falling down a cliff had not been the only dangers I had escaped. At the top of the field I found a man feeding his pigs. I stood there, an incongruous figure in my flying-suit with my parachute draped over my arm, but the farmer did no more than glance in my direction. 'I saw yer come down,' he said in a conversational tone, 'I'll give yer a lift to the village when I've finished feeding these y'ere pigs.' And so he did.

After he had ejected Tony Doyle's aircraft had continued to fly for a short time before coming down in the sea approximately three miles from the coast. Despite an extensive search, however, no wreckage was ever found. The Board of Inquiry that was set up to investigate the accident could only state that it had probably been caused by an uncontained explosion in No.1 engine, which had led to an intense in-flight fire. Some items of engine debris from the explosion during the high-speed run were found on the airfield at Exeter.

Having had its canopy torn off by jet blast the previous year, T.4 XM992 of 111 Squadron was involved in another unfortunate incident on 14 July, although this time it was all of its own making. On completion of an instrument flying sortie XM992 returned to Wattisham and was being taxied back to dispersal when the brakes failed due to a hydraulic failure. Unfortunately this occurred as the Lightning was being turned towards other aircraft and it was impossible to prevent it hitting one of the squadron's single-seaters and also coming into contact with another. The T.4 received Cat.3 damage in the collision and the two other Lightnings were assessed as Cat.2.

The next Lightning barrier engagement took place at Leconfield on 3 August when XN786 of 92 Squadron was returning from a high-level interception sortie. On landing the pilot had to contend with a crosswind and had difficulty keeping straight on the runway with the braking parachute streamed as his aircraft tried to weathercock into wind. The use of differential brake had little to no effect so to prevent his aircraft going onto the grass the pilot jettisoned the parachute. He continued braking but the level of deceleration was not enough to stop the Lightning going into the barrier. As with previous barrier engagements the level of damage was considerable and XN786 did not return to service for almost five months.

By now Lightning incidents were beginning to follow a regular pattern and on 6 August there was another open cockpit flight. Before take-off from Akrotiri the pilot of XN776 of 19 Squadron opened his canopy for ventilation but had to close it again due to fumes from the aircraft ahead. In the event he decided to leave the canopy slightly open but when it was his turn to line up with the runway he forgot to lock it shut and did not notice the canopy unlocked warning light. The canopy was ripped off at about 140 knots and, as was now customary, it hit the tail on its way. The pilot continued the take off and landed safely after burning off fuel.

At Wattisham 111 Squadron lost one of its F.3s in September when Flight Lieutenant Hedley Molland was returning after a high-altitude interception exercise. The following is his account of what happened as given to the Board of Inquiry:

On 29 September I was briefed by Squadron Leader J. Mitchell and authorised myself to fly Lightning Mk.3 aircraft XP739 on an exercise of simulated high flying attacks against a Canberra target aircraft. The weather was checked and conditions were cloud base 4,000 feet minimum and visibility over 10 miles. I taxied out, took off and climbed to Flight Level 360. Just before levelling off the cabin pressure warning came on and the cabin altimeter showed 22,000 feet at Flight Level 360 instead of about 18,000 feet. Use of the de-mist lever rectified the malfunction.

I carried out three radar attacks using reheat on all attacks. My fuel state at the beginning of the last was 1,800lbs on each side. I started the recovery with a fuel state of 1,200lbs per side about fifteen miles north of the dive point. I requested a straight letdown to Point Alpha for a visual re-join and started to descend 30 miles from Point Alpha on a heading of 240 degrees Magnetic. I selected airbrakes out, throttled back to idle/fast idle and descended at 0.90 Mach converting to 375 knots. Between 15,000 and 20,000 feet I selected airbrakes in and continued descending at 375 knots. I passed Point Alpha, 18 miles on the runway extended centre line at about 8,000 feet. At some time before this I was told to change UHF frequency to Stud 6 for Wattisham radar surveillance. At the same time I selected low sensitivity on the IFF.

At about 5,000 feet I selected airbrakes out and steepened the descent to maintain 375 knots. At this stage I was in visual contact with the ground. I was cleared to descend to 1,500 feet so I did not level at 3,000 feet but started easing out of the descent in order to level off at 1,500 feet. As I reached the level position I increased power to about 80 per cent rpm on both engines. As rpm neared 80 per cent a light flashed on the Auxiliary Warning Panel (AWP). I looked down but the light had gone out. As I was looking at the AWP, the FUEL 1 warning light came on. I checked that No.1 engine rpm were below 85 per cent. At the same time I transmitted an R/T call and I think I said that I would be doing a straight-in approach instead of a circuit. I then looked back at the AWP and noticed that the FUEL 2 warning light was also on. On looking back at the No.1 engine rpm I noticed that it was dropping below 50 per cent. I opened up the No.1 throttle and when the engine did not respond I informed base that my No.1 engine had flamed out.

I then noticed that I had all the indications of an AC failure and checked No.2 engine rpm, which were dropping. I opened No.2 throttle and when the engine did not respond I transmitted that I had a double flame-out. While making this call I pressed the relight buttons. My fuel state at this time was 900lbs per side and I prepared for a possible ejection. I lowered the seat and checked the aircraft trim by letting go of the stick. The nose of the aircraft dropped so I trimmed back to what I thought was a level attitude. At about this time I became conscious that the attention-getters were flashing and the audio warning was operating. I cancelled these and noticed that a generator failure was indicated on the Standard Warning Panel (SWP). Simultaneously I noticed Needham Market dead ahead so I turned the aircraft five to ten degrees to starboard. I heard base asking if I was still with them and informed them that both re-lights had been unsuccessful and that I was ejecting.

I checked my height and speed from standby instruments and found I was between 1,000 and 2,000 feet at about 250 knots. Without adjusting the straps or moving my feet from the rudder pedals, I pulled the seat pan handle. The hood left the aircraft immediately. During the one-second, delay which seemed a very long time, I became aware of the audio warning. I did not see if there was anything more indicated on the SWP. I heard a bang, felt the acceleration, and the seat tumbling. Almost immediately I felt the jerk of the main parachute deploying. I noticed the aircraft approximately 200 yards ahead. It was in a slight descent with the nose up and the wings gently rocking. It appeared to be intact and I was struck by the absolute silence. I landed in a field near a road and was driven to a nearby farm where I telephoned Wattisham,

informed them of my position and requested an ambulance as my
back and neck were rather stiff. The ambulance took me to Ipswich
hospital for an X-ray.

After Flight Lieutenant Molland ejected, his aircraft continued in a
gentle descent for another 3 miles before striking the ground in a gliding
attitude. Upon impact it disintegrated and caught fire. At the time of
the accident there was still ample fuel on board (800lbs per side) but
despite this both engines had flamed out. The Accident Investigation
Branch concluded that the fuel starvation was most likely caused by
the DC fuel transfer pumps not transferring fuel to the collector tank
to supply to the fuel-draulic booster pumps. The precise reason for the
fuel not being transferred, however, could not be established. From
what remained of the fuel system no definite fault could be found and
although the switches operating the DC fuel pumps were suspected, it
was not proven that they had been faulty. At the time of the accident
XP739 was less than a year old and had flown only 180 hours.

Although Flight Lieutenant Molland was not blamed in any way for
the accident by the Board of Inquiry – indeed he was commended for
his coolness when confronted with a difficult situation – it did consider
that the flight profile used in the descent may have contributed to the
fuel starvation. It was noted that XP739 had already flown three sorties
on the day of the accident and in each of these the descent was quite
different to that flown by Flight Lieutenant Molland. In one case the
aircraft had been descended in a nose-up attitude and in the other two the
aircraft had been flown level for a time before the throttles were opened.
In all of these cases the fuel collector boxes would have been filled
under the influence of gravity so that when the throttles were opened
there was sufficient fuel available. In Flight Lieutenant Molland's case
he had carried out a nose-down descent and immediately after levelling
out had made a demand for more fuel by advancing the throttles. The
combination of insufficient fuel in the collector boxes and an inefficient
DC fuel system meant that not enough fuel was available to supply the
demand of the engines and so they both flamed out.

No more Lightnings were lost during the remainder of 1965 although
there were several incidents. On 21 October Lightning T.4 XM994 of
226 OCU took off with the starboard fuse panel unfastened, which
promptly tore off causing Cat.3 damage. A week later F.3 XP762 of 111
Squadron suffered a seized port brake and ended up on the grass at

the side of Wattisham's runway, although damage was relatively minor (Cat.2). On 16 November there was another case of a stuck nose-wheel that affected XN783 of 92 Squadron, which was being flown by Flying Officer John Rooum on a radar exercise. The sequence of events was virtually identical to the previous cases and the accident was once again caused by a small screw in the nose-wheel shock absorber assembly, which had worked loose allowing the ring nut to unscrew and extend the nose oleo. As a result the leg could not be moved to the down position.

The final Lightning mishap of the year affected T.5 XS419 of 226 OCU which suffered a landing accident on 16 December. This was caused primarily by the braking parachute, which candled shortly after being deployed. As it appeared that the aircraft was heading for the barrier, the captain (Flight Lieutenant Ed Durham) applied port brake to steer the aircraft onto the grass but it unfortunately hit a number of obstacles before coming to a halt. The result was Cat.3 damage and four months in the repair hangar.

By the end of 1965 there were six squadrons fully operational on the Lightning plus 226 OCU. The increased number of aircraft in service was reflected in a 35 per cent increase in the number of flying hours by Lightnings compared with the previous year. Total flying hours for 1965 were 22,130 and there were nine major accidents resulting in an overall accident rate per 10,000 flying hours of 4.1. This represented a slight improvement on the previous year and compared favourably with other RAF fast jets. Indeed the statistics for the Javelin showed a further worsening of its accident rate, which continued the trend of the previous five years. Total flying hours for the Javelin were 19,187 but there were twenty majors during 1965 so that the rate per 10,000 hours was 10.4. To some extent this trend can be explained by the fact that the Javelin's role had expanded, as it was now in use in the Far East in connection with the Indonesia/Malaysia confrontation where it was often flown at low level. However, as the Lightning was a much newer aircraft, such a low accident rate for what was also an extremely complex machine was highly commendable; the Hunter's accident rate for 1965 was 4.2.

Chapter 3
Enter the F.6

Although most pilots loved the Lightning, the meagre fuel capacity of the early variants was a major concern. This problem was finally addressed with the F.6, which featured a much enlarged ventral fuel tank and with increased use of in-flight re-fuelling (together with the use of overwing ferry tanks) the Lightning force was transformed; this increased flexibility allowing long-range deployments and the option of basing aircraft abroad. The new version of the Lightning was first delivered to a new Lightning squadron, No.5, which had disbanded as a Javelin unit at Geilenkirchen in Germany in early October 1965 before being resurrected at Binbrook the following day under the command of Squadron Leader Les Hargreaves. The first F.6 did not arrive until 10 December and only three had been delivered by the end of the month, although a full complement of aircraft had been received by March 1966.

Although the Lightning's safety record for 1965 had shown further improvement, the new year got off to the worst possible start when Flying Officer Derek Law of 56 Squadron was killed in XR721. Having been airborne for thirty minutes, Flying Officer Law began a practice diversion to Bentwaters but his No.1 engine seized whilst approaching the glidepath. At this point he was at about 1,700 feet and decided to return to Wattisham, which was 18 miles away. About one minute later he informed base that his No.2 engine would give no more than 90 per cent power and, as he was unable to maintain height, he was ejecting. Shortly after this the Lightning crashed in a field and Law was killed.

The investigation that was set up to find the cause of the accident concluded that the No.1 engine starter had not disengaged after engine start-up and that this had eventually disintegrated sending debris into the intake. This had been ingested by the engines which, after a period of time, led to failure of the No.1 engine and reduced power on No.2. A particularly tragic finding of the inquiry was the fact that Flying Officer Law had attempted to eject but had been prevented from doing so by failure of the canopy to jettison, which stopped the seat from firing. The only course of action remaining was to carry out a forced landing. This was carried out with considerable skill but the constant jolting as the aircraft ran along the ground was sufficient to dislodge the canopy, the departure of which allowed the ejection seat to fire. Flying Officer Law's body was found a short distance from the aircraft, the cockpit of which was completely intact.

Another canopy was lost on 21 February when XN775 of 19 Squadron was taking off. The pilot had been scrambled as the No.2 in a pair for an air defence exercise but his leader signalled that he was having trouble starting his engines. The No.2 then took his hand off the canopy lowering lever and signalled back that he would get airborne by himself. He taxied out but unfortunately did not check the shoot bolts or the canopy lights. During the take-off run the canopy broke away and hit the fin causing considerable damage to the leading edge. The next Lightning incident took place on 14 March when a pilot of 56 Squadron was returning to base in XP743 after an in-flight refuelling exercise. As the aircraft was at a relatively high all-up weight he crossed the undershoot area at a speed of 180 knots IAS before gradually reducing power as he rounded out. On touch-down the tail cone hit the runway resulting in Cat.3 damage, which took three months to repair.

The next day another Lightning came down in the North Sea when Captain Al Petersen USAF, who was on an exchange posting, had to eject from XM190 of 226 OCU. His flight only lasted three minutes and shortly after taking off as No.2 of a pair for a tactical exercise, he received a Reheat 1 fire warning. As the No.1 engine was shut down the Fire 1 warning also illuminated and the fire extinguisher was activated. Captain Petersen then began to turn away from land and as he did so the Reheat 2 warning came on. This was then followed by a Fire 2 warning and Petersen ejected over the sea at a speed of 220 knots IAS and a height of 7,000 feet. The crash investigation was hampered by the fact that only a relatively small amount of wreckage was recovered from the sea, although it was noted that the pieces that were trawled up did not show any sign of fire damage. This led some to believe that the fire warnings may have been spurious.

Another of 226 OCU's F.1As was written off on 6 May in what was to be the first of several spectacular take-off accidents for the Lightning force. The aircraft involved was XM213 and the unfortunate pilot was Squadron Leader Paul Hobley. As was customary on take-off the undercarriage was selected up shortly after the aircraft became airborne but on this occasion it sank back, the tail hit the runway and the result was one Lightning careering along on its ventral tank, which soon split open. Fuel from the ventral then caught fire to make the scene even more dramatic and the Lightning continued across the perimeter track before finally stopping 20 yards inside a farmer's field. Squadron Leader Hobley was completely unhurt in the incident and the fire was extinguished by the fire crews. At the time of its demise XM213 had flown a total of 886 hours.

On 11 May it was the turn of the crash crews at Wattisham to demonstrate their skills following a landing accident to XP747 which was being flown by Flying Officer Stuart Pearse of 56 Squadron. After carrying out a high-level practice interception, the recovery was made with the help of TACAN but on touch-down both main wheels were locked and the tyres burst. After a short period the port wheel started turning but the starboard wheel remained locked and this caused the aircraft to swing off the runway. Once onto the grass the port wheel hit an obstruction and the undercarriage leg collapsed, the aircraft eventually coming to a stop on its port wing. XP747 had a lengthy lay off and did not fly again until February 1967. At Leuchars hangar space was soon being taken up by 23 Squadron's T.5 XS417, which was damaged Cat.3 in an explosion on the ground on 3 June. As the captain was going through his pre-start cockpit checks there was a loud bang, the forward equipment bay panels were blown off and there was extensive internal damage. It was considered that AVPIN vapour had been present due to bad drainage and lack of ventilation and that it had been ignited by the electrical installation.

Three days later another two-seat Lightning was damaged when T.4 XM971 of 226 OCU suffered a hot gas leak. A student pilot had been briefed for a re-heat take-off and climb, but at about 25,000 feet the aircraft yawed severely to starboard. The pilot applied full port rudder trim but this had no noticeable effect. He cancelled re-heat before levelling the aircraft at 31,000 feet but noticed that the No.1 engine nozzle was stuck between cruise and the Stage 1 re-heat position. He increased power on No.1 engine to 100 per cent but the nozzle did not move. As the aircraft began to yaw again he reduced No.1 engine power to slow/idle, issued a PAN call and recovered to base before making a precautionary landing. It was discovered that the No.1 re-heat pipe and the rear fuselage had been damaged by a hot gas leak.

Another tail scrape occurred on 27 June when a relatively inexperienced pilot on his first tour with 111 Squadron returned to Wattisham early after a radar malfunction in XR716. Rather than burn off fuel he elected to land at a high all-up weight despite the fact that the air was turbulent and there was a 20 knot crosswind. The result was that he landed heavily, short of the runway threshold and damaged the tail cone.

As far as 226 OCU was concerned, 1966 was proving to be a year to forget as another aircraft was lost on 1 July. Flying Officer Geoff Fish took off from Coltishall at 1602 hours in XS453 for a solo radar exercise with a Canberra but after the first attack the cockpit filled with smoke. On depressurising the cockpit the smoke disappeared and a return was made for a precautionary landing. After selecting airbrakes and flaps, however, Flying Officer Fish was unable to lower the undercarriage although the services pressure was normal. Having let Air Traffic know of his predicament the Tower was able to confirm that the undercarriage was only partially down. Eventually Fish was joined by another aircraft flown by Wing Commander Mick Swiney who watched as the T.5 was put through a series of manoeuvres, but although the undercarriage appeared to come down when 'g' was applied, it returned to its half-way position as soon as the 'g' was removed. The emergency lever for undercarriage operation was pulled but this had no effect.

By the time that fuel was down to 400lbs per side the decision was made to eject. A rescue helicopter was already in position near Cromer but after climbing to 10,000 feet Fish was advised to check his straps during which he noticed that one of the attachment lugs was not connected to the quick-release box. He was advised to go through the strapping-up procedure again and by the time this was complete he was very low on fuel and No.1 engine had flamed out. It was important for him to eject before No.2 engine did the same, thereby avoiding any control problems. In the event the ejection was entirely straightforward and he was picked up after spending a short time in the water.

The next barrier engagement occurred at Geilenkirchen on 6 July when Flight Lieutenant Rick McKnight of 92 Squadron lost his braking parachute when landing on a wet runway in XN768. The level of damage was consistent with previous incidents of this nature as the top cable cut into the fuselage spine. This accident was soon followed by the loss of another canopy, this time on XP741 of 111 Squadron. The incident occurred on 19 July when a pilot was conducting a practice QRA scramble at night. Having closed the canopy he went through his pre-take-off checks as he taxied out but missed the hood check. However, when he did the control checks, he monitored the AWP for a hydraulic warning and also checked that there was no canopy warning. Unfortunately during the take-off run the canopy lifted and broke away to hit the fin. After becoming airborne the pilot checked that the canopy handle was fully down and he then burnt off fuel before landing. When this incident was investigated it was found that the pilot had put the canopy handle down before the canopy had been fully closed.

The fifth Lightning write-off of the year took place off Seahouses on 24 August and involved XP760 flown by Flight Lieutenant Al Turley of 23 Squadron. Turley was an extremely experienced Lightning pilot having previously been on the staff of 226 OCU at Middleton St George. On this particular day he was to fly with Flight Lieutenant Tony Aldridge on a practice interception of four Hunters flying at 35,000 feet. It had previously been agreed that the pair would shut down their No.2 engines at a pre-determined altitude to conserve fuel before continuing the climb under GCI control. The Hunters were eventually picked up on the Lightning's AI radar but Turley had extreme difficulty in relighting his engine. After his third attempt the Reheat 1 and 2 fire captions illuminated and these were accompanied by the audio warnings. He throttled back No.1 engine and made an emergency call but his aircraft then pitched up violently to an angle of about 70 degrees. There was a dramatic loss of speed, which quickly led to a stall and spin. Despite his perilous situation Turley still tried to recover the aircraft and his natural curiosity in trying to understand what had happened nearly led to him delaying his ejection until it was too late. He eventually ejected at a height of 5,000 feet during which he sustained back injuries and was picked up by helicopter having spent about forty minutes in his dinghy.

On 22 August four Lightnings of 111 Squadron arrived in Akrotiri for a two-month detachment. All went well until 27 September when Flying Officer Graham Prichard became the next member of the Lightning fraternity to fly into the barrier on take-off in XR714. He was the No.4 in a stream take-off but the re-heat on the No.2 engine was unserviceable. Unbeknown to him the No.2 engine nozzle was also fully open so that when full dry power was selected the thrust was considerably less than it should have been; the cockpit nozzle indications were also unserviceable. As was normal on a stream take-off there was considerable turbulence generated by the aircraft ahead so that the strip airspeed indicator fluctuated dramatically, which forced Prichard to use the standby ASI up to a speed of 120 knots indicated. With the strip ASI showing 175 knots, Prichard lifted his aircraft off the ground, also noting the position that the Lightning ahead of him had become airborne and delaying his lift-off accordingly. Unfortunately his aircraft sank back onto the runway and once again the fuel in the ventral tank provided a spectacular, thankfully brief, trail of fire as the Lightning sped along the runway. As it did so Prichard was busy shutting down both engines, which he managed to do before the aircraft went into the barrier. He was completely unhurt in the incident and although XR714 was initially assessed as Cat.4, it was eventually made Cat.5 and was gradually stripped for spares before being dumped.

The first accident to involve a Lightning F.6 took place on 27 October at Binbrook when Captain J. Barr USAF of 5 Squadron ended up in the barrier in XR763, when his braking parachute failed after landing on a wet runway. On this occasion the level of damage was rather less than on previous occasions and it was assessed as Cat.2. The penultimate incident of the year occurred on 16 November shortly after Flight Lieutenant Dan Gurney of 23 Squadron had taken off for his first night solo in a F.3 (XP736). A fire warning led to a rapid return to base and a safe landing after just fifteen minutes in the air. On this occasion the warning had been the result of a hot gas leak between the engine and jet pipe, which was the result of a fatigue crack in the pipe.

The final accident of 1966 took place at Leconfield on 13 December when XM214 was on an air test following a major overhaul. On a previous air test by a test pilot from 60 MU the re-heat had worked satisfactorily but on a second air test in which the undercarriage operation was to be timed there was a sudden deceleration shortly after lift-off. At the time the test pilot had just pressed his stopwatch and was changing hands on the control column prior to writing the figure on his knee pad. Assuming that there had been a double re-heat auto cancellation, he pulled both throttles out of re-heat but, realising that the aircraft was about to settle back onto the runway, he selected full re-heat. The aircraft accelerated and climbed away but not before rubbing its tail and ventral tank on the runway surface. Once safely airborne the pilot jettisoned the ventral, carried out a handling check and completed a precautionary landing. Repairs took just over five months to complete and XM214 was returned to 226 OCU on 24 May 1967.

During 1966 the Lightning force had suffered a total of fifteen major accidents compared to nine in the previous year, but as total hours had increased to 28,263 the rate per 10,000 flying hours was not significantly higher at 5.3. In contrast the accident rate for the Javelin worsened once again with eighteen majors in 16,290 hours, resulting in an overall rate of 11.0. In terms of cost, however, each Lightning that was written off cost £606,000 compared to £260,000 for each Javelin. The majority of major accidents on the Lightning were put down to pilot error at 49 per cent with the rest attributable to technical defects and other causes. In 1966 the Hunter force flew a total of 45,628 hours with twenty-one majors resulting in an accident rate of 4.6. During the year three Hunters were written off at a cost of £101,000 apiece. Although its safety record bore favourable comparison with other types, the number of special occurrence reports that had to be issued for the Lightning was significantly higher. On average, thirty-eight reports were raised on the Lightning per 10,000 flying hours, which compared with fifteen on the Hunter and twenty-two on the Javelin. About 80 per cent of all SORs raised for the Lightning and Javelin were for technical issues with the remainder comprising servicing and pilot errors and hazards.

The first major accident of 1967 occurred on 2 January when T.4 XM971 of 226 OCU crashed not long after taking off from Coltishall. The aircraft was under the command of Squadron Leader Terry Carlton with Flight Lieutenant Tony Gross as student. The following is the account of the flight as submitted by Flight Lieutenant Gross to the Board of Inquiry:

On the 2nd of January at 1200 hrs I was briefed by my instructor, S/L Carlton, for a dual radar exercise in Lightning XM971. Before walking out to the aircraft my instructor and I were informed by the squadron operations officer that the aircraft XM971 had experienced nose-wheel shimmy on take-off on the previous sortie. I then carried out the pre-flight external checks, which were satisfactory. Having read that morning a Fighter Command Flight Safety article on the subject of foreign object damage I paid particular attention to the main air intake including the radar bullet. I then strapped in and carried out the normal checks before starting, started the engines and taxied to Runway 22. The AI.23 radar was switched on before starting engines. We took off on Runway 22 and at about 500 feet I switched on the radar transmitter but I did not look at the B Scope at this point. During the take-off when the nose-wheel was on the ground we experienced moderate nose-wheel shimmy which continued during retraction of the undercarriage but ceased when the undercarriage was locked up.

I climbed on a heading of 360 degrees with all cockpit indications normal. At about 8,000 feet I unfolded the AI visor, switched from auto-range to AI, selected search on the long-range scale and the presentation appeared to be normal. Very shortly afterwards I heard a sharp explosion, which came from the front of the aircraft. S/L Carlton immediately took control of the aircraft, throttled back and turned towards Coltishall. I checked the engine indications and they were normal at idle/fast idle. A short discussion followed and we agreed that the most probable cause of the explosion was a burst nose-wheel and S/L Carlton informed the approach controller that we were returning to base.

During the descent I selected AI transmitter off, auto-range mode and then the main AI switch to off. I looked at the B scope and saw the picture collapse into the left-hand bottom corner. The picture normally takes up to fifteen seconds to collapse but I got the impression on this occasion that it collapsed almost immediately after switching off. Also during the descent I remember my instructor checking both engines up to about 85 per cent and the engine indications were normal. We continued the descent at idle/fast idle and at about 3,000 feet S/L Carlton told the local controller of our intention to fly past the Tower for a visual check of the aircraft, especially the nose-wheel. At this time the rate of descent was reduced and at 250 knots I lowered the flaps, and at 220 knots I lowered the undercarriage. Operation of these services was satisfactory and S/L Carlton informed the local controller that we had three green lights.

At about 1,000 feet S/L Carlton levelled the aircraft and opened the throttles. S/L Carlton then said 'I am having trouble with the No.1 engine'. I noticed the throttle fairly well open but the rpm was only about 70 per cent. I then looked at the No.2 engine JPT gauge and noticed the needle showing maximum gauge reading. The speed was still falling and we were losing height. S/L Carlton transmitted a brief Mayday call and advised the local controller that we would have to eject. I attempted to tighten my lap straps and S/L Carlton ordered me to eject. I reached for the top handle and failed to grasp it at the first attempt but quickly located it and pulled the blind. The ejection sequence worked correctly and I landed safely. I realised that I had hurt my back during the ejection and I believe this may have been due to the fact that I deliberately moved my kidney pad slightly to fit under the rubber roll of my immersion suit when strapping in for reasons of comfort. I was wearing a Mk.1 helmet, immersion suit, anti-g suit and Mae West and leg restraint garters.

Squadron Leader Terry Carlton described the last moments of the flight as follows:

At about 1,500 feet I started to level off for a downwind circuit height of 1,000 feet. Simultaneously I opened up the No.1 engine to parallel it with the No.2. As I opened the No.1 engine I noticed the JPT rising rapidly past about 700 degrees C with scarcely any increase in rpm. I immediately throttled back the No.1 engine to control the JPT. I then opened up the No.2 engine from about 75 to 80 per cent and its JPT rose rapidly towards the limit of the gauge with again scarcely any increase in rpm. These were the only indications of engine malfunctions. There were no other warnings present at any time. At about 1,200 feet I told F/L Gross to prepare himself for a possible ejection. The speed was falling and the nose trim was fully up. With the speed still falling through about 180 knots I raised the flap to reduce drag but the speed continued to fall. At about 1,000 feet with the speed falling through 175 knots I transmitted a Mayday call on local frequency informing the Tower that I was about to bale out. I ordered F/L Gross to bale out, which he did at 700 feet and 170 knots. When he was clear of the aircraft I baled out at an estimated 500 feet and 160 knots. My ejection was perfectly satisfactory, and apart from coming down uncomfortably close to some high tension cables, it was uneventful.

The crash site was two-and-a-half miles east of Coltishall. The aircraft had come down in an approximately level attitude although shortly before hitting the ground it had clipped a tree that detached the starboard aileron and damaged the wing tip. On impact the aircraft disintegrated and there was a substantial post-crash fire. However the cockpit section remained largely intact as it had broken off at the transport joint at the cockpit rear pressure bulkhead. This meant that the radar bullet pressurisation installation in the forward equipment compartment was undamaged and could be examined.

Although the pilots had suspected that the nose-wheel had burst, examination of the wreckage showed this to be intact but that the radome was missing and the AI scanner was damaged. The radome was eventually found 7 miles from the crash site. The compressor blades of both engines showed damage consistent with the entry of loose articles and it was also noted that the exhaust units and jet pipes of both engines were coated with fused aluminium deposits, which indicated that severe damage to the compressors had occurred before the crash. Pieces of the AI radar scanner were also found in the engine compressors.

It was concluded that the accident had been caused by over-pressurisation of the radar bullet and detachment of the radome due to overstressing (the overpressurisation was the result of defects in the reducing valve and pressure relief valve). The loss of power on both engines resulted from damage caused by the entry of debris from the radar scanner into the engine compressors. It was also noted that the radar bullet had been changed twice in the two weeks immediately before the accident. At the time of the crash XM971 had flown a total of 689 hours.

Two months later there was another Lightning loss when F.3 XP699 of 56 Squadron crashed on 3 March. The pilot was Flying Officer Stuart Pearse who had been involved in a landing accident at Wattisham the previous year when both main wheels had locked and he hit obstacles after leaving the runway. This accident was altogether more life-threatening, however Pearse was able to eject safely and later gave evidence to the Board of Inquiry;

At about 1300 hrs on Friday, 3 March 1967 I was briefed to fly Lightning F.3 XP699. S/L Stuart-Paul, my flight commander, briefed me to carry out a flight re-fuelling and practice interception sortie. S/L Stuart-Paul himself authorised the flight and at about 1330 hrs I walked out to the aircraft. I took off at about 1345 hrs. I climbed out to meet my tanker aircraft and carried out one wet and six dry contacts. Finally I took on a full load of fuel and left the tanker. I then carried out a practice interception with another Lightning as target. As I was closing in on my target the AC failure light appeared on the auxiliary warning panel. I took the normal action and when I pressed the AC reset button the AC came back on line. At about this time I noticed that my ventral tank was slow to feed, and because of my position I decided to re-join the tanker aircraft. Having re-joined the tanker I took on a full load of fuel. On this occasion the sequence in which the tanks filled up as indicated to me by the refuelling lights was unusual in that the flap lights stayed on after all the other lights had gone out.

I came back towards the Wattisham Dive Circle and re-filled before descending. The re-fuelling light indications were as on the last re-fuelling. Because I suspected a non-feeding ventral I did a slow let-down at 250 knots. At 10,000 feet I cycled the undercarriage in an attempt to clear the ventral valve. After this the ventral appeared to feed correctly. I carried out a GCA and remained in the Wattisham circuit until the ventral was empty. I then asked for a practice crash diversion to Wethersfield. This went entirely according to plan and I eventually overshot about one mile from the threshold of runway 28 at Wethersfield. On overshooting I opened up the throttles to about 90 per cent and selected airbrakes in and flaps and undercarriage up. At about one third of the way down the runway and at about 400 feet above ground level I opened up the throttles to full cold power. As the No.1 throttle reached the full cold power stop, it slipped into reheat. As the No.1 throttle was in the reheat position, I advanced it to the full reheat position as this is the approved method for handling the reheat.

At this stage I commenced a starboard turn, the reheat had stabilised, and about five seconds after the initial selection, I cancelled reheat. Both the selection and cancellation of reheat were normal. At this time I was at about 1,000 feet above ground and at approximately 325 knots. About one second after cancelling reheat, the Fire 2 attention-getters and bells and the Fire 2 extinguisher button came on. I cancelled the attention-getters. I then moved the throttles to idle/fast idle and moved the No.2 throttle to the high pressure cock closed position. I was about to select the No.2 fuel cock switch to the closed position when the attention-getters came on and the bells sounded. On looking at the standard warning panel I found that I now had a Reheat 1 warning in addition to the Fire 2 warning. At this stage I looked at my engine instruments, it was a quick glance and I gained the impression that the No.1 and

No.2 jet pipe temperature gauges were in a position, which would correspond to temperatures of 650 degrees C and 550 degrees C respectively.

My recollections of my actions are rather confused but to the best of my knowledge my next action was to press the No.2 fire extinguisher button. Whilst waiting to see if the Fire 2 caption would go out I noticed that the Fire 1 caption and Fire 1 extinguisher button had come on. Since the Reheat 1 caption had illuminated, the attention-getters had been flashing and the bells sounding continuously. At this stage I felt I had no option but to abandon the aircraft. My last impression was that I had the following lights on – both fire extinguisher switch lights, Fire 1 and Fire 2 captions and Reheat 1. Just before I abandoned the aircraft I made the following call on the radio 'Three nine, aircraft on fire, abandoning aircraft'. I cannot recall which frequency I was on for certain, but it must have been either Wethersfield GCA frequency or Wattisham approach frequency.

When I started the ejection sequence my height was approximately 1,500 feet and speed 300 knots. I initiated the ejection sequence by pulling the seat pan firing handle. I was aware of a rush of air and an impression that the canopy lifted only about 2 inches and then I blacked out. Just before I blacked out I had the impression that the aircraft had entered cloud. My next recollection was hanging in the parachute and just emerging from the bottom of cloud. I saw the aeroplane about 150 yards from me and level with me. The aircraft flew past me from left to right, wallowing, and with a nose-up attitude. The aircraft then descended below me and fell towards the ground like a falling leaf. As it flew past me I saw black smoke of a medium density coming from the jet pipe area. The smoke was like that of an American aircraft taking off. I saw no flames coming from any part of the aircraft on the way down until it hit the ground. I parachuted down safely into a ploughed field about 200 yards upwind from the now crashed aircraft.

The ejection was not straightforward as during the ejection sequence and parachute deployment damage was caused to the drogue box and the pilot's helmet; Flying Officer Pearse suffered minor head injuries as a result. His parachute was severely torn during deployment but, thankfully, it did not affect his safe descent.

The Board of Inquiry found that the accident was caused by a fuel leak in the No.2 engine bay. This was then ignited when it came into contact with a hot spot in the No.2 engine bay and was responsible for the Fire 2 warning. The burning fuel then found its way along known paths from the No.2 engine bay to the No.1 reheat area and also the No.1 engine bay. This initiated the Reheat 1 and Fire 1 warnings. The AIB report into this accident showed that the leak had come from a fatigue fracture of a fuel-draulic pipe to No.2 engine. As the fuel in this pipe was pressurised to some 2,000 psi any crack would lead to a very serious leak of fuel. It was also noted that the spontaneous ignition temperature of aviation kerosene in an enclosed and inadequately ventilated space could be as low as 214 degrees C.

Following the leak in the No.2 engine bay, fuel could easily drain into the No.1 engine bay and reheat area via inadequate sealing of fire zones and openings for control rods and pipes, etc. This leakage of fluid from one engine zone to another in the Lightning was not unknown and ignition of this free fuel was considered to be the reason for the fire warnings in both engine compartments. In places the tone of the AIB report showed a certain amount of exasperation at the situation with the Lightning with reference to yet another fire resulting in abandonment and loss of the aircraft. It was also noted that RAF records showed that there had been fifty-five cases of fire in Lightning aircraft since 1964 and twenty-two of these had been attributed to fuel or hydraulic oil leaks. Due to the various points of high temperature that existed in each engine bay the ignition of any free kerosene or hydraulic oil was almost a certainty. It was also a fact that, with the existing fire extinguishing system, fires in both engine bays at the same time could not be dealt with effectively. The fire extinguishers could only be used in one engine bay or the other and no extinguisher was provided for the hot jet pipe areas.

The AIB report also mentioned that the fuel-draulic pipe to No.2 engine in the Lightning had given repeated trouble in service due to fuel leakages, mainly at the welded joints. Although a modified pipe had been introduced (Lightning modification 4200 introduced a one-piece steel pipe that had increased flexibility and eliminated the rigid elbow connections), the AIB questioned whether this would be an effective remedy. Their concern was down to the fact that the pipe needed to be stressed so that it could be fitted and the suggestion was put forward that this built-in stress was likely to contribute to and accelerate fatigue cracking. The vibrations and pressure pulses that also contributed to fatigue were also still present. In the case of XP699 there had been six instances of fuel leaks from the fuel-draulic flexible pipe on No.2 engine between August and November 1966. On each occasion the pipe failed after a short life and was replaced. It was a Fighter Command requirement that checks for leaks be made after every turn-round and after flight servicing. At the time of the accident mod.4200 had not been embodied on XP669.

In the case of the accident to XP699 no control problems were experienced that could be attributed to the engine fire, but the AIB said that it was disturbing that the aluminium control rod to the Power Control Unit for the tailplane was still a feature of the Lightning. This passed through fire zone 3, the hot jet pipe, which was a non-fireproof area. The consequences of failure of this rod had been dramatically demonstrated on 13 December 1962 when test pilot George Aird had been forced to eject from XG332 on the approach to Hatfield. On this occasion an engine fire had resulted in failure of the control rod to the tailplane and this had caused the aircraft to pitch up violently. Aird ejected at very low level and survived albeit, with two broken legs having landed in the middle of a large greenhouse. The accident to XG332 was similar in many respects to that of Al Turley in XP760 on 24 August 1966. Even though this potential problem had been identified five years before, modification work comprising a steel rod and fittings instead of aluminium alloy (which was likely to fail in a very short time when attacked by fire) had yet to be implemented for all Lightning aircraft.

The next Lightning accident took place at Coltishall on 7 March when T.5 XS454 of 226 OCU was landing after a radar exercise. The aircraft was being flown by Flight Lieutenant Mike Graydon with Flight Lieutenant Bob Offord as instructor. After a ground controlled approach a landing was carried out, which at first appeared to be normal but as the braking parachute was deployed the main undercarriage legs began to retract. Although they did not retract completely the aircraft ended up sliding along the runway on its ventral tank. The engines were shut down and gradually the Lightning began to swing to the right, eventually coming to a halt just off the runway. Although the damage was assessed as Cat.3 it would be another six months before XS454 was back with the unit. At Binbrook XM164 of the Fighter Command Trials Unit lost its canopy on take-off on 17 March resulting in Cat.3 damage. FCTU had taken over the duties of the Air Fighting Development Squadron, which had been disbanded on 1 February 1966.

On 17 April there was another case of a serious fuel leak on a Lightning. This involved XM184 of 226 OCU, which was being flown by Flight Lieutenant Gerry Crumbie who had been chosen as the display pilot for the OCU. Having carried out a practice aerobatic display in clear airspace he returned to Coltishall, but on checking his fuel state he noticed an asymmetry of 600lb, so throttled back on the engine that had the lower reading. When he joined the circuit at Coltishall the runway controller saw that the Lightning was trailing what appeared to be white vapour and this was still evident when the aircraft landed. By the time that it was halfway down the runway, smoke and flames could be seen coming from the port side of the rear fuselage. Flight Lieutenant Crumbie was advised of this but almost at the same time Fire 1 and Reheat 1 and 2 warnings appeared on the standard warning panel. After stopping his aircraft, Crumbie shut down the engines before pressing the No.1 engine fire extinguisher button, switching off all the electrics and jumping down to the ground. As XM184 was not fitted with Firestreak missiles Crumbie was faced with a straight drop of about 12 feet and slightly injured a foot on landing, although this did not stop him putting as much distance as possible in the shortest amount of time between himself and his burning aircraft. The conflagration was put out by the station crash crews but the fire damage was such that XM184 never flew again and was eventually stripped for spares.

Not all fire warnings were caused by fuel leaks, as was demonstrated to a pilot of 29 Squadron on 21 July when flying XP694. No.29 Squadron had begun to fly Lightnings on 10 May 1967. During the climb out on a training flight he received a Reheat 1 caption on the standard warning panel. He immediately closed the No.1 engine HP cock but the light remained on and he was about to jettison the ventral tank when it finally went out. The aircraft was returned to Wattisham and, apart from the braking parachute failing to deploy, it was landed without further incident. An investigation was carried out and it was found that there had been a hot gas leak caused by a crack in a welded seam in the jet pipe. It was noted that this type of failure was not unusual and was most likely the result of local stress conditions brought about by vibration of a very high frequency.

Having suffered damage to its tail in a heavy landing the previous year, XR716 of 111 Squadron was involved in a similar accident on 31

August. The post-flight inspection of the aircraft revealed that the tail bumper had been pushed up into the rear fuselage. Further investigation showed that the base of fuselage frame 62 was dented to a depth of ¾ inch and distorted to a distance of 6 inches. Both bumper support beams and the bumper carrier plate were also distorted. Repairs were carried out on site and took three-and-a-half months to complete.

In the space of six days in early September two more Lightnings were to be lost including the first F.6. This was XR766 of 23 Squadron, which crashed in the North Sea about 50 miles east-north-east of Leuchars on 7 September. At the time it was being flown by Squadron Leader Ron Blackburn who had already successfully completed a supersonic practice interception when he was asked if he would act as a target for another Lightning flown by Flying Officer Paul Reynolds. Both aircraft were at 34,000 feet and, to make the exercise as realistic as possible Squadron Leader Blackburn commenced a hard evading turn to port using full cold power. When IAS had reduced to 250 knots the nose of the aircraft was allowed to fall below the horizon and a downward aileron turn was performed. At 25,000 feet, at an IAS of about 210 knots, the wings were levelled and back pressure applied to the control column to reduce the rate of descent. At this stage the nose of the aircraft pitched up sharply and yawed to the right. The controls were centralised but this action failed to prevent the aircraft from entering a spin to the left at about 22,000 feet.

Squadron Leader Blackburn took the normal spin recovery action but the aircraft failed to respond. After two or three turns with the controls in the normal spin recovery position, full pro-spin control was applied for two turns, after which full anti-spin control was again applied for two or three turns. Finally, in an attempt to break the stability of the spin, in-spin and out-spin aileron was adopted for three or four turns, but again without success. By this time the aircraft was approaching 8,000 feet and Squadron Leader Blackburn made the decision to eject. Having announced his intention by R/T he grasped the face blind handle and abandoned his aircraft, which continued to spin until it hit the sea. Blackburn was eventually picked up safely by helicopter after spending nearly an hour in his dinghy. The Board of Inquiry was of the opinion that the aircraft might have been saved if the controls had been held in the spin recovery position for longer than two or three turns, although there was nothing in Pilot's Notes at the time to suggest that this might be the case. Ron Blackburn later described the spin as being flat, with the nose very near to the horizon, which might explain the aircraft's reluctance to come out of the spin.

By now some of the older Lightning F.1s had been modified to act as supersonic targets and several had been delivered to Target Facilities Flights (TFF), which had been set up at Lightning bases. One such was XM136, which had previously flown with AFDS, 74 Squadron and 226 OCU and was now with the Wattisham TFF. By 13 September it had flown 742 hours but was to be the next to suffer from an in-flight fire which was now becoming an increasingly serious problem for the safe operation of Lightning aircraft.

At the time of the accident the aircraft was being flown by Flight Lieutenant Jock Sneddon, who had been briefed to act as target so that another Lightning could carry out a high-level subsonic practice interception. After take-off the aircraft was climbed to 26,000 feet at 100 per cent rpm (full cold power) and for the remainder of the climb to 36,000 feet the power was reduced to 95 per cent rpm. About two minutes after levelling at 36,000 feet the attention-getters and bells activated and the Reheat 1 caption came on. No.1 engine was closed down and the fuel to that engine was switched off before Flight Lieutenant Sneddon made a PAN call. He then made a hard descending turn to port through 360 degrees with airbrakes out and No.2 engine throttled back to idling rpm, but he could see no external evidence of fire. During the turn he noted that the readings on the JPT gauges to both engines were normal. He was just about to consider jettisoning the ventral tank when the attention-getters and bells came on once more to announce a Reheat 2 warning.

By this time the aircraft was at 12,000 feet and Flight Lieutenant Sneddon made a radio call announcing his attention of flying towards the coast where he said he would eject. With the airbrakes out, No.1 engine flamed out and No.2 engine at idling rpm, he put his aircraft into a gentle climb and decided that he would eject when indicated airspeed had reduced to 250 knots. Shortly afterwards the port wing dropped, the rate of roll being similar to an out-of-trim condition, which had existed at the top of the climb and which had been corrected by a combination of rudder and aileron trim. On attempting to correct the wing drop, Sneddon also made a fore-and-aft movement on the control column, during which he discovered that control to the tailplane had been lost. The attitude of the aircraft became progressively more nose up and the angle of bank increased to 45 to 50 degrees. By now indicated airspeed had dropped to 260 knots and Sneddon successfully ejected himself by means of the seat pan firing handle.

Although XM136 came down on land, the wreckage was extensively damaged by fire which made it impossible to determine the precise cause of the fire in the air. However, from examining the remains, it appeared that there had been an intense fuel fire in the fuselage area just forward of frame 57 and that this fire had burned through the control rod to the tailplane. It is interesting to note that once again there had been a significant pitch up when control had been lost. In its report on the accident to XP699 the AIB stated that when the control rod to the tailplane failed, the power control input valve, which was spring-loaded, did not fail safe. In fact the tailplane was immediately and automatically powered to an extreme angle (aircraft nose up) with consequent loss of control. During the investigation into the loss of XM136 the power control unit was found to be at this extreme limit. The AIB also made mention of Pilot's Notes in which Lightning pilots were recommended to 'look for signs of fire, i.e. smoke, flame, control system malfunction, etc', concluding that this was unreasonable if a pilot received a Reheat 1 warning or a persistent fire warning on his panel. It was also stated that it was against design requirements that an essential flying control rod should pass through a non-fireproof area.

A rather unfortunate, and completely unnecessary, accident took place on 26 October when four of 23 Squadron's Lightning F.6s were operating from Sola in Norway. As Flying Officer Tony Ellender was taxiing along the side of the runway in XR725 his aircraft began to sink through the concrete surface to a depth of 30 inches causing damage to the port undercarriage and part of the fuselage. It transpired that only the centre part of the runway was to be used but this information had not been passed on to the RAF detachment. An airbag was used to prevent the aircraft sinking deeper and thus causing further damage and it was eventually lifted out by a crane. After inspection it was discovered that the amount of damage was not as great as had been feared and temporary repairs allowed XR725 to be flown back to Leuchars a week later (wheels down) where a permanent fix was made.

On 31 October the Wattisham barrier was in use again when XP741 of 111 Squadron was returning from a night sortie. Weather conditions were not good with a crosswind component from the port side of almost 15 knots and a wet runway. The aircraft touched down within 100 yards of the threshold at around 155 knots IAS and at first the amount of braking action appeared to be as expected. By the time the halfway point in the runway had been reached, however, the level of deceleration was not what it should have been and the pilot was having increasing difficulty in preventing the aircraft from weather-cocking into wind. With about 500 yards remaining the Lightning was getting dangerously close to the left-hand edge of the runway and the pilot decided to jettison the brake parachute. Although the aircraft stayed on the runway the pilot had no choice but to engage the barrier at a speed of around 70 knots, which caused Cat.3 damage.

The final Lightning incidents of 1967 involved a tail scrape on landing to XP754 of 111 Squadron on 28 November and another canopy departure on take-off the following month. The latter incident took place at Leuchars on 14 December when Captain Frank Pieri USMC of 23 Squadron was taking off at night in XR767. The usual procedure after this type of accident was for a team to enter the runway to retrieve the canopy and any debris before the aircraft was recovered, but on this occasion there was no sign of the canopy. When the aircraft eventually landed it was discovered that the hood had managed to wrap itself around the leading edge of the fin, to which it was firmly attached.

During 1967 there had been a total of thirteen major accidents to Lightning aircraft, which was a reduction on the previous year when there had been fifteen. There were five accidents in which aircraft were completely written off (the same as 1966) but there were no fatalities. Due to the fact that total flying hours were significantly higher at 36,000, the overall accident rate for the year was down at 3.6. This compared with an accident rate of 5.9 for the Hunter and 6.2 for the Javelin. In fact the accident rate for the Lightning had fallen below that of the Gnat T.1 advanced trainer, which for 1967 was 4.5. Although the reduction in the accident rate for the Lightning was encouraging, the number of aircraft rendered Cat.5 was becoming a concern, as were the number of in-flight fires and fire warnings. It would not be long before problems posed by this type of hazard would begin to threaten the viability of the Lightning force and lead to questions as to how long it could continue in its role as the UK's premier interceptor.

Chapter 4

The Lightning Worldwide

By the beginning of 1968 the Lightning force had reached its peak with nine operational squadrons and the OCU. No.11 Squadron was re-formed on the Lightning F.6 at Leuchars on 1 April 1967 and, as has already been mentioned, 29 Squadron became the last Lightning unit when it came into being at Wattisham on 10 May 1967. Although it had been designed primarily as a point defence interceptor to protect the UK from attack by bombers armed with nuclear weapons, the Lightning was now capable of being operated anywhere in the world. No.74 Squadron was now based at Tengah in Singapore, from where it would deploy as far as Australia, and 56 Squadron had moved to Akrotiri in Cyprus in May 1967 to become part of Near East Air Force. In RAF Germany Nos.19 and 92 Squadrons were based at Gutersloh near the border with East Germany as part of 2nd Allied Tactical Air Force. The UK-based squadrons comprised Nos.11 and 23 at Leuchars, No.5 Squadron at Binbrook and Nos. 29 and 111 Squadrons at Wattisham. In addition there were Target Facilities Flights at Binbrook, Leuchars and Wattisham that operated small numbers of Lightning F.1s to provide targets for the resident squadrons.

From the flight safety aspect 1968 got off to a bad start as there were four major Lightning accidents in January alone. The first accident took place on the 9th and was another case of a failed take-off. This one took place at Geilenkirchen and involved F.2 XN728 of 92 Squadron. Two weeks later the unit moved to Gutersloh to join 19 Squadron. The pilot was Flight Lieutenant (later Air Chief Marshal Sir) David Cousins and the take-off run appeared normal up to the point of lift off, the engines having been set to 100 per cent cold power. The aircraft became airborne at 170 knots IAS but shortly after selecting undercarriage up Cousins became aware that it was settling back onto the runway. A quick check of the engine instruments showed that the rpm for No.2 engine was dropping below 70 per cent. As was becoming customary in this type of accident the ventral tank split and left a fiery trail as the

Lightning sped along the runway before eventually coming to a stop. The level of damage was rated as Cat.4 and repairs were carried out at Warton where the opportunity was taken to convert the aircraft to F.2A standard. At the time of writing this aircraft is a familiar landmark, although perhaps not for much longer, on the A1 where it crosses the East Coast Main Line near Newark.

The next in this sequence of accidents occurred on 16 January and was another barrier engagement at Wattisham. The pilot on this occasion was Flying Officer Dave Bramley of 29 Squadron who was returning to base at night in XP765 after a practice diversion to Manston. Almost everything conspired against Flying Officer Bramley as there was a strong crosswind and the runway was also flooded. He then suffered a braking parachute failure and this was compounded by defective wheel braking. Despite the fact that the Lightning went into the barrier at a relatively slow speed substantial damage was caused, in particular to the fuselage spine. The next day another Lightning T.5 of 226 OCU (XS423) had its undercarriage collapse on landing at Coltishall in similar fashion to the accident to XS454 the previous year.

The last Lightning accident in January 1968 took place on the 24th when F.6 XS900 of 5 Squadron crashed 6 miles south-east of Lossiemouth. The pilot was Flight Lieutenant Stuart Miller who had just taken off to return to Leuchars, but as he pulled into a climb his aircraft was shaken by two loud bangs and the attention-getters announced a Fire 1 warning. Cancelling reheat on both engines, Miller shut down No.1 engine and manoeuvred his aircraft back towards Lossiemouth as he activated the fire extinguisher. By now the Lightning was in a dive, but as the control column was moved back there was no response. The dive gradually became steeper and as a progressive stiffening of the control column could be felt Miller decided that his only course of action was to eject. He abandoned his aircraft by using the face blind handle and landed safely. During the take-off run a number of ground observers had noticed that XS900 appeared to be venting fuel from somewhere near the ventral tank. In addition there was a glow in the jet pipe area indicative of a fire. Although much of the evidence was destroyed when the aircraft crashed it was thought that a fuel leak had resulted in a fire in No.1 engine and this had eventually led to failure of the control rod to the tailplane causing loss of control in the pitching plane.

The Lightning F.6 was powered by two Rolls Royce Avon 301 turbojets each rated at 12,690lb, static thrust or 16,360lb, in reheat.

XG312 of the development batch was used for trials of the Lightning's AI.23 radar.

A Lightning F.1 displays shock wave formation when flying at near-sonic speed at low level.

Lightning F.1A XM183 of 56 Squadron after one of its two barrier engagements.

A Firestreak missile is hoisted into place on a Lightning F.1 of 74 Squadron.

Nosewheel malfunctions caused a number of accidents. This is Lightning F.2 XN774 of 19 Squadron which was brought down on a foam-covered runway at Leconfield on 15 October 1963.

Lightning F.1A XM191 of 111 Squadron which was damaged Cat.5 on 9 June 1964 after an engine fire.

A neat echelon formation of Lightning F.1As of 56 Squadron.

The ghosting effect of gun firing is demonstrated by Lightning F.1A XM214. This aircraft was damaged Cat.3 on 13 December 1966 when the tailcone and ventral fuel tank came into contact with the runway on take off.

Lightning F.1A XM171 before delivery to 56 Squadron. This aircraft had an in-flight fire in the No.2 engine on 5 March 1965 but it was successfully extinguished and a safe landing was made.

Lightning T.4 XM973 suffered an undercarriage collapse at Binbrook on 22 January 1963.

The remains of Lightning F.3 XP704 of 74 Squadron which crashed at Leuchars on 28 August 1964. The pilot, Flight Lieutenant Glyn Owen, was killed.

A close up of the nose markings of Lightning F.2 XN769 of 92 Squadron.

The tail and fuselage spine of 92 Squadron Lightnings were painted dark blue.

Lightning F.2s of 92 Squadron.

A formation break by Lightning F.3s of 23 Squadron. The nearest aircraft (XP751) survived until 22 October 1986 when it had an engine fire during service with the LTF. Although it was landed safely, it was not flown again.

A view of the shattered remains of Lightning T.4 XM971 of 226 OCU which crashed on 2 January 1967.

After Lightning F.3 XP699 crashed due to an in-flight fire on 3 March 1967, all that remained was the tail section.

A Lightning F.3 of 74 Squadron low over the sea.

Lightning F.6s and a T.5 of 5 Squadron at a typically wet Binbrook.

Lightning F.6 XR761 of 5 Squadron. This aircraft was lost on 8 November 1984 due to an in-flight fire. The pilot, Flight Lieutenant Mike Hale, ejected safely.

After surviving a barrier entry on 19 August 1963 with 74 Squadron, Lightning F.1 XM145 went on to serve with the Leuchars TFF.

During its service life the Lightning T.5 was constantly plagued with undercarriage problems. XS418 is seen at Stradishall on 23 August 1968 after the starboard leg collapsed on landing.

F.1 XM147 of the Wattisham TFF was one of a number of Lightnings to lose its rudder in flight. This incident occurred on 27 November 1969.

XM147 ended its days as a decoy at Wattisham before being used as a target at Pendine ranges.

The tail section of Lightning F.6 XS896 of 74 Squadron which crashed at Tengah after an engine fire on 12 September 1968.

Lightning F.1A XM169 is seen here with 23 Squadron in 1973 for TFF duties.

After serving with 56 Squadron, Lightning F.1A XM180 flew with 226 OCU.

Although it is seen here in the markings of 226 OCU (65 Sqn), F.1A XM189 had an excursion off the runway during a night take off on 19 January 1962 when with 111 Squadron.

Lightning F.3 XP703 of 29 Squadron takes to the grass at Wattisham.

F.3 XR751 of the LTF during an aerobatic display at Waddington in 1980

Seen at Mildenhall in 1981 with 11 Squadron, T.5 XS417 later served with the LTF and was involved in a landing accident on 13 March 1984 in which a tyre burst and the ventral tank was ripped off.

Lightning F.6 XR773 was the first aircraft to experience an engine titanium fire on 22 February 1968 when serving with 74 Squadron at Tengah.

Although the Avon was an extremely reliable engine it did have certain problems, one of which led to an accident involving XR773 of 74 Squadron on 22 February. The aircraft was being flown by Flying Officer Trevor MacDonald Bennett, who had just returned to the squadron after a serious road accident and although he had been cleared to fly, he was still not 100 per cent fit. Indeed this was to be his first sortie in an F.6 for more than six months. The intention was for him to fly a practice diversion to Changi, which was to be followed by aerobatics and general handling before returning to Tengah. When he was on the approach to Changi, however, he felt a severe vibration and noticed that the No.1 engine rpm was dropping rapidly with an associated rise in the jet pipe temperature. He then heard a loud bang (described in the accident report as a 'positive clank') and assumed, correctly, that the engine had seized. The HP and LP fuel cocks for No.1 engine were closed but there was no indication of fire on the cockpit warning panel.

Flying Officer MacDonald Bennett landed safely at Changi despite the fact that he did not have the services of a braking parachute as the doors for this were operated hydraulically via No.1 engine. Shortly after landing large quantities of white smoke issued from the air intake and the No.1 engine jet pipe and flames could be seen in the region of the ventral tank. The emergency services were soon in action and the fire was attacked from all directions and put out. After the aircraft was recovered No.1 engine was removed for inspection. A number of torched holes could be seen in the compressor outlet casing and it was suspected that there had been a titanium fire in the rear stages of the compressor. When the vibration was first noticed the Lightning had been in the air for about thirty minutes, was at an altitude of 1,000 feet with the No.1 engine rpm in the range 90 to 95 per cent.

A more thorough examination of the failed engine confirmed that a titanium fire had occurred in the rear of the compressor and as a result the engine was damaged beyond repair. The fire had not been contained within the engine and a total of fifteen holes were burned in the compressor casing. The primary cause of the fire was the fatigue failure of a stage 5 titanium stator blade due to high stress levels. This had caused severe secondary damage in the rear of the engine which had then been further damaged by fire. Although there had been four previous cases of failure of a stage 5 stator blade in the Avon 301 this was the first confirmed case of a titanium fire. Avon Mod 3497

introduced steel blades for stator stages 5 and 6 instead of titanium to
reduce blade deflection in operation and give increased fatigue life.

Towards the end of March there were two incidents in quick succession
involving Lightning T.5s of 226 OCU. The first was yet another
undercarriage failure, this time affecting XS455, the accident taking
place at Wattisham on the 25th when Flight Lieutenants Chris Rowe
and Tony Gross were landing. After touch-down the port undercarriage
collapsed and the aircraft went off the side of the runway. This was
the third such incident and was to result in a temporary grounding of
the T.5 as the undercarriages on all aircraft were checked. Flying was
allowed to resume on the 28th but the day after there was a rather
different type of emergency involving XS457. As the aircraft was taking
off it was heard making a strange noise and appeared to be trailing
smoke. The noise was eventually heard by the crew and on reaching
25,000 feet the No.1 engine was set to idle. Not long after an explosion
occurred and the Fire 1 and Reheat 1 warning captions came on. No.1
engine was shut down and after a short period of time the warning
lights went out and a safe landing was made at Coltishall. The fire was
caused by a fuel leak and considerable damage was caused to systems
in the No.1 engine bay.

The next Lightning incident also involved a fire warning and took
place on 3 April. As XP749 of 111 Squadron was climbing through 7,000
feet the pilot received a Reheat 2 warning. However, after No.2 engine
was throttled back, the light went out and the return to Wattisham was
without further incident. It transpired that a hot gas leak had occurred
as a result of failure of a welded seam in the reheat pipe and that this
had caused damage to the airframe. Repairs were carried out on site
and XP749 was returned for service towards the end of July. On the
same day Flying Officer Vic Lockwood of 5 Squadron was flying XS926
when, shortly after take off, he received a warning that there was a fire
in the No.1 engine bay. He immediately carried out the appropriate
emergency drills and the fire was extinguished. As his aircraft was still
heavy with fuel, however, he had to make an overweight landing but
this was successfully carried out and he was later recommended for a
good show.

The Lightning force suffered its first fatality for fifteen months on 29
April when Flying Officer Al Davey of 5 Squadron was killed in XS924
prior to carrying out a low level in-flight re-fuelling demonstration
at Scampton. Having taken off from Binbrook, he was about to join

up with a Victor tanker on the port wing station when his Lightning suddenly pitched up to an angle of about 60 degrees. This caused a significant loss of speed so that the aircraft stalled and dropped its port wing before crashing 4 miles south-west of Binbrook. The subsequent investigation into this accident found no reason for the sudden pitch up. It was suggested that turbulent air from the Victor's wing may have led to loss of control but as the pitch up had been of a violent nature this was considered unlikely. The most likely cause was a failure in tailplane control but the reason could not be established. As Flying Officer Davey had made no attempt to eject it was thought that he may have blacked out during the pitch up manoeuvre, a theory that was backed up by the fact that he was not wearing an anti-'g' suit. At the time of the accident Flying Officer Davey had only been married for four weeks.

One of the more unusual Lightning accidents occurred on 21 June when Squadron Leader Arthur Tyldesley, who was a member of No.42 Lightning Conversion Course at 226 OCU, was taxying back to dispersal at Coltishall in XM188. Although the landing was entirely straightforward, Tyldesley was soon faced with a difficult situation as the brakes failed on his way back to the apron. Having negotiated one bend he then had nowhere to go, although his method of stopping the aircraft was unorthodox to say the least as he ran into the offices at the side of No.1 Hangar at an angle of about 30 degrees. At this stage he was running on No.2 engine having shut down No.1 after landing but unfortunately as the Lightning struck the building the No.2 throttle moved forward to about 70 per cent power and then jammed. The Avon engine proceeded to suck debris in through the air intake, anything from furniture and loose items in the offices to bricks and mortar that had been dislodged in the collision. Squadron Leader Tyldesley in the meantime had vacated the cockpit by stepping onto the flat roof of the office block before giving the impression of running around in a state of panic. The rapidly deteriorating situation was quickly sorted by the intervention of the Rolls Royce representative who managed to shut down No.2 engine before it consumed the entire building. Not surprisingly, this proved to be the end for XM188 as it never flew again.

On 23 August XS418 of 226 OCU became the fourth Lightning T.5 to suffer an undercarriage collapse on landing. On this occasion the aircraft was being flown by Flight Lieutenant Henryk Ploszek with Senior Aircraftman (SAC) D. J. Hewitt as passenger in the right-hand seat. The spate of landing mishaps with the T.5 had led to accusations of pilot error as it was thought that pilots in the left-hand seat had inadvertently operated the undercarriage retraction instead of the similarly placed brake parachute lever. As a result an instruction had been issued stipulating that the brake parachute could only be deployed from the right-hand seat where there was no undercarriage lever that could be inadvertently pulled. The accident to XS418 took place at Stradishall where it was due for static display after a flight from Coltishall. SAC Hewitt was a member of the turn round team and had been briefed to operate the brake parachute after landing. Flight Lieutenant Ploszek gave the following evidence to the Board of Inquiry that was set up to investigate the accident:

The transit sortie was uneventful and I arrived overhead Stradishall at approximately 1645 hrs, overweight for an immediate landing. I therefore decided to practise some circuits to ensure a good landing. I have previously landed on runway 07 at Stadishall in Hunter aircraft and I was aware of the unusual approach to the threshold. This was confirmed by my circuits. I carried out five circuits, the third one being a reheat overshoot. The undercarriage, flaps and airbrakes were operated in a standard manner and at no time were any abnormalities noticed. After these five circuits my weight was suitable for a landing and I decided to aim for a touchdown speed between 156 and 160 knots. If I misjudged it I would overshoot or if I was at all unhappy I would consider a roll before making another approach.

The final circuit was normal and speed on finals was 175 knots reducing to 165 knots in the dip. During this stage I checked three greens, flaps down and airbrakes out, and my standby ASI was reading 180 knots with the main ASI reading 175 knots. With the power reducing I approached the threshold slightly higher than I intended but I did not correct this at such a late stage as I was preparing for a reasonably large round out on the uphill slope of the runway and I did not want to strike the tail in a steep nose up attitude with an excessive sink rate. The aircraft touched down half way down the ORP and did a short skip. I throttled back to idle/idle and waited for the aircraft to settle with the nose-wheel on the ground but hesitated in calling for the parachute as I thought that I had misjudged the speed and that it would be prudent to roll. However on checking the speed, which was around 157 knots, I reassured myself that it was satisfactory and decided to call for the parachute, instinctively moving my hand forward towards the port 'chute handle in case the airman fumbled and I had to pull it quickly.

At this moment there was a lurch and I gripped the throttles. At first I thought that a tyre had burst but then realised that the aircraft had settled starboard wing down and that the undercarriage must have collapsed. I immediately stopcocked No.1 engine; at the same time I remember seeing the undercarriage lever in the fully down position but I did not notice the undercarriage lights. I then remembered the braking 'chute and decided to pull it myself as things were happening rather quickly. The aircraft started a swing to starboard, which I could not correct. I then stopcocked No.2 engine and started to look ahead for obstructions. As the aircraft slowed down I started opening the canopy and told the airman to get out. This he did when the aircraft came to a rest, jumping from the right-hand side of the cockpit, which was quite close to the ground. I also unstrapped from my seat, but as there was no fire I bent down and switched all the gang bar switches off and made both seats safe. By this time the fire crews had arrived and I vacated the cockpit down a ladder.

Having submitted his evidence to the Inquiry it is interesting to note that the first question Flight Lieutenant Ploszek was asked related to whether or not he had touched the braking parachute lever before the aircraft lurched to starboard. Clearly pilot error was still uppermost in the minds of some, but the fact that Ploszek had not streamed the brake parachute until after the starboard wheel began to collapse ruled out pilot error in this case and suggested that there was an unknown technical defect that had probably also caused the three other cases of undercarriage collapse as well. An inspection of the undercarriage ruled out any structural failure and, as in the previous cases, the exact cause of the incident could not be determined. It was considered, however, that what evidence there was pointed to an obscure and transient malfunction, which caused an UP selection to be made to the undercarriage system, almost immediately followed by a return to the original DOWN selection.

No.111 Squadron experienced another barrier engagement on 2 September during a detachment to Malta, the unfortunate pilot on this occasion being Flying Officer Ted Girdler. On landing at Luqa in XR715, brake parachute failure led to the parachute being jettisoned on the runway and an overshoot being initiated. Unfortunately for Girdler he was about to have one of those days as after his second attempt at landing he experienced brake failure. The barrier was quickly raised and the Lightning entered it at a speed of around 40 knots ending up with the usual Cat.3 damage.

There was further tragedy on 12 September when Flying Officer Pete Thompson, a former Cranwell cadet who had only joined 74 Squadron four weeks before on his first tour, was killed when his aircraft crashed after catching fire as he was in the circuit to land at Tengah. He was flying F.6 XS896 (call sign Mission 59) and was No.2 to his flight commander, Flight Lieutenant Peter Carter, who described what happened to the Board of Inquiry:

> I was leader of a pair for a reheat take off, cold power climb to Flight Level 360, practice interception under Gombak control at or around Flight Level 360 against subsonic targets, a pairs let-down to Point Alpha (18 miles from touch-down on the extended centreline of Tengah runway) and finally, depending on fuel, either a pairs GCA to land or a pairs run in and break for landing. We took off in close formation at 1100 hrs and the sortie was flown without incident to Point Alpha. At this time I asked Mission 59 for a fuel check and his reply Joker plus 100 signified he had 2,500lbs remaining. As this fuel was sufficient for a pairs GCA and overshoot into the circuit, I elected to do this and declared my intention to ATC and Mission 59. A normal GCA was flown and a standard pairs overshoot initiated from the runway threshold. I increased power to 90 per cent rpm, in cruise nozzles, on both engines, called and selected in turn, divebrakes in, wheels up, flaps up and as the speed increased through 250 knots, called and executed a reduction in power to 87 per cent on both engines.
>
> We changed frequency to Local Control and, at the end of the runway, started a climbing turn on to the downwind leg, using 40-45 degrees bank at 250-260 knots. At about 1,000 feet, with about 30 degrees to go to the runway reciprocal, 59 disappeared from the view in my mirror and made an R/T call that I understood to be; 'I have Reheat Fire 1 and 2 captions illuminated'. He said that he was turning underneath and inside me, so I selected maximum

cold power and cleared his path high and to the right. I transmitted a Mayday call on Local frequency and asked the Tower to confirm that they were aware of the emergency. From my position above and slightly ahead of 59, I checked his aircraft for signs of fire and saw none. 59 made an R/T call indicating that he intended to land and I instructed him to stopcock both engines when on the runway.

I then watched him fly what appeared to be a normal downwind leg. At the point where I would have expected him to start his finals turn I saw the aircraft start to roll, I think to the right. It rolled through nearly 360 degrees and entered what was obviously a flat, upright spin to the left. I saw that the wheels were down and I had the impression that the flaps also were in the down position. As soon as he entered the spin I shouted over the R/T: 'Get out! Get out! Get out!' The spin continued for at least two turns before I saw the canopy separate from the aircraft. I then saw the seat leave the aircraft and both drogues deploy. The aircraft struck the ground and the seat and drogue 'chutes entered the trees at a shallow angle very soon afterwards and only a short distance away. I saw no sign of the pilot separating from the seat.

The Lightning struck the ground in a near horizontal attitude with a low forward speed, but with a high rate of descent. It disintegrated on impact and the body of Flying Officer Thompson was found about thirty yards away. This particular accident was similar to a number of previous crashes in that an in-flight fire had taken hold in the region of the reheat jet pipe on the bottom of the fuselage and had then burnt through the control tube sleeve, thereby disconnecting the pilot's control of the tailplane. One of the most disturbing aspects of this accident, however, was the fact that Mod 2537 had been embodied on XS896, which was supposed to prevent loss of tailplane control in a fire situation. The aluminium alloy control tubes had been replaced by stainless steel but the end fittings were still of light alloy. A further mod eventually cured this. In the words of the accident investigation: 'It is considered highly probable that the fire melted the light alloy internal sleeve of the joint in the stainless steel tubing.' This caused a disconnection in the rearmost section of the push/pull tube system operating the tailplane Powered Flying Control Unit (PFCU).

After the sad loss of Pete Thompson the last thing 74 Squadron needed was to be faced with the same circumstances again. Although they both had happy endings, two incidents on 9 October set the nerves jangling. The first involved Flight Lieutenant Jim Jewell who had a Reheat 1 warning shortly after take-off in XS927. Reasoning that this might have been caused by a fuel leak from No.2 engine, he shut this one down and thankfully the warning went out. He landed safely at Tengah although as his aircraft was still heavy with fuel, he ended up taking the RHAG (rotary hydraulic arrestor gear). The second incident affected XS921 and was a compressor failure in the No.2 engine that was caused by FOD (foreign object damage).

With XR715 of 111 Squadron still under repair at Luqa in Malta after its trip into the barrier on 2 September, the unit then lost the services of its T.5 for a short period of time when XS450 had a barrier engagement at Wattisham on 29 October. The damage on this occasion was not as severe as normal in this type of accident and was rated as Cat.2. The final Lightning accident of the year was another Cat.5 write off when F.1A XM174 of the Leuchars Target Facilities Flight crashed at Balmullo just to the west of the airfield. The problem once again was an engine fire that resulted in loss of control, however, on this occasion the pilot (Flight Lieutenant E. Rawcliffe) was able to eject safely.

Despite the fact that the accident statistics for the Lightning for 1968 showed an increase on the previous year with fourteen majors, the rate per 10,000 flying hours was only slightly higher at 3.9. In both years the number of aircraft written off as a result of accidents amounted to five. However 1968 had proved to be a bad year in terms of fatalities with two pilots losing their lives compared to none in 1967. In contrast the new year of 1969 was to be the best yet as regards the Lightning's safety record, although unfortunately this was to prove to be the calm before the storm.

The first accident of note in 1969 did not occur until 16 June when XP737 of 29 Squadron had a fire in No.1 engine. It was being flown by Flight Lieutenant Mike Bettell at the time, but he was able to make a safe landing back at Wattisham. An unusual incident took place on 10 July when XR752 of 11 Squadron was on a radar training sortie out of Leuchars. When the aircraft was being flown at 40,000 feet and a speed of Mach 1.15, the Standard and Auxiliary Warning Panels notified the pilot that the main air turbine had failed. The standby inverter and generator functioned correctly but severe vibration was experienced during the return to base to the extent that the pilot had difficulty in focusing his eyes on his No.2. After landing it was found that the Air Turbine Gearbox (ATG) had seized and there was secondary damage to the support struts. There was also damage to frames 54 and 54A, together with skin damage, which in total amounted to Cat.3. An investigation by Dowty Rotol confirmed that the ATG had failed in both the turbine and gearbox assemblies as a result of overheating, which was in excess of 300 degrees C. This was due to an extremely rare fatigue failure of the air cooling pipe.

Another Lightning was damaged by fire on 16 July, although the circumstances of this accident were rather different. The incident involved XP740 of 111 Squadron, which had just landed at Wattisham after a training sortie. The pilot turned off the runway and went through his post landing checks, which included shutting down No.1 engine and setting the No.2 at fast idle. Not long after the Standard Warning Panel operated and the Reheat 1 and 2 captions illuminated. The pilot immediately shut down No.2 engine and switched off the electrical systems but by this time he could see smoke in the region of the port airbrake. As he left the aircraft the fire crews arrived and the fire was quickly put out. Although the emergency crews had responded extremely quickly Cat.3 damage was still caused, which was mainly to the rear fuselage on the port side, in the vicinity of the airbrake and air turbine. It was discovered that hydraulic oil under pressure had come into contact with the jet pipe as a result of a failed seal near the port airbrake. A lack of cooling air after No.1 engine had been shut down was enough for the oil to ignite.

An unusual incident took place on 28 August when XS923 of 5 Squadron was damaged Cat.3 when three of the fins of the Red Top acquisition missile it was carrying broke off in flight. It was realised that something was wrong when a fuel leak was observed by the marshaller as the aircraft was returned to dispersal, leading to rapid engine shutdown by the pilot (Flying Officer Chris Coville). On inspection it was found that damage had been caused to the fuselage, wing leading edge, ventral fin and tailplane on the port side. The fins from the missile were eventually discovered by the side of the runway having broken off during a 4g break for landing. On checking back through the records, these revealed that the Red Top had been carried in the air for 250 hours and as a result of this incident a requirement was made that all acquisition rounds were to have their wing attachment plates replaced after 100 hours.

It had been some time since a Lightning had been damaged on start-up but XR758 of 74 Squadron received Cat.3 (later upgraded to Cat.4) damage on 17 September during a four-aircraft detachment to Darwin in Australia. Flight Lieutenant Trevor MacDonald Bennett had started both engines and was accelerating No.2 engine to fast idle rpm when he heard (and felt) a muffled explosion from the rear of the aircraft. In response he immediately shut down both engines and made safe all switches before leaving the cockpit. The internal damage was extensive, the sequence of events beginning with the venting of a large amount of fuel from the starboard wing tanks during ground refuelling. The fuel then entered the fuselage at an aperture between frames 39 and 40 and vaporised in the intense heat, creating an explosive mixture near the hot air pressure reducing valve. As No.2 engine was accelerated to fast idle rpm the increasing pressure burst a seal in this valve, releasing hot air under pressure that ignited the fuel vapour. The explosion started above the fire roof of the No.1 engine bay, continued up the starboard side distorting frames 41, 42 and 43, through to the inner skin area, ripped the intake skin away from the frames and burst along a rivet seam. The force also tripped the inertia switches initiating the fire bottles and cut off all electrical supplies. A Special Technical Instruction (Lightning 325) issued two months later called for sealing of the aperture at the wing to fuselage forward attachment to eliminate fuel seepage into the No.1 engine bay. XR758 was eventually airlifted back to Warton for repairs and was then issued to 23 Squadron.

The only Lightning to be lost during 1969 was XS926 of 5 Squadron, which crashed in the North Sea on 22 September during an air combat training exercise. This was the lead aircraft of a pair and was flown by Major Charlie Neel USAF. The first of a series of manoeuvres was carried out at 25,000 feet in an area 40-80 miles east of Flamborough Head and was completed successfully. The second phase of the practice combat saw the two aircraft gradually reduce height to 15,000 feet and this ended with XS926 in a hard turn to starboard with the No.2 aircraft to his left. Major Neel then reversed his turn in an attempt to join up with the No.2 but as he did so he felt the airframe buffet suddenly increase and he lost control. At this time he was approximately 500-700 yards astern of the No.2 and in a position where his aircraft would have been affected by the wake turbulence coming off the other Lightning.

With speed falling alarmingly, XS926 flicked to the right and eventually settled into a spin to the right with an indicated airspeed of 120 knots. The standard recovery action in a spin was to apply full opposite rudder while holding the control column central and then slightly forward with the engines set to idle/fast idle rpm. Although the aircraft seemed to be responding to these control inputs, by now height was down to 10,000 feet which was 5,000 feet below the recommended ejection height when in a spin. Major Neel finally ejected at a height of 9,000 feet and was eventually picked up by a rescue helicopter which was assisted by the pilot of an F-4 Phantom which happened to be in the area at the time. The subsequent Board of Inquiry found that the accident had been caused by mishandling, that was made worse by the effects of turbulence from the aircraft in front. This was the second accident caused by an inadvertent spin and the Inquiry recommended that the whole subject of limit manoeuvre be given detailed attention throughout all phases of Lightning training, starting at the OCU. Poor Charlie Neel was also criticised by the Inquiry for his attire as at the time of the accident he was wearing a USAF flying helmet and flying boots. The AOC-in-C made it quite clear that flying clothing was not a matter for individual judgement.

The next mishap took place on 27 November when XM147 of the Wattisham TFF was acting as a target. The brief was for the pilot to carry out a dive from 25,000 feet at a steady indicated airspeed of 600 knots. When he was descending between 10,000 and 5,000 feet he felt a slight yawing of the aircraft, which he attributed to the fact that the aircraft was in the transonic region at the time, but on landing it was discovered that the rudder was missing. Cat.3 damage was caused to the fin skin and the rudder mounting brackets. It was thought that rudder damper flutter or wear at the top hinge may have caused the eventual failure of the top hinge rudder assembly due to fatigue. Although it was thought that failure of the rudder damper was the primary cause of the accident, as the rudder was not recovered the condition of the damper could not be established.

During the year there had only been six major accidents to Lightning aircraft with one Cat.5 loss and no fatalities. As total flying hours amounted to 36,000, the accident rate per 10,000 flying hours was significantly lower than previous years at 1.7. This was well below the projected figure, as the forecast from 1965 onwards had been for an accident rate of 3.0. However, as already intimated the number of Lightning accidents was about to show a sharp rise, in particular the number of aircraft that were lost as a result of crashes due to in-flight engine fires. This situation was to lead to a comprehensive review of Lightning operations as at one stage it appeared that there would not be sufficient aircraft to maintain a credible air defence capability until that role was taken on by the McDonnell Douglas Phantom.

Chapter 5

The Engine Fire Epidemic

At the beginning of 1970 the Lightning force was still at the peak of its power with nine first-line squadrons and the Operational Conversion Unit. The OCU at Coltishall had become an extremely large organisation and in the twelve-month period from September 1970 the unit operated a total of thirty-seven Lightnings, comprising ten F.1As, four F.3s, eleven T.4s and twelve T.5s. At Gutersloh in RAF Germany Nos.19 and 92 Squadrons were now flying the much improved F.2A, which featured the enlarged ventral fuel tank. Many pilots regarded this to be the best Lightning of the lot, especially as it retained its gun armament, unlike the F.6, which had to be modified so that two 30mm Aden cannon could be fitted in the forward section of the ventral pack at the expense of 170 gallons of fuel. The decision to remove the gun armament from the Lightning had been taken with the F.3, a move that was widely condemned at the time.

By now it had been some time since a Lightning had lost its canopy on take-off but it happened once again early in the year and, as on the last occasion, the culprits were 23 Squadron. On 26 February XR752 was halfway down the runway when the canopy started to lift. As the pilot was committed to taking off by this stage the hood was ripped off and on this occasion managed to damage the fuselage spine as well as the leading edge of the fin.

The first serious accident of the year was a particularly tragic one as the pilot managed to eject successfully but subsequently died of exposure before he was picked up from the North Sea. On 4 March Flying Officer Graham Clarke and Flight Lieutenant Tony Doidge (call signs Kilo 15 and 16 respectively) took off from Leuchars in the late afternoon to carry out low level practice interceptions. Towards the end of the sortie Flight Lieutenant Doidge in XS918 received a Reheat 1 warning and this was followed almost immediately by a Reheat 2. Flying Officer Clarke manoeuvred his aircraft to check for signs of fire and, although at first he could not see any, as he flew to the left of XS918 he could see the glow of a fire in the No.1 engine jet pipe. He advised Flight Lieutenant Doidge to eject who did so at 1900 hrs at around 10,000 feet and approximately 9 miles from the coast. Unfortunately Clarke lost sight of his No.2 as he descended on his parachute and then had to return to Leuchars as he was low on fuel.

By this time the rescue helicopter had been scrambled but in the gathering gloom it did not come into visual contact with Flight Lieutenant Doidge. As the SAR helicopter was already in the air, the pilot of another Lightning was advised to observe where XS918 crashed instead of looking for its pilot as he descended on his parachute. The search was continued but without success and it was not until 0100 hrs the following morning that the body of Flight Lieutenant Doidge was picked up by a local lifeboat. The Board of Inquiry noted a number of deficiencies in his survival equipment including the fact that his immersion suit had been modified without authority to make it more comfortable to wear. This involved removing the integral rubber boots and replacing them with wrist seals so that ordinary socks and flying boots could be worn, which allowed water into the suit. It was also noted that he had insufficient clothing underneath his immersion suit to provide adequate thermal insulation but this was rendered somewhat irrelevant by the fact that the suit was not watertight. Two other crucial lapses were that he had lost his Personal Survival Pack during his descent and had removed the battery of the Search and Rescue Beacon (SARBE) locator from the Mae West instead of the beacon itself so that there was no signal for a rescue helicopter to home onto. The Board also highlighted several other more minor failings.

As Flight Lieutenant Doidge had ejected just before dark, the helicopter had very little time to locate him and this task was made virtually impossible as his SARBE was not working. His aircraft had been seen to crash in the sea between Anstruther and the Isle of May and although the nearest lifeboat was alerted immediately this was located at Broughty Ferry, which was approximately 20 miles from the crash site. As the ejection had taken place over the Firth of Forth it is likely that Flight Lieutenant Doidge had come down somewhere not too far away. From the small amount of wreckage that was eventually recovered it was thought that the fire might have been caused by hydraulic oil from the No.1 Controls or a services system in Fire Zone 3 (the jet pipe area).

No.74 Squadron had another start-up fire on 6 April when Flying Officer Paul Adams was about to fly XS928. It appeared that a valve in the AVPIN starting system did not close and so AVPIN drained down to the starter exhaust, which was situated under the port flap where it burnt with an invisible flame. Fuel then leaked from a jammed overwing vent valve (a common problem) and, having been heated by the sun as it flowed over the upper surface of the wing, ignited when it came into contact with the AVPIN flame. The level of damage was assessed as Cat.4 and XS928 was eventually airlifted back to the UK where it joined XR758 at Warton for major repair work.

There was another case of a hot gas leak on 7 April when XP756 of 29 Squadron was climbing to altitude to begin a practice interception exercise. The first indication of trouble was a Reheat 1 warning when the aircraft was at 25,000 feet although, after the standard actions were taken, the light went out after about thirty seconds and remained off for the rest of the flight. On landing at Wattisham it was discovered that the No.1 intermediate jet pipe had split, which had allowed hot gases to damage part of the structure at the rear of the aircraft.

Another aircraft was lost to fire on 7 May when Flying Officer Stu Tulloch of 111 Squadron ejected from XP742 during an exercise involving supersonic interceptions. As he was in a starboard turn at 28,000 feet and a speed of Mach 1.0, the Standard Warning Panel lit up with Reheat 1 and 2 warnings and these were joined soon after by a Fire 1 warning. Flying Officer Tulloch throttled both engines but as the warnings stayed on he wasted no time in ejecting, his aircraft crashing into the sea off Great Yarmouth. During the ejection he sustained slight injuries and was rescued from his dinghy by helicopter after approximately twenty-five minutes in the water.

Finding the reason why an aircraft crashed was not easy when it went down into the sea as it was often difficult, if not impossible, to find the wreckage. In the case of XP742, however, sufficient evidence was found to establish that there had been a titanium fire in No.1 engine, which had then broken through the compressor casing. It was also discovered that there had been a serious fuel leak in Fire Zone 1 of the No.1 engine bay although the source of the leak could not be established as not enough wreckage was recovered. Having started in Fire Zone 1, the fire then quickly spread to Fire Zones 2 and 3 and led to the warnings that were conveyed to Flying Officer Tulloch.

No.1 engine was examined by Rolls Royce, whose task of finding the cause of the titanium fire was not helped by the severe damage that the engine had sustained as a result of the fire and also by the effects of having been immersed in sea water. It appeared, however, that a failure had occurred in a stage 7 stator blade or blades. Debris was then passed through the engine in the course of which a group of titanium stator blades ignited. The reason for the blade failure could not be established with any degree of certainty, although there was a possibility it may have been caused by Foreign Object Damage as there was evidence of FOD on rotor blades in the early stages of the compressor. It will be recalled that a titanium fire had occurred over two years before resulting in Avon Mod 3497 to replace titanium stator blades at compressor stages 5 and 6 with steel blades. This modification was still being embodied as engines were returned for overhaul.

No.74 Squadron had another AVPIN fire on 15 May when XS897 was being prepared for a sortie resulting in Cat.2 damage to the electrics in the fuselage spine. However, much worse was to follow. On the night of 26 May Flying Officers John Webster and Dave Roome were carrying out practice interceptions at low level over the Malacca Straits. Flying Officer Webster in XR767 was acting as target and after a number of successful interceptions at 5,000 feet, clearance was given to descend to 1,000 feet. Nothing more was heard from Webster and it was later assumed that he had flown into the sea. Despite an extensive search of the area only a small piece of debris from his aircraft was found.

Also on 26 May another of 29 Squadron's F.3s had a hot gas leak when XP745 was departing Wattisham with two other Lightnings. The first sign of trouble came when the re-fuelling panel lights came on during inverted flight, although a thud was felt at the same time. Not long after the pilot became aware that his pitch control was restricted and immediately returned to base together with another aircraft. In the descent the Reheat 1 warning light came on but after the appropriate actions were taken it went out again. A safe landing was eventually made and it was discovered that once again the No.1 intermediate jet pipe had split which had led to hydraulic oil igniting. The Cat.3 damage that the aircraft had sustained took over two months to repair.

Due to the prodigious power of its Rolls Royce Avon engines, the Lightning was capable of flying some extraordinary aerobatic manoeuvres including what was termed the rotation take-off. This involved raising the undercarriage as soon as possible after becoming airborne, holding the aircraft down to gain speed and then moving the control column sharply back to bring the nose up to an angle of 60-70 degrees. Aerodynamic lift was replaced by thrust from the engines as the aircraft appeared to go up in a vertical climb. Although it was spectacular, this particular manoeuvre had to be finely judged and the minimum entry speed that was required was 260 knots IAS with no more than a 3g pull. Most Lightning pilots performed a rotation take-off at some point in their careers but it was to lead to tragedy at Tengah on 27 July.

Flying Officer Roger Pope and Flight Lieutenant Frank Whitehouse of 74 Squadron were scheduled to fly as a pair and both decided to perform rotation take offs. Roger Pope was first away in XS927 with Frank Whitehouse following a few seconds later in XS930. Shortly after the latter rotated into the climb his aircraft was seen to enter what appeared to be a spin to the left and having attained a height of only 600 feet it crashed in the jungle just beyond the runway. Although Whitehouse attempted to eject there was insufficient time for his parachute to open and he was killed. It seemed that the pull that Whitehouse had made on the control column had been well in excess of 3g but there was another factor involved. To prevent the problem of fuel venting, ventral fuel transfer had been inhibited when on the ground and so with a lengthy taxy and hold at the end of the runway the fuel used would have come from the wing tanks. With a full ventral on take off, CG would have been further aft than it would otherwise have been, resulting in decreased stability in pitch. Although there was a funeral and cremation for Whitehouse in Singapore, his ashes were flown back to the UK and interred at Cranwell where he had been a student in September 1963.

The degree of instability that was produced by a CG that was near the aft limit was particularly hazardous when extreme manoeuvres were carried out at low level as in an aerobatic routine or a rotation take-off. Squadron Leader (later Air Commodore) Ken Goodwin, who was one of the first Lightning pilots with the AFDS and was later on the staff at LCS, came across this problem but found that it was not given due credit by some who should have known better:

One of the special qualities of the Lightning was the spectacular rotation take-off, which included a 220-knot, 60-degree climb into a wing-over. Whereas it was claimed the Lightning would not pitch up because of its notched delta configuration, I thought otherwise, and gave evidence to this effect to a Board of Inquiry into a fatal display accident. At a practice display at Wattisham I was delayed for take-off and, unbeknown to me, I was using main tank (wing) fuel without a transfer from the ventral tank. A rotation take-off left me with an aft CG and a continuing pitch up with the control column fully forward. I was able to use rudder and gentle aileron to get a wing-over going and the nose coming down laterally. I am quite certain we lost two pilots and aircraft through uncontrolled pitch up. Sadly, the Board of Inquiry was highly sceptical of my evidence.

The Tigers' run of misfortune was to continue as another aircraft was lost the following month, although on this occasion the pilot managed to eject with only minor injuries. On the night of 12 August Flying Officer Mike Rigg was returning to Tengah in XS893 after a low level interception sortie. When downwind at 1,500 feet he selected undercarriage down but was then confronted with a port main gear red. He re-cycled the undercarriage before applying roll, yaw and 'g' to his aircraft but the undercarriage leg still refused to come down. The emergency system was activated but again without success and as his fuel state was becoming critical, Rigg had no alternative but to climb up to 12,000 feet and eject. Although the ejection was straightforward, his parachute descent was less so as he got the impression that he was falling out of his parachute harness. Several of the harness attachments were positioned abnormally high on his body, to the extent that he had difficulty in breathing. Only by pulling himself up in his harness was he able to breathe normally. After landing in the sea he was picked up by a SAR helicopter.

The crash investigation was again hampered by a lack of wreckage so that the findings had to be based on a certain amount of supposition. It was eventually concluded that the failure had been caused by the door locking latches not opening fully on the down selection. Of equal concern was the traumatic parachute descent that the pilot had experienced. Normally the Martin Baker Mk.4BS ejection seat had a barostat system where the main parachute opened at 10,000 feet but on Far East Air Force Lightnings the barostat had been set to 5,000 m (16,400 feet) before delivery, to allow for flight over mountainous regions en route. When Mike Rigg ejected at 12,000 feet there would have been no deceleration before the parachute opened and it was thought that the high loads generated had resulted in the failure of stitching that joined the harness crutch loops to the bottom cross strap. As a result of this accident the barostat mechanism in the ejector seats of FEAF Lightning aircraft were set to the normal setting of 10,000 feet.

On 9 September another Lightning pilot was killed in an accident that in recent years has taken on a degree of notoriety. The unfortunate pilot was Captain Bill Schaffner USAF who had joined 5 Squadron two months before on an exchange posting. He was an experienced pilot who had completed two tours of duty on the F-102 Delta Dagger and at the time of the accident had accumulated 121 flying hours on the Lightning, of which eighteen hours were at night. He also had a Green Instrument Rating and was rated as limited combat ready after his eight weeks on the squadron. This was rather a short period in which to have achieved this flying category but it reflected his previous fast jet experience. The limited aspect referred to the fact that he had not been cleared for full visual identification (visident) missions as he had not completed his training in this respect.

On the 9th a Tactical Evaluation (TACEVAL) was called in which Captain Schaffner was cleared to participate as it was understood that operations would not include the shadowing or shepherding of other aircraft operating at low level. He was ordered to his aircraft at 1834 hrs and the scramble came at 1947 hrs but as he was taxying out to the runway he was recalled. His fuel was replenished but there was a mix up as regards turn round servicing as he did not request any which was against standing instructions. The engineering officer-in-charge of the aircraft ordered a full turn round to be carried out but this was delayed and had not been completed when Schaffner was scrambled again at 2025 hrs. He took off five minutes later and climbed to 10,000 feet but at this time he was still unaware of the type of target he was about to be allocated or the height at which it was operating. In fact the task had just been changed by the TACEVAL team to a shadowing and shepherding operation, which Schaffner had not been cleared to participate in.

The targets were Shackleton aircraft that were flying at a cruising speed of 160 knots at 1,500 feet which was the minimum height authorised for this type of exercise. The minimum speed that a Lightning could be flown for visident procedures was 200 knots as referred to in the Lightning squadron training syllabus, and although shadowing and shepherding was an unusual request, it was included in the war task of

Lightning squadrons and so was theoretically subject to TACEVAL. At 2039 hrs Schaffner was given a target that was 28 nautical miles away and was ordered to accelerate to Mach 0.95. He was given various heading alterations until he made a R/T call to say that he was in contact. It was noted by the controller that his voice sounded strained as though he was being affected by 'g'. At 2041 hrs Schaffner's aircraft was seen above and behind the Shackleton by the pilot of another Lightning who had just broken away from the target. The navigation lights of the Lightning were then picked up by the crew of the Shackleton, but by now it appeared to be quite low. A minute later a R/T call to Schaffner from control went unanswered, which prompted the implementation of emergency procedures, but despite an immediate search by the target Shackleton and an air/sea search the next day there was no sign of aircraft or pilot.

From calculations provided by the Board of Inquiry and expert sources, the general location where the Lightning had come down was ascertained and it was found nearly two months after the accident by a Royal Navy minesweeper. Despite having been flown into the sea the aircraft was substantially complete except that the port wing had broken off and some fuselage panels were missing. Having survived contact with the water the Lightning had sunk at a minimal rate of descent and had settled gently on the sea bed in a tail down attitude. Although the cockpit canopy was still attached, it was not closed and there was no sign of the pilot. Examination of the wreckage showed that the aircraft had hit the sea at low speed, in a tail down attitude and with a low rate of descent. Both throttles were in the reheat gates, there was a nose-up trim of six degrees, the undercarriage was up, flaps down and the airbrakes were out. It appeared that Schaffner had attempted to eject but the canopy had not blown off as its gun cartridge had received only a light percussion strike and had not fired. After the aircraft hit the water he had tried to manually abandon the aircraft but the conclusion was that he had drowned during or after this attempt. The light percussion strike on the canopy gun cartridge occurred because of negligent servicing in that the firing unit was incorrectly seated as a result of damaged screw threads. Although the non-release of the canopy prevented Schaffner from ejecting, it is likely that he would not have survived in any case as his use of the seat would not have been within its operating limits.

In recent years the story of this accident has been taken over by those fond of conspiracy theories and UFOs. This has mainly come about as the aircraft was recovered from the sea in a relatively complete state but with no pilot in the cockpit. For some it could only mean one thing, an alien abduction. Increasingly imaginative stories emerged of Captain Schaffner intercepting an object travelling at over 500 mph (fast for a Shackleton), which was also giving off an intense bright blue light. Radar operators had apparently then seen the two radar traces merge before separating again, one disappearing off the screens at an estimated speed of 20,000 mph. Of course, such a fanciful tale would not be complete without accusations of an official cover up and lost reports. Sadly this twisting of the truth in relation to the events of 8 September 1970 has tended to trivialise a tragic event in which a fine airman lost his life.

The seventh (and last) Lightning to be lost in 1970 was T.4 XM990 of 226 OCU which crashed near Coltishall on 19 September. This was Battle of Britain Open Day and one of the highlights of the show was to be a sixteen-aircraft formation flypast. To get sixteen aircraft in the air all at once was an ambitious target considering the Lightning's serviceability rate and XM990 was the second of two airborne spares, also having the role of whipper-in for the formation. The aircraft was to be flown by Flight Lieutenant John Sims with Flight Lieutenant Brian Fuller in the right-hand seat. With one Lightning having dropped out before take-off, another then had an AC failure in the air so that XM990 was required to take up the vacant place in the formation. This was flown successfully but after the break for landing one of the F.1As (XM180 flown by Flight Lieutenant Eric Hopkins) burst a tyre on the runway so that some aircraft from the formation had to divert to Wattisham. They returned to Coltishall later in the day but after turning left onto the downwind leg of the circuit John Sims found that he had to move the control column to the right to prevent the port wing from dropping.

At first Sims and Fuller thought that they could get the aircraft back on the ground, but the problem then became much worse and it was soon obvious that they would have to eject. Unfortunately they were still at circuit height so Sims moved the throttles into full cold power and began to climb. However, there was a progressive worsening of lateral control to the point that he was unable to prevent the Lightning from rolling to the left. To maintain the climb he pulled on the control column when the aircraft was upright and pushed when it was inverted. In such fashion he managed to climb to about 2,000 feet before ordering Brian Fuller to eject. As the Lightning was rolling constantly this was not easy but, by initiating the ejection sequence when the aircraft was approximately 90 degrees from wings level, he timed it correctly so that he came out when it was upright. John Sims had a much more difficult job as he was now being badly affected by slipstream from the open cockpit and as soon as he released the controls the nose of the aircraft began to drop. He then had difficulty grasping the top handle but eventually managed to eject himself and came down in some trees. Although Brian Fuller was back in the air just four days later, John Sims suffered back and neck injuries that took six months to heal.

About a month before the accident XM990 had received a scheduled inspection in which work was carried out on the port and starboard aileron Powered Flying Control Units (PFCUs). The work involved the removal and replacement of life-expired PFCUs on the port wing and was completed over a period of nine days. The investigation into the accident discovered that two bolts to the valve input lever of the port aileron PFCU had been inserted head-down but that the slotted nut and split pin had not been fitted. As a result the bolts had eventually fallen out and this led to the port aileron being able to travel upwards beyond its normal range. The use of full starboard aileron and full right rudder within their normal maximum limits of deflection were not enough to counteract the rolling induced by the excessive deflection of the port aileron.

This particular incident caused much controversy at the time as XM990 had been flown twice after the servicing work had been carried out and on each occasion the pilot involved had noted various unserviceabilities, these including what he considered to be a slight problem with the aircraft's autopilot. As nothing untoward was seen during subsequent ground inspections, the aircraft's service and flying logbook (Form 700) was annotated that, although it was deemed to be fit to fly, it was not to be flown in formation. Unfortunately Flight Lieutenant Sims only became aware of this when he was already in the cockpit immediately before start-up (the formation leader had no idea that XM990 had a flight restriction). This put Flight Lieutenant Sims in an extremely difficult position and he only decided to continue as he was the No.2 spare and, in theory, should not have been required, but Lightning serviceability being as it was, he was soon called upon to take up a position in the formation. Had the control problem occurred when in formation it is likely that a mid-air collision would have occurred involving two or more aircraft Even though there were more Lightnings at Coltishall than anywhere else, it was still an extremely difficult task to get sixteen aircraft in the air at the same time so another factor in this accident was undoubtedly the desire to put on a good show, even if it meant cutting a few corners to have the requisite number of aircraft available.

There was another incident of fuel venting on 5 November when XN794 of 19 Squadron had completed a scramble start during an exercise. The aircraft had only taxied a few yards when the Fire 2 caption illuminated. In response the pilot shut down both engines and operated the fire extinguisher before vacating the cockpit. It was discovered that fuel from the port wing vent valve had entered the fuselage and had then been ignited by the hot No.2 starter exhaust pipe. On this occasion, however, the flash fire that resulted did not cause any damage.

The final incident of 1970 was a bird-strike to XM139 of the Wattisham TFF on 10 December. The aircraft was hit shortly after take-off and the intake duct was damaged, some debris was ingested by No.1 engine, which suffered severe indentations of the compressor blades. Although bird-strikes were an ever present hazard, the Lightning was affected rather less than other RAF types due to its predominantly medium-to-high level role. The bird-strike rate per 10,000 flying hours for the Lightning for the last three years had been 9.0, 5.5 and 6.4. In comparison the figures for the Hunter were 11.0, 21.2 and 8.2 and for the Canberra 17.0, 26.1 and 22.9. Due to its ultra-low level role the aircraft that was most prone to bird-strikes was the Buccaneer, with a strike rate of 43.1. The accident to XM139 was in fact only the fourth bird-strike to result in Cat.3 damage since the entry of the Lightning into squadron service in 1960.

During the year there had been twelve major accidents to Lightning aircraft and with a total of 39,000 flying hours the rate per 10,000 hours was 3.1. Although this compared favourably with previous years, a total of seven aircraft had been written off, which was two more than in the 1966, 1967 and 1968 when there had been five in each year. The Cat.5 accidents had resulted in four fatalities, which was double the previous highest figure of two, which had been recorded in 1966 and 1968. Unfortunately this trend towards higher losses was to be continued in the first few months of 1971.

The Lightning force did not have to wait too long for its first fright of the year when Flight Lieutenant Russ Morley of 29 Squadron had a fire warning in XP765 on 11 January. The incident took place at night as the aircraft was climbing through 18,000 feet and involved a Fire 1 warning. The standard actions of shutting down the engine, jettisoning the ventral tank and operating the fire extinguisher were taken as a return was made to Wattisham where the aircraft was landed safely. Once again the fire had been caused by a fuel leak but by Lightning standards it was of a relatively minor nature and did not cause serious damage.

A pilot of 74 Squadron had a similar experience three days later when flying XR761, but in his case it was a Reheat 1 warning. The warning flashed as he was flying at 11,000 feet and, as it stayed on after he had carried out his Fire Drills, he gave a Mayday call. On returning to base a visual inspection was made by the pilot of another aircraft who reported that he could see what appeared to be fuel leaking in the vicinity of the No.1 jet pipe. The warning light eventually went out after about ninety seconds and the remainder of the flight was uneventful. Once on the ground it was discovered that the leaking fluid was actually hydraulic oil that was covering the jet pipe area. This had come from a connection in the hydraulic line to the airbrake and had caused a flash fire in Fire Zone 3 at frame 55.

On 23 January XR727 of 23 Squadron was landing at Leuchars after an air test when a large flock of birds was seen to rise off the runway near the touch-down point. The pilot initiated overshoot action but was unable to avoid flying through the birds and he heard a slight bump on the underside of the aircraft. The undercarriage and flaps were left down and a further circuit was flown followed by a precautionary landing. Subsequent examination of the aircraft revealed that there had been two bird-strikes, one in each undercarriage bay. Although the port side was undamaged, the starboard side sustained damage to the D-door aperture amounting to a dent in the main skin and cracking on rib 15. Just before this incident the runway controller had fired a number of cartridges to scare the birds off the runway, but the birds that did the damage came from an unseen flock that rose from the undershoot area. Although seemingly innocuous, bird-strikes could cause serious damage and in this case it was assessed as Cat.3, which resulted in XR727 being out of action for nearly three months. Bird-strikes were a particularly hazard at Leuchars as the runway was so close to the sea.

The first Cat.5 accident of 1971 occurred on 25 January when Captain Bill Povilus USAF of 29 Squadron had to eject from XP756 during a night interception sortie off the coast of East Anglia. After climbing to

35,000 feet Captain Povilus was given information on his first target and had just engaged reheat when there was Reheat 1 warning. After carrying out the emergency drills and transmitting a Mayday call he was given a course to steer for Wattisham by Control, but as he turned onto the required heading he noticed that the indication on the main airspeed indicator/Mach meter was dropping to zero. There was then a dramatic deterioration in control response. At first he became aware that movement of the rudder pedals completely lacked resistance and had no effect on the aircraft's motion. On checking the services hydraulic pressure he saw that it was reading lower than normal and was fluctuating. Then, as the nose of the aircraft began to drop, there was no response to backward movement on the control column. At this point Povilus ejected and although he received minor injuries, the ejection was successful and he was rescued by helicopter after spending two hours in his dinghy. The delay was down to the fact that a USAF helicopter had to be called as Royal Air Force SAR helicopters were not night-capable.

Unfortunately the remains of XP756 were not found so the Board of Inquiry set up to investigate the accident was unable to establish a positive cause. However, from the pilot's evidence of the symptoms of the fire, the Board reasoned that there was a strong probability that the fire was caused either by a hydraulic leak from the services pressure or return pipelines or by failure of a fuel coupling in the fuel transfer pipe that passed through Fire Zone 3.

Another Lightning went down on 28 January when F.2A XN772 of 92 Squadron crashed near Diepholz in Germany after entering a spin during an air combat training exercise. The aircraft was being flown by Flying Officer Pete Hitchcock as No.2 to Flight Lieutenant Jim Watson in a 2 versus 1 practice combat at low supersonic speeds at 35,000 feet. When the singleton aircraft (flown by Flight Lieutenant Rich Rhodes) was picked up at a range of 5 nautical miles and closing fast, Watson called for a break to starboard, but during this turn XN772 flicked into a spin to the right that had not been recovered by the time the aircraft was passing through 15,000 feet, at which point Flying Officer Hitchcock ejected. The Lightning continued to spin until it crashed in open country and was largely destroyed in the ensuing fire. An additional hazard was the fact that a number of 30mm HE and ball shells, both exploded and unexploded, were found scattered around the crash site. The requirement to carry live ammunition during training flights by

Lightnings of RAF Germany was subsequently cancelled. Hitchcock made a safe parachute descent and landed safely some distance away.

Unfortunately he came in for some adverse comment during the Board of Inquiry as regards his handling of the aircraft, some of which was unjustified. One of the greatest criticisms of the Lightning's stall/ spin characteristics was the fact that it had virtually no stall warning and, therefore, no spin warning. The moderate airframe buffet that became evident at high angles of attack occurred at speeds well above the stall (around 215 knots IAS) and changed very little right down to the stall itself, which, depending on weight and configuration, took place at about 115 knots IAS. As the aircraft would have to be flown well within the buffet boundary in order to manoeuvre effectively during air combat, it would clearly be difficult for the pilot to know precisely how close to the stall he was. Even considering the above it did appear that Pete Hitchcock's break had been rather too aggressive. His subsequent use of rudder to assist the turn and the application of aileron to arrest the yaw that this created only served to aggravate the situation.

He was also criticised for his actions once the aircraft was in the spin, the Board stating that the most likely cause of the failure to recover from the spin was that the pilot had not maintained the correct recovery action long enough for it to have the desired effect. However, it appeared that the Lightning had entered a flat spin from which recovery was virtually impossible. This was backed up by photographs of the crashed aircraft that showed it had hit the ground in a flat attitude with virtually no forward speed. Although much of the fuselage had been destroyed by fire the fin and rudder were clearly recognisable and were level with the ground. In the remarks made by the AOC-in-C at the end of the report, although he accepted that Flying Officer Hitchcock had been negligent, he did recognise that the Lightning had to be flown in a part of the flight envelope where little margin existed between successful manoeuvre in combat and an inadvertent spin and he therefore considered the pilot's negligence to be excusable. During the course of the investigation into this accident four cases of inadvertent spins were admitted by Lightning pilots from Gutersloh that had not previously been reported. Despite this accident, the F.2/F.2A still had the best safety record of all Lightning variants. Including XN772 there had only been two Cat.5 write-offs whereas the total for all other marks at this time amounted to thirty-nine.

The next serious incident involving a Lightning took place on 31 March and very nearly resulted in another ejection. The aircraft was XM172 of 226 OCU, which was taking part in a cine-weave exercise when a double hydraulic failure occurred. On levelling at 8,000 feet the controls seized but the pilot decided not to eject, instead he pulled back sharply on the control column and it suddenly became free again at which point the HYD 2 light went out. A return was made to Coltishall using minimum control movements and just before the aircraft was landed the HYD 1 light also went out. The cause of this incident was put down to heavy aeration of hydraulic fluid in the No.1 and 2 systems.

The next in-flight fire was not long in coming and occurred on 26 April when T.4 XM996 of 226 OCU was being flown by a student pilot. A Fire 1 warning was received during a full-power climb and the pilot shut down No.1 engine and switched off the fuel before his instructor took control of the aircraft. After the ventral tank had been jettisoned (by now these were in rather short supply) and the No.1 extinguisher was operated the warning went out after about fifteen seconds. An airborne check by the pilot of another Lightning revealed that although fuel appeared to be venting from the area where the ventral tank had been, there was no sign of fire.

On return to Coltishall an examination of Fire Zones 1 and 2 revealed the presence of hydraulic oil and tests showed that this had come from a flexible pipe that had failed. The hydraulic oil had then found its way from Zone 1 to Zone 2 where it had collected in the hottest part, adjacent to the rear fire wall. Because of the attitude of the aircraft in the climb, the drainage holes in Zone 1 had not dispersed the fluid and a lack of complete sealing between the two fire zones had allowed transfer of the fluid to take place.

Two days later another Lightning was lost when F.6 XS938 of 23 Squadron crashed shortly after taking off from Leuchars as a result of an engine fire. The aircraft was flown by Flying Officer Alistair McLean who had been tasked with carrying out practice interceptions with a Canberra. Having departed Leuchars on runway 09, Flying Officer McLean accelerated to 430 knots IAS and was passing 3,000 feet when the attention-getters came on and the Fire 2 caption illuminated. This was followed shortly afterwards by a Reheat 2 warning and McLean quickly shut down the No.2 engine and pressed the fire extinguisher button. By this time he was at 5,000 feet and during a turn back towards Leuchars the Fire 2 warning went out but was replaced instead by a Reheat 1 warning. With the situation rapidly worsening McLean made a R/T call that he was ejecting and he abandoned the aircraft at a height of 6,000 feet. As he had taken off at 2134 hrs it was almost dark by the time he parachuted into the sea – a few minutes later and he would probably have had to spend the night in his dinghy. This was due to the fact that the SAR helicopter would not have been able to make a rescue at night. As it was, the helicopter found him almost straight away and he was winched aboard before the light finally went.

Although the RAF attempted to find all Lightning aircraft that went into the sea, the level of success of these operations varied dramatically. The hunt for XS938 went better than most and the wreckage was located two days after the crash at a depth of 90 feet about 5 miles west of Bell Rock by HMS *Bildeston*, a Royal Navy minesweeper. In fact the search was successfully concluded only a few hours after it had begun. The main structure and both engines were then salvaged by RFA *Dispenser* by 4 May and these were sufficient to establish the source of the fire. The RAF was particularly keen to find the cause of the accident to XS938 as this aircraft had been through the Fire Integrity Programme that was supposed to reduce the number of Lightning in-flight fires (see Chapter Six).

From the wreckage that was recovered within the first week of the salvage operation it was ascertained that the source of the fire had been in the area of the No.2 engine fuel-draulic pump, probably as a result of a massive fuel leak. Although the fuel-draulic pumps were not brought up during the initial salvage operation, it was concluded that the flexible hose from the pump had failed. A painstaking search was continued for the next two months, during which the fuel-draulic pumps and hoses were eventually recovered from the sea bed. Examination of these components revealed that the fuel leak that caused the fire had in fact originated from a gasket fitted between the fuel-draulic pump and the flexible hose. During the course of the crash investigation it was established that the fuel leak was of the order of 25 gallons per minute. As a result of these findings action was taken to fit new gaskets to all Lightning aircraft on a top priority basis.

By now it had been nearly eight years since a Lightning had been involved in a mid-air collision but this particular hazard was about to reappear in the long list of Lightning accidents. On 26 April four Lightning F.3s of 111 Squadron flew to the French Air Force base at

Colmar for a detachment that was due to last ten days. During their stay in France the Lightnings exercised with locally-based Mirage IIIs but on 3 May, when returning to Colmar, one of a pair of Mirages that had been carrying out dissimilar combat training with two of 111 Squadron's aircraft collided with XP752 flown by Flight Lieutenant Tony Alcock. The accident occurred after the Mirage pilot had declared that he was low on fuel and had broken away from a formation comprising Alcock and the other Mirage (the second Lightning had lost contact in cloud by this stage). Having separated from the other two aircraft the Mirage then flew towards them again and the underside struck the Lightning in the cockpit area causing severe damage to the right-hand side of the nose and removing the canopy. In addition the No.1 engine seized and there was a failure of the AC electrical system so that the main instruments and radio did not function.

After the collision Flight Lieutenant Alcock attempted to eject but found that he was unable to do so. Having carried out a control check, however, he realised that his aircraft was still responding normally and on seeing the Mirages in the distance he followed the two French Air Force aircraft in to land, by which time he was extremely low on fuel (the Mirage that was involved in the collision also landed safely). The Board of Inquiry into this accident concluded that the pilot of the Mirage, having left the formation, had then failed to keep a proper distance and had thus caused the collision. It was also noted that there had been much confusion in the air due to the use of both English and French during radio calls (the pilot of the Mirage involved in the collision was French whose English was poor, although the pilot of the other Mirage was an RAF officer who was on an exchange posting and was bilingual in English and French).

A week later on 10 May yet another aircraft crashed as a result of an in-flight fire. On this occasion it was 56 Squadron that suffered the loss, although happily the pilot ejected and survived. This was Flight Lieutenant Bob Cole who was taking part in a night continuation training exercise in XP744. Having taken off from Akrotiri he was just levelling off at 15,000 feet when there was a Fire 2 warning. As Flight Lieutenant Cole was in the process of carrying out his emergency drills for an engine fire, the attention-getters went again to announce a Reheat 1 warning. At this point he gave a Mayday call and after heading back to base he jettisoned the ventral tank, at which point the Fire 2 warning went out, although the Reheat 1 remained.

As if Bob Cole's workload was not high enough already, the attention-getters then went off again and the Fire 2 warning came back on, together with a Reheat 2 warning. Not long after he felt the fore-and-aft control column movement stiffen, which meant that he had no alternative but to eject. Having informed control of his intentions he ejected at a height of 9,000 feet and was rescued from the sea by a SAR helicopter. Unfortunately his aircraft came down in very deep water and very little wreckage was found. In view of this the investigation into the accident was not able to establish a positive cause although it concluded that the fire had probably originated and been fed by a severe fuel leak within the No.2 engine bay.

By now the number of Lightning engine fires was rapidly reaching a crisis and there was to be no let-up in the immediate future. On 21 May it was the turn of Flying Officer Graham Clarke of 29 Squadron to experience a problem shortly after taking off from Wattisham in XP708, although on this occasion use of the fire extinguisher successfully put out a fire in No.1 engine. It is interesting to note that the ventral tank that was jettisoned as part of the emergency drills travelled for some distance before landing harmlessly in a garden. Due to its shape the ventral acted like a lifting body and actually 'flew' quite well.

Before the end of May there was still time for another Lightning to be lost. This took place on the 26th shortly after Flight Lieutenant Ali McKay of 5 Squadron had taken off from Binbrook in XS902. This aircraft had spent the last six months at 60 MU at Leconfield undergoing a rather protracted major service, which included being snagged several times when flown by the resident test pilots after work had been carried out. On arriving back at Binbrook it was flown on an acceptance check, which was uneventful, and it was then returned to the line. On its second sortie of the day, as Flight Lieutenant McKay was turning onto the departure heading, the Fire 2 warning activated, but as he was carrying out the appropriate fire drills for this emergency the Reheat 1 and 2 captions also came on. Continuing to climb on No.1 engine only, Flight Lieutenant McKay made for the coast to avoid built-up areas and his plight was monitored by another Lightning flown by Flight Lieutenant Merv 'Masher' Fowler who radioed that he could see a brilliant white flame coming from the rear of his aircraft. The control column and rudder pedals then began to move without any input from the pilot, a sure sign that control was about to be lost. Once over the sea McKay wasted no time in ejecting himself by using the face blind handle to become the latest in a long line of Lightning pilots to qualify to be a member of the Caterpillar and Goldfish Clubs. Although he was quickly rescued from the sea, unfortunately he suffered major back injuries during the ejection and it would be several months before he was able to fly again.

Once again there was an unfortunate lack of evidence as no wreckage was ever found. The Board of Inquiry thus had very little to go on, other than the testimony of the pilot, but the sequence of fire warnings was virtually the same as those in the crash of XS938 four weeks before. In view of this it was assumed that the cause of the accident was a fierce fire in the rear fuselage resulting in failure of the controls. There was another similarity to the loss of XS938 in that XS902 had also been through the latest fire integrity modification programme, which was of considerable concern.

The accident statistics for 1971 up to and including the loss of XS902 showed a further worsening of the Lightning's safety record, as in this period there had been eight major accidents that included five Cat.5 write-offs. As total flying hours up to 26 May amounted to 17,000, the overall accident rate was now up to 4.3. This was the highest figure since 1966 and was significantly above the projected figure of 3.0, which it had been assumed the Lightning would have achieved at the end of 1965 and maintained for the rest of its service life. The only bright spot was the fact that there had been no fatalities thus far in 1971. The most worrying aspect of the accident figures was the high number of aircraft that were complete losses. Since the beginning of 1970 twelve aircraft had been destroyed and of these eleven were F.2A, F.3 and F.6 machines as operated by the front-line squadrons. It was also disappointing that the trend in accidents due to fire was rising at a time when most aircraft had been modified in accordance with the Fire Integrity Programme.

Chapter 6

Lightning Accident Review

The recent spate of Lightning accidents led to a comprehensive review of its accident rate since its entry into service, with particular emphasis on the number of aircraft that were being lost to in-flight fires. As the Lightning was scheduled to remain in service until its gradual replacement in the air defence role by the McDonnell Douglas Phantom in 1974/75, the high loss rate was becoming critical. Although the Phantom was already in service it was being used mainly in the strike/attack role, a task it would continue to fulfil until the arrival of the Anglo-French SEPECAT Jaguar.

The problem of in-flight fires in Lightning aircraft had been known about from the very beginning and had eventually led to a Fire Integrity Programme in the late 1960s, which it was hoped would lessen the risk of aircraft being lost to fire. The design of the Lightning had been optimised for performance with particular emphasis on high levels of acceleration, together with a rapid climb rate and the ability to fly at high supersonic speeds at altitude. To generate the high levels of thrust needed, a twin-engine design had been adopted in which the engines were mounted one above the other and staggered, which had the effect of reducing frontal area, which in turn reduced drag. No.1 engine was mounted low in the fuselage with No.2 mounted above and to the rear of No.1. This meant that No.2 engine was positioned above the No.1 jet pipe so that any fuel or hydraulic leak from this engine was likely to find its way into the hot Fire Zone 3 area of the No.1 jet pipe due to inadequate sealing. To try to prevent this Lightning aircraft were sent to maintenance units in a rolling programme where a product known as Viton was applied to the floor of the No.2 engine bay. This was a synthetic rubber material that gave excellent heat resistance (200 degrees C) and was resistant to fuel and oils. As previously noted, however, Lightnings continued to be lost to in-flight fires even after they had passed through the Fire Integrity Programme.

A report was compiled on the Lightning's safety record and covered the period from its entry into service to 11 May 1971, with accidents analysed by causes and by marks of aircraft in order to detect any possible trends. Comparisons were also made with a number of other RAF types. In addition fire accidents and incidents were analysed thoroughly for the period January 1970 to 11 May 1971. These dates were used due to a lack of earlier data. An assessment was also made of the risk to the pilot in terms of abandonment and mortality, and the likely level of future write-offs was also assessed.

Since the entry of the Lightning into service there had been a total of 110 accidents, of which forty led to the aircraft being written off. Aircraft fires were the main cause, resulting in 30 per cent of all accidents and 37.5 per cent of all write-offs. Pilot error accounted for 29 per cent and 22.5 per cent respectively and other technical causes accounted for 21.8 per cent and 25 per cent. This left other causes and unknowns for the remaining 19.2 per cent and 15 per cent. A breakdown of accidents by mark showed that, overall, the F.1/F.1A was involved in the most accidents with thirty which represented 30 per cent of the total. Next in line were the F.3 and F.6 which were in practically equal proportions with twenty-five and twenty-four respectively (25 per cent of total accidents). These three marks together accounted for 82 per cent of all accidents due to fire with the F.3 alone being responsible for 33 per cent.

In the case of write-offs, the same three marks accounted for 85 per cent of all cases with the F.1/F.1A contributing the largest proportion with fourteen (35 per cent). Write-offs due to fire did not involve the F.2 and T.4. In this category the largest proportion was represented by the F.3 with six cases (40 per cent). This was followed by the F.1/F.1A with five (33 per cent) and the F.6 with four (27 per cent). It was thus concluded that fires were the largest single cause of all Lightning accidents and write-offs with the F.3 being the mark that was most prone to fire accidents.

In addition to breaking Lightning accidents down by mark, the report also looked at a timeline and here it was noted that fire accidents had become more prominent since 1966, with the exception of 1969 when there were only two fire accidents and no write-offs as a result. Since 1969 there had been five write-offs due to fire, of which three involved the F.3 with the other two being F.6s. It was noted that the same two marks were involved in all eight fire accidents. It was clear that fire accidents and write-offs had been on the increase since 1966 and that there had been a revived upsurge since 1969. When the total number of accidents was broken down into cause groups it was found that in recent years, accidents caused by pilot error or technical causes (other than fire) had shown a downward trend while other causes had remained constant. On a cumulative basis fires were the largest single cause of all accidents, and had been since 1967 in the case of write-offs with a recent upward trend.

At the time of the report, in the case of write-off rates, only the F.1/ F.1A and T.5 showed a definite downward trend that had been indicated since 1968 for the F.1/F.1A and 1966 for the T.5, which was very soon after its introduction to service. However, in the case of cumulative write-off and accident rates due to fire, although the F.1/F.1A was now showing a downward trend, its overall rates were still the highest at 1.18 and 2.1 (per 10,000 hours) respectively. The upward trend for the F.3 had been particularly pronounced since 1969 and in the case of fire accidents the F.3 had shown a 50 per cent increase. Although the trend for the F.6 was also upward, the trend for the F.3 was described as alarming. It was concluded that, of the different marks of Lightning, only the F.1/F.1A and T.5 were showing any sign of improvement.

Although the Lightning's recent problems were giving cause for concern, overall its accident rate compared favourably with other types including the Javelin, Hunter and Buccaneer in terms of accidents and write-offs. However, in some cases the causes of these accidents varied considerably. A comparison was made of the write-off rates of the Lightning, Hunter and Javelin based on cumulative flying hours in which it was discovered that the proportion of write-offs due to fire for the Javelin (36.1 per cent) was actually very similar to that of the Lightning at 37.5 per cent. In the case of the Hunter the figure was only 9.7 per cent. A comparison of write-offs due to pilot error showed the Lightning in the best light with 22.5 per cent, which compared with 27.8 per cent for the Javelin and 40 per cent for the Hunter. Write-offs caused by other technical issues were similar for all three aircraft. The comparison with the Hunter therefore showed the greatest differences, the Lightning being nearly twice as good from the pilot error aspect, but four times worse in terms of fires.

With regard to the Lightning's recent accident history, the most important part of the report was its findings in relation to fire hazards. The breakdown of fire accidents looked at the marks involved, whether the occurrence took place on the ground or in the air, the type of fire, stage of flight, the use of reheat and whether the aircraft had passed through the Fire Integrity Programme. In all marks of Lightning most of the fire incidents occurred during the climb or when under cruise combat conditions when high power settings were being used with corresponding higher temperatures within the fire zones. However, no link could be established between fire incidents and the use of reheat due to the fact that in 66 per cent of in-flight fires the use of reheat was not recorded.

Of all the real fire warnings that had occurred, 75 per cent involved No.1 engine and the prevalence of Fire 1 and Reheat 1 warnings was common to all marks of Lightning. With regard to hot gas leaks, however, these were recorded in equal numbers for each engine installation with three quarters resulting in either a Fire 1 or a Fire 2 warning. As well as real fire warnings, there were numerous spurious fire warnings on the Lightning and 75 per cent of these resulted in Fire 2 and Reheat 2 warnings. The marks that were most likely to receive spurious warnings from the No.2 engine were the F.3 and T.5.

Not surprisingly the most common causes of actual fires were fuel leaks and hydraulic oil leaks with each contributing 30 per cent to the total of all fires. These two causes accounted for all fires in the F.6 and 45 per cent of those in the F.3. The only actual fire to occur in a T.4 also resulted from the burning of hydraulic oil. The F.3 and F.6 were the only marks to have suffered from engine titanium fires. Of particular concern was the fact that of the nineteen airborne fire accidents and incidents in 1971, fourteen occurred in aircraft that had been through the latest Fire Integrity Programme and two thirds of the aircraft involved in actual fires in the air had had the fire integrity modifications embodied. The only mark of Lightning that did not have an accident or incident to a fire modified aircraft was the F.2/F.2A.

As has already been recorded, fires also occurred on the ground and of these 75 per cent occurring during start-up. Once again they were most prominent in the F.3 and F.6. During the period under review there were two cases of hot gas leaks on the ground, one occurring during taxying in a T.4 and the other during start-up in an F.6. There were also six spurious warnings that were evenly split between start-up and taxying. The main causes of fires on the ground were AVPIN (58 per cent) and fuel venting (33 per cent) with all of the AVPIN fires occurring on start-up. The mark that was most affected by fuel venting was the F.6 with three cases out of four resulting in fires. The occurrence of fires on the ground in aircraft that had had the fire integrity modifications fitted was less than in the air at 33 per cent.

When the analysis of fire incidents was widened to include those from January 1970 it was found that there had been twenty-six in all of which eighteen had been through the Fire Integrity Programme. Having tabulated the figures for this period an estimate was then made of likely aircraft losses in the future. Assuming that the write-off rate remained the same it was calculated that by 1976 a further twenty-six would have been lost of which half would have been F.3 and F.6 aircraft. Thereafter it was estimated that losses would have been two aircraft per year. The risk to the pilot was also calculated. Assuming a four-year tour on the Lightning force, the chances of a typical pilot, flying some 320 sorties a year (20 hours per month), being involved in an aircraft fire leading to abandonment were estimated at 6 per cent with a subsequent risk of mortality of 1.5 per cent. When all accidents were taken into consideration there was a 17 per cent chance of having to eject during a typical tour with a 4.25 per cent risk of mortality.

From the report into the Lightning's safety record it was clear that the marks that were most at risk from in-flight fires were the F.3 and F.6. Although five F.1/F.1A aircraft had been lost as a result of fires, this mark had shown a significant improvement since 1968 whereas the figures for the F.6, and particularly the F.3, had shown a worsening trend. The most likely reasons for this situation were given in an Air Ministry memo dated 23 September 1971. It was believed that there were several engineering features of the F.3 and F.6 that were responsible, at least in part, for their poor fire record.

The F.3 and F.6 were both powered by Rolls Royce Avon Mk.300 series engines which, when operating at ground level and full military power (without reheat), ran at carcass temperatures about 20 degrees C higher than the Mk.200 series engines as fitted in other marks of Lightning. It was also noted that the surface temperatures of some parts of the Mk.300 series engine were higher than the spontaneous ignition temperatures of fluids passing through the engine bays. Another difference of the Mk.300 series Avon compared to the Mk.200 series was the fact that the former employed a high pressure fuel-draulic system that had been prone to defects that had caused fuel to leak into the engine bays. This was mainly due to the very high fuel pressures involved. The engines of the F.3 and F.6 were also fitted with a Hot-Streak reheat initiator unit that had also been susceptible to faults in which fuel had been spilt into the engine bay areas. Paradoxically, although theses three features were also incorporated in the two-seat T.5, the fire record of this mark was the complete opposite of the F.3 and F.6. From an engineering point of view this was impossible to explain, although it was thought that the T.5's role as a trainer may have accounted for its better record as regards in-flight engine fires.

During the official correspondence on this matter it was noted that Coltishall's record of engine fires in Lightning aircraft was considerably better than all other Lightning stations. This was put down to the particular mix of aircraft that was flown from the Norfolk base. Although its complement of aircraft amounted to thirty-seven, at the time of the report it only operated four F.3s. As has already been noted, this was the variant that was most prone to engine fires. Although Coltishall still operated ten F.1As, this mark had shown a considerable improvement in its fire record in recent years.

The success, or otherwise, of the Fire Integrity Programme was a matter of considerable debate, although it appeared to have been effective regarding the earlier marks of Lightning, clearly there was still a way to go with the F.3 and F.6. As such it was agreed that further work should concentrate on the differences between the two sets of marks, i.e. the higher engine bay temperatures, the fuel-draulic system and the Hot-Streak reheat ignition, and that weaknesses that could not be readily cured should be contained.

The weaknesses in the fuel-draulic system were identified as the repeated breaking of a flange joint, the inadequacy of a gasket that had been employed, and the susceptibility of a flexible pipe to damage through bending and its liability to fatigue as a result of large ripples in pressure. By mid-1971 action was in hand to bring about improvement on all three counts. A problem had also been identified on the low-pressure fuel system on a F.6 aircraft and improved seals were to be fitted that were capable of withstanding temperatures of 200 degrees C. A method to box in this part of the fuel system was also proposed to act as a heat shield and to contain and drain away any leakage. Also at this time large-bore overboard fuel drains were due to be flight-tested, which were intended to drain fuel should a massive leak occur. Attention was also focused on the hydraulic system which had been the cause of a number of in-flight fires. Hitherto the system had not been subject to periodic replacement, but it was now clear that bonded seals in the hydraulic system, deteriorated due to heat. Because of this the existing seals were scheduled for replacement by improved seals within a year. In the meantime Viton tape was used to minimise spray from leaks.

A number of recommendations were made with regard to the engines and these included examination of the jet pipe areas to check for cracks following a recent hot gas leak in a F.6. Ultimately it was proposed that the intermediate jet pipe be replaced by one of a new material. The programme for substituting steel outlet guide vanes for titanium to prevent titanium fires was underway and a cyclic fatigue test of the Hot-Streak reheat ignition system was being carried out. Flight trials were also due to start with fuel additives that were intended to show up fuel and hot gas leaks. Servicing was also being reviewed and a new system of service training had recently been set up so that technicians who had not previously worked on the Lightning were given the best possible background to ensure fire integrity. This knowledge was also to be passed to the squadrons. In addition, there had been a review of all outstanding modifications and these were placed in strict order of priority in the fire integrity context.

The Fire Integrity Programme was thus continuing and in time, with a greater knowledge of the problems that affected the Lightning, the number of fire incidents was gradually reduced. Had the number of accidents as a result of fire continued at the levels recorded in 1970/71 however, as one writer put it, it would probably have resulted in the aircraft's premature demise. This would have been an extremely serious situation and may well have resulted in a gap in air defence capability before this role was taken on in the main by the Phantom. In the early 1970s the version of the Phantom as flown by the RAF also had major problems relating to its Rolls Royce Spey engines.

Chapter 7

Picking up the Pieces

With the imminent withdrawal of British forces in the Far East the Lightning force was about to see its first contraction when 74 Squadron was disbanded on 31 August 1971. The unit's F.6s were flown to Akrotiri where they were taken over by 56 Squadron. The trip to Cyprus was via Gan in the Maldives, the leg from Gan to Akrotiri being flown direct in eight hours with the aid of multiple hook-ups with tanker aircraft. In most other respects the distribution of Lightning squadrons in what was now No.11 Group, Strike Command, remained the same, except that in March 1972 No.11 Squadron left Leuchars to begin a long-standing partnership with 5 Squadron at Binbrook.

The first incident after the publication of the review on Lightning accidents occurred on 16 June 1971 when XS455 of 5 Squadron was damaged Cat.3 by a lightning strike. The aircraft had taken off from Binbrook for a weapons instructional sortie and was climbing when it flew through fairly thick, but non-turbulent, cloud for about thirty seconds. The crew were not aware that their aircraft had been hit and it was only after landing that they realised what had happened. As a result of a lightning strike the fin tip had been torn away and there was bowing of the skin. A number of rivets had also been pulled out on both sides of the fin and the upper aerial probe was broken into three pieces and the access panel had buckled outwards. A new fin had to be fitted by 60 MU at Leconfield and XS455 was returned for service six weeks later.

There was another case of fuel venting leading to a fire on the ground on 23 June when XR723 of 11 Squadron had just begun to taxy prior to a familiarisation exercise. The accident took place at the Royal Danish Air Force (RDAF) base at Skrydstrup during a four-aircraft detachment. The exercise was to have involved two of the Lightnings and two RDAF Hunters, but shortly after XR723 began to move the pilot of the other Lightning called to say that it was venting fuel in large quantities.

Almost immediately the leader of the Danish formation radioed to say that the Lightning was on fire. On looking behind, the pilot of XR723 saw flames coming from his wing and so shut down both engines and brought his aircraft to a halt. During his shut-down checks he noticed that the Fire 1 warning had illuminated so he operated the No.1 fire extinguisher before making all electrics safe and abandoning the cockpit.

The fire was centred on the starboard fuselage and wing root and was eventually contained by ground personnel before it was finally extinguished by the emergency fire crews. After hosing the aircraft down with water the ground crew towed it back to dispersal with two fire vehicles in attendance. On arrival at the pan, several panels were removed from the aircraft and it was discovered that there was a fire in the No.2 engine bay. This was quickly put out by the firemen who had accompanied the aircraft.

The fuel that had flowed out of the wing tank had come via the vent valve in the starboard wing. The precise cause of the fuel venting could not be determined, although it was considered to be the result of either a faulty fuel valve or a sticking float switch. Another possibility was a transient electrical fault. The fuel that had been used to refuel XR723 was JP4, which was highly volatile. The ignition of the fuel most probably occurred in the muff covering No.1 engine to intermediate jet pipe joint. The fuel had gained entry to the muff via its outlet pipe to the side of the fuselage, which was unprotected from the ingress of vented fuel. The burning fuel at this point then ignited the external fuel that was on the wing of the aircraft and the fuel that had also passed into the No.2 engine bay. It was likely that the fire in the No.2 engine bay had not been extinguished during the initial fire operations and was still burning as the aircraft was being towed back to its dispersal point.

In the aftermath of this accident a recommendation was proposed to position the Flight Re-fuel/Normal switch to Flight Refuel during engine-start, taxying and take-off to minimise the risk of fuel venting. However, this was rejected by the AOC-in-C of No.11 Group as this procedure could lead to a dangerous CG change prior to take off. This method had been adopted by 74 Squadron in the Far East and was thought to have been a contributory factor to the take-off accident to XS930 in which Flight Lieutenant Frank Whitehouse had been killed.

Although the loss of Lightning canopies on take-off had featured regularly in various Flight Safety publications over the years, it was unfortunately still happening, although perhaps not to the extent of the mid-to-late 1960s. Once again it involved a F.2, this particular mark being responsible for the majority of occurrences in this category of incident. The accident took place at Gutersloh on 24 June when F.2A XN780 of 92 Squadron was taking off after a simulated operational turn-round in front of a VIP audience who were thus treated to rather more than they had anticipated. The canopy was ripped off at a speed of around 135 knots IAS and hit the fin as it came away as well as causing damage to the fuselage spine adjacent to the canopy pivot points. The take off was continued normally and after burning off fuel to reduce weight to an acceptable level for landing, the aircraft was recovered safely. During his take-off checks the pilot had failed to lock the hood, a possible contributory factor being that the canopy warning light daylight cover had not been selected to the Day position. The number of canopy-related incidents with the F.2/F.2A may have been due to the lack of a canopy warning light on the Standard Warning Panel, which was a feature on other marks of Lightning.

The next fire-related loss of a Lightning was not long in coming and once again it involved a F.3. No.29 Squadron flew to Cyprus in early July for a four-week detachment but on the 8th XP705 crashed into the Mediterranean about 35 miles south of Akrotiri. At the time the aircraft was being flown by Flight Lieutenant Graham Clarke on the second of two one-to-one fighter combat sorties with a rapid turn-round in between. The first sortie was uneventful and after taking off on the second, the two aircraft (the other was flown by Flying Officer George Fenton) climbed to 20,000 feet for a yo-yo exercise with XP705 acting as the target. The first part of the exercise involved two 360-degree starboard turns and was completed without any problems. On repeating this exercise in a turn to port, Flight Lieutenant Clarke allowed his aircraft to descend to 16,000 feet with speed falling to 250 knots IAS. He then engaged reheat on both engines to gain altitude and maintained speed at 250 knots IAS. At this stage both reheat systems were working normally. With reheat still lit, Clarke then turned again to port and, as he passed the other Lightning on a reciprocal heading, he demonstrated an escape manoeuvre by levelling his wings and pushing the control column fully forward to apply zero 'g' for maximum acceleration.

About two-to-three seconds after pushing forward on the stick, Clarke heard a 'Whoomph' and his aircraft kicked gently. His initial thought was that there had been a reheat malfunction but shortly afterwards the audio warning sounded and the attention-getter flashed to announce a

Reheat 1 fire warning. The appropriate fire drills were performed and a Mayday call was made, by which time a restriction in the fore-and-aft control of the Lightning could be felt, although the other control responses were as normal. In the next few seconds there was a gradual stiffening of the control response in pitch and a few seconds later this was followed by the audio warning sounding again as the Reheat 2 caption illuminated. As he was now faced with two reheat warnings and the imminent loss of control in pitch, Clarke made one final Mayday call. Having lowered his seat and kicked the rudder pedals away, he ejected at a speed of 230 knots IAS and an altitude of 13,400 feet.

Flight Lieutenant Clarke's ejection was observed by his playmate (Flying Officer Fenton) who continued to watch XP705 as it spiralled steeply downwards, trailing grey smoke from the No.1 jet pipe until it eventually crashed in the sea. The ejection itself was relatively straightforward, although there were moments of anxiety. As the seat fired, Clarke felt his head move forwards and was aware of the canopy arch dropping away below him. Once clear of the aircraft the seat tumbled violently leading to concern that the drogue parachutes had not deployed, but this only lasted for a short time and the main parachute opened with a resounding crack. The relief of the rapid deceleration was, however, quickly replaced by a sharp pain as the harness tightened between his legs. During the long descent Clarke did not have much time to admire the view as he had great difficulty in detaching his oxygen mask and then found that his Mae West would not inflate. It was only after several increasingly desperate double-handed tugs that the life-jacket was eventually inflated (the cord had been misrouted). After coming down in the sea, he inflated his dinghy and a Whirlwind HAR.10 helicopter of 1563 Flight from Akrotiri arrived about twenty minutes later to winch him aboard. During the short trip back to Cyprus, Graham Clarke had a shocking experience (literally) when the crew of the Whirlwind plugged his helmet, which was still full of sea water, into the helicopter's intercom system. On arriving back at Akrotiri he was taken straight to hospital where a check-up revealed that he had not suffered any injuries.

As the Lightning had crashed in deep water (some 6,500 feet), a salvage operation was not possible so there was no material evidence available to the Board of Inquiry for it to come up with a positive cause of the airborne fire. Despite a lack of wreckage it was concluded that the most likely cause of the accident was a fuel leak from the main refuelling and transfer gallery, which led to fuel pooling on the floor of the No.1 engine intermediate jet pipe area of Fire Zone 3. It was considered that the application of negative 'g' had caused this fuel to be thrown onto a hot surface leading to an explosion and fire in the No.1 jet pipe. It was also likely that the explosion would have caused further damage to fuel lines in the affected area. After a short time the fire spread into Fire Zone 3 of the No.2 engine causing the Reheat 2 warning. It was also felt that inadequate drainage of the fuselage was a contributory cause to the accident.

The Board acknowledged that the fire integrity of Lightning aircraft continued to be the subject of the closest study and was high priority at all levels. It noted that numerous measures were being formulated and introduced to stem the hazard and these included improvements to the low-pressure fuel system couplings that were a known high risk source of leakage together with fluid drainage of the fuselage. At the time of the accident BAC Warton was carrying out a further analysis of all Lightning airborne fire accidents that had occurred in 1971 with a view to determining the causes of these fires more precisely. Immediately after the accident the AOC-in-C No.11 Group issued a signal advising Lightning pilots to avoid negative 'g' manoeuvres whenever reheat was selected pending the outcome of the Board of Inquiry findings. However, this was subsequently withdrawn when no evidence was forthcoming that this had been the primary cause of the accident.

The next Lightning mishap was a barrier entry to XN792 of 92 Squadron on 6 August. During a training flight a HYD 1 failure occurred and the pilot returned to Gutersloh for an overweight precautionary landing. As a result of the hydraulic failure the braking parachute did not deploy, so the pilot used maximum braking until 500 yards before the end of the runway, by which time he already had his arrestor hook down so as to take the runway RHAG (the release of brakes was in accordance with standard procedures). However, the arrestor hook did not engage with the RHAG and despite applying maximum braking once again, the pilot was unable to prevent his aircraft from going into the barrier at a speed of about 30 knots. Unfortunately there was a malfunction with the barrier and part of it struck the aircraft spine and crushed the AVPIN tank, which caused a fire. As a result the aircraft was damaged Cat.3 but the pilot was uninjured.

It was discovered that the HYD 1 failure had been caused by a fracture to a hydraulic pipe connection to the No.1 Control system pressure filter, which was probably the result of a broken filter bracket. It was also considered that the failure of the arrestor hook to engage with the RHAG was due to the wire bouncing after being trampled by the aircraft's main wheels. The wire had then knocked the hook violently upwards causing damage to the underside of the fuselage; it was noted that about 3 per cent of all attempted Lightning RHAG engagements were unsuccessful.

On 16 September another mid-air collision occurred, which was the third occasion that Lightning aircraft had been involved in this type of accident. The collision took place during a formation practice by nine Lightnings of 92 Squadron before a display that was scheduled to be part of an Open Day at Gutersloh. After take-off the aircraft formed up into a diamond-nine formation and performed a number of turns and a flypast at Gutersloh before climbing to 5,000 feet to practise reversal turns. These were effectively shallow wing-overs as bank angles were no more than 75 degrees and the maximum pull force on the control column was 2½g.

Former Red Arrows pilot Flight Lieutenant Terry Kingsley was flying XN727 in the No.6 position in the centre of the formation directly behind the leader. As the formation began to roll for a third wing-over, Kingsley became aware that his aircraft was being affected by the presence of another to the extent that it was impossible for him to maintain his position. Almost immediately his Lightning was hit by XN774, which was being flown by Flight Lieutenant John Bryant in the No.8 position, which was to his right and behind. The port wing of Bryant's machine struck Kingsley's starboard wing and both aircraft were ejected upwards and out of the formation. With both aircraft out of control for a time it appeared that Bryant rolled around Kingsley's machine so that for a brief moment they were in a very close mirror formation.

As a result of the collision XN727 suffered a badly-damaged starboard wing in which use of the aileron had been lost, a bent fin (with restricted rudder movement) and a damaged tailplane. Although Kingsley was just able to control his aircraft, because of the damage to the starboard wing and aileron he was unable to turn right and was reduced to flying in a series of left-hand orbits. Also, the damaged tailplane meant that he had to hold the control column fully forwards just to maintain level flight. Having carried out a slow speed handling check, Kingsley was able to adjust his constant left-hand turn so that he was eventually in a position to land. Despite the fact that he had extreme difficulty in keeping straight and had greatly restricted control in pitch he managed to bring his aircraft in for a successful landing. John Bryant's Lightning had corresponding damage to its port wing but he too was able to land safely at Gutersloh. During the collision Terry Kingsley suffered a back injury due to the shock load that was transmitted through his aircraft. The damage to both aircraft was assessed as Cat.3 and in time they were returned to service.

During close formation flying it is imperative that aircraft maintain their positions as accurately as possible as any deviation is likely to lead to contact with the wing tip vortices coming from other aircraft flying in positions immediately ahead. This problem had been identified at least ten years before during formation displays by Hunter aircraft and it had also been experienced with the first Gnat aerobatic teams. As the Lightning was considerably bigger and heavier, the amount of disturbed air flowing off the wing was of a much greater intensity so that its potential effect on other aircraft flying a few feet away was significantly worse. The trailing vortices were also stronger if, as in this case, the formation was carrying out a turn. It appears that the Lightning flown by John Bryant was affected by wake turbulence to the point where it became uncontrollable and hit the aircraft flown by Terry Kingsley. During the briefing it had been agreed that the reference for pilots to maintain their position in the formation would be line astern, not echelon, and it was felt that this may have been a factor in the collision. Indeed the station commander at Gutersloh, Group Captain Mike 'Dusty' Miller, was of the opinion that the formation leader would have been better advised to instruct the pilots in the No.7 and No. 8 positions to obtain their reference in echelon. If this had been the case John Bryant would have used Terry Kingsley's aircraft as a reference and not the No.2 flying directly ahead of him.

On 22 September another Lightning pilot lost his life in an accident that proved to be one of the most difficult for the investigators to determine the cause. A pair of F.3s from 29 Squadron took off from Wattisham to carry out supersonic practice interceptions over the North Sea. The interceptor was XP736 flown by Flying Officer Phil Mottershead, who was directed by Control for a 90-degree crossing contact where the target aircraft approached from right to left (the target aircraft had taken off seven minutes before XP736 so that it could be positioned to commence its attack run towards the coast at a height of 40,000 feet and a speed of

Mach 1.1). Flying Officer Mottershead was ordered to increase speed to Mach 1.3 and when the target had crossed some 8 to 10 miles ahead of his aircraft the controller called for a left turn onto the target's course.

Having rolled out behind the target aircraft at a range of about 4 miles, Flying Officer Mottershead began to close but not long afterwards he made a Mayday call that was largely indistinguishable. On hearing this radio message the pilot of the other aircraft began a turn to port in an attempt to make visual contact and saw condensation or wing tip trails in a spiral pattern just before XP736 disappeared into cloud at about 32,000 feet. There were no further radio transmissions and the aircraft eventually disappeared from the radar screens, although a faint (and apparently stationary) return was noticed, which it was later thought might have been the aircraft's canopy after it had been jettisoned.

Very little wreckage from XP736 was recovered from the sea and the body of Flying Officer Mottershead was never found. The canopy was picked up and it was clear that it had been jettisoned before impact with the sea. From this scant piece of evidence, however, it was concluded that there had been a failure in the interconnecting cable between the canopy and the seat, which would have prevented Mottershead from ejecting. Although the Board of Inquiry had very little evidence on which to base its findings, it was considered that the accident had probably been caused either by a control malfunction or inertia cross-coupling, or possibly by a mishandled emergency situation.

No.92 Squadron lost another aircraft to long-term repair on 23 September when XN730 suffered an undercarriage malfunction. The aircraft was being flown by Flight Lieutenant Norman Barker, who became aware that something was amiss when he noticed a port undercarriage red shortly after take-off. A visual inspection was carried out by Flying Officer Mike Johnson, who reported that the port wheel had castored and appeared to be at an angle of about 45 degrees to the fore-and-aft axis of the aircraft. After a period spent burning off fuel, during which Flight Lieutenant Barker was eventually able to get three greens after much manoeuvring, he attempted a landing in the early stages of which the port undercarriage leg collapsed. Thankfully the aircraft remained upright and eventually came to rest with substantial damage to the left wing and underside. This was repaired on site but XN730 was not ready for its return to 92 Squadron until June of the following year. The failure was caused by a fracture of the toggle-link pin on the port main undercarriage, which was a known defect on the Lightning.

On 30 September one of the ex-74 Squadron Lightning F.6s (XR764) that had recently been handed over to 56 Squadron crashed into the Mediterranean approximately 35 miles south-east of Akrotiri. The aircraft had already been in the air not long before the accident sortie and this trip had been completed without any problems. On the second sortie, after a standard reheat take off and climb to 1,000 feet with speed increasing to 450 knots IAS, the rest of the climb was carried out in full cold power, but when passing through 24,000 feet the Reheat 1 warning caption illuminated. The pilot (Flight Lieutenant Richard Bealer) immediately reduced power on both engines, turned back towards Akrotiri and went through his reheat fire drills. As he was still doing these, however, he noticed a stiffening of control in pitch and the Reheat 2 warning also came on. A few seconds later the Reheat 1 warning went out, but as the Reheat 2 warning remained, Flight Lieutenant Bealer put out a Mayday call. Around two minutes after making this call and with his situation unchanged, Bealer ejected himself from his aircraft by means of the face blind handle.

As he had ejected at approximately 22,000 feet, Bealer had a seemingly endless wait before the barostat mechanism activated the seat release and main parachute at 10,000 feet. His descent into the sea was uneventful apart from a close encounter with his wingman (Flying Officer Al Bryan) who was desperately trying to locate his position. After spending around half-an-hour in the sea in his dinghy, Bealer was picked up by SAR helicopter and returned to Akrotiri. His Lightning crashed in the same general position as Flight Lieutenant Graham Clarke's XP705 four months before and the depth of water in this area once again meant that a salvage operation was out of the question. It was fairly obvious that fire had occurred within the reheat zones but the cause could not be established. XR764 had been through the Fire Integrity Programme in August 1970 when it was still with 74 Squadron. At the time of the accident it had flown a total of 982 hours.

Although it did not result in an accident, a pilot of 111 Squadron had a potentially disastrous in-flight incident on 5 October while flying XP741. During a climb in echelon port formation in full cold power and at Mach 0.90, his Lightning suddenly rolled hard to port as the aircraft were climbing through 18,000 feet. He was able to regain control to wings level by using full right aileron trim and minimal force on the control column. At the time the auto-stabilisers were engaged and the pilot found that normal control was restored when these were disengaged.

However, when the auto-stabs were re-selected the same symptoms were reproduced. As a result of this control problem the mission was aborted and the aircraft returned to Wattisham. The fault could not be reproduced during ground investigation and no conclusive evidence of the cause could be found. An actuator socket on the port aileron was found to be defective and it was thought that it might have been contaminated with fuel at some point. It was considered that an intermittent electrical break had occurred at this socket allowing the actuator to become de-restricted. The comment was made that if this eventuality had taken place when the aircraft were flying in echelon formation to starboard then the outcome would probably have been the loss of two or more aircraft.

It had been some time since a Lightning had sunk back onto the runway during take-off but on 29 October it happened for the fourth time and this particular accident was probably the most spectacular yet. On this occasion the scene was Wattisham and the unfortunate aircraft was XR711, which was being flown by Flight Lieutenant Eric Steenson of 111 Squadron. The intention was for three aircraft to carry out a stream take-off with five seconds between each machine and as the Lightnings approached the runway they lined up in echelon formation. The lead aircraft flown by Squadron Leader John Hawtin took off normally but Flight Lieutenant Steenson in the No.2 position did not (the No.3 Lightning of Flight Lieutenant Dennis Brooks also got airborne without any problems).

With Squadron Leader Hawtin accelerating down the runway, Flight Lieutenant Steenson applied full cold power and noted that the rpm and jet pipe temperatures were both normal, although the No.2 engine nozzle was slightly late to close. He then selected full reheat and his aircraft quickly picked up speed along the centre of the runway. At a distance of 900 yards from the runway threshold, just before the calculated lift-off point, the aircraft touched its tail bumper and ventral fin on the runway, leaving a mark some 50 feet long. The aircraft then skipped for a further 50 feet before settling on the ventral tank.

The aircraft continued to slide on its belly for the remaining 1,560 yards of runway and by good fortune it stayed level, although at one stage the port wing tip scraped the ground and the machine gradually settled forward onto its nose. About 1,000 yards from the threshold, burning fuel from the ruptured ventral tank started to spill onto the runway and continued to burn on the runway surface. As it shot down the runway with seemingly undiminished speed the Lightning entered the centre of the barrier. The force was such that the bottom cable broke but fortunately the top one held although it cut deeply into the base of the aircraft's fin. It finally came to rest some 500 feet past the barrier and Flight Lieutenant Steenson, who was completely unhurt, was able to vacate the cockpit using the normal hood opening system. It was later concluded that XR711 had become airborne at too low a speed and with the undercarriage already selected up before a safe climb-away had been established the aircraft was able to sink back onto the runway.

As a result of the accident the other two Lightnings of Squadron Leader Hawtin and Flight Lieutenant Brooks had to be diverted to Coltishall. In addition to rendering one Lightning Cat.5, Eric Steenson also made quite a mess of the Wattisham runway as it was discovered that fuel from the ventral tank had soaked into the friction course. This caused the parts of the runway top surface so affected to break up when it was cleared for use once again. After the accident XR711 was stripped for spares before ending up on the Wattisham dump. It was finally scrapped in 1975.

Although in general 1971 had been another difficult year for the Lightning, in particular the number of in-flight fires, there were at least some signs towards the end of the year that a corner had been turned. The following is the official view of the fire situation at this time:

1971 as a whole has been a disappointing year with regard to Lightning fire occurrences compared with 1970 when the resurgence of the problem first became apparent. In 1971 there were eight Lightning fire accidents, including six write-offs, as against five fire accidents and two resulting write-offs in 1970. The eight fire accidents for 1971 represent 8.3 per cent of the total number of RAF aircraft accidents for the year and, as such, were the single major cause of accidents resulting from technical defects. Although the year taken as a whole presents a poor record of Lightning fires, the trend for the latter part of 1971 is much more encouraging. All of the year's fire accidents occurred during the first three quarters of the year, the worst periods being from April to June with four accidents and July to September with three accidents. Since no Lightning fire accidents have occurred since 30 September 1971, the fourth quarter was the first to be free for a whole year.

These initial signs of a possible long term improvement in the situation have been apparent also in the reduced number of fire incidents in the fourth quarter. Only three incidents involving actual fire occurred in the final quarter compared with six in the first and five in each of the second and third quarters. Also, all three fires were engine starter exhaust fires, which happened on the ground during start-up; no airborne incidents involving actual fire have been reported since September 1971. Hot gas leaks accounted for three incidents in the final quarter, which thus showed no major improvement over previous quarters. Spurious fire warnings decreased to two in the final quarter from six in the previous quarter. Although the decrease is a welcome sign, previous records show that such reductions in numbers of spurious warnings can be short-lived and any reduction would have to be sustained over several consecutive quarters to indicate a permanent improvement in the situation. In addition to the incidents mentioned above, one other was reported that is still under investigation, making a grand total of nine fire incidents for the quarter – three fewer than the preceding quarter.

The fourth quarter's return of Lightning fire accidents and incidents provides what could be the first concrete evidence of the effectiveness of the improvements made to the fire integrity of the aircraft. However, the improved record should be viewed with cautious optimism only, for the statistical sample derived from a single quarter is small. Should the improvement continue well into 1972, it could be considered that the long-awaited breakthrough had finally been achieved. These early signs are most encouraging, and it is hoped that the continued efforts of all currently involved in resolving the fire problems of the Lightning will ensure that the downwards trend seen at the end of 1971 continues in the months ahead.

The first notable accident of 1972 was a barrier engagement on 14 February at Binbrook as a result of an aborted take off. The aircraft involved was XS455 of 5 Squadron, which apparently suffered a control problem during the take-off run. Having raised the nose-wheel, the pilot checked further back on the control column at a speed of approximately 170 knots IAS to set up the necessary attitude for lift off, but as he did so he noticed a control restriction in pitch. He immediately made the decision to abort take-off and lowered the nose-wheel back onto the runway before operating the parachute and applying maximum braking. At the same time he adjusted the throttles to idle/idle before shutting down No.1 engine. Although these actions were carried out with the utmost haste, the pilot could not prevent the aircraft going into the barrier at relatively high speed. For once the damage was minimal (Cat.2) and XS455 was soon returned to the line.

No.29 Squadron's run of bad luck continued two days later during a practice interception at night. The aircraft concerned were XP698, which was being flown by Flight Lieutenant Paul Reynolds and XP747, flown by Flight Lieutenant Paul Cooper. The exercise required interceptions to be carried out at supersonic speeds and the sortie was uneventful until the recovery phase. As there was thick cloud extending up to 20,000 feet, after the exercise had been completed the pre-flight briefing had included for the two aircraft to form-up above cloud in close formation so that the cloud layer could be penetrated safely. The two aircraft made for the Wattisham dive circle and at this stage Flight Lieutenant Reynolds saw the lights of the other aircraft on his starboard side. He then turned to his right and flew over XP747, which was then seen again on his port side. Not long after, whilst flying at 34,000 feet and a speed of Mach 0.90, Flight Lieutenant Reynolds began his descent but shortly afterwards the two aircraft collided, the impact being extremely violent and both aircraft immediately went out of control.

Paul Reynolds tried to move the control column back to prevent a nose-down pitch but he found that there was no control response in the fore-and-aft sense. With speed increasing rapidly and his aircraft in a steep dive, Reynolds ejected by using the face blind handle. His only injury was to his left elbow as he had missed the ejection handle with his left hand and his arm flailed badly in the slipstream (it is possible that his aircraft may have been supersonic when he ejected). His parachute opened at 10,000 feet and, having come down in the sea, he was eventually rescued by a Dutch fishing boat. Sadly, nothing more was heard from Flight Lieutenant Cooper and his body was never found. Both aircraft came down in the sea about 60 miles east of Harwich but despite an extensive search, no wreckage was discovered. This accident highlighted the difficulty of forming up in formation at night as even with lights displayed it was not easy for a pilot to appreciate how far away an aircraft was. Although cloud penetration in close formation was routinely carried out, closing up with another aircraft at night so that it could be followed in cloud was fraught with danger and, as on this occasion, occasionally catastrophic. Paul Cooper was ex-Cranwell and had been on the same course as Pete Thompson, who had lost his life with 74 Squadron in September 1968.

A unique accident took place at Gutersloh on 24 February when Flying Officer Geraint Harries of 92 Squadron was landing in XN787. After touch-down the aircraft began to swing to starboard and by its general behaviour it was assumed that the starboard tyre had burst, a not uncommon occurrence. Having used differential braking to keep straight, Harries brought the Lightning to a rather abrupt halt on the runway, but it later transpired that the starboard wheel had come adrift (it was eventually found about 500 yards away on the station golf course). During the landing roll the aircraft had been supported on its right-hand side by the starboard brake disc, which was considerably reduced in size by the time that the aircraft finally stopped. Fortunately very little damage was caused and XN787 was soon returned to the air.

There was another case of a lightning strike on 27 March and the unfortunate aircraft on this occasion was XN726 of 19 Squadron. Considerable damage was caused to the ventral tank, the fuselage skin and internal structure. The control runs to the tailplane were also damaged. Although the aircraft was initially assessed as Cat.3 it was subsequently reclassified as Cat.4, the level of damage being of sufficient magnitude for it to be returned to Warton for repairs. These took nearly two years to complete and XN726 did not fly again until 12 March 1974.

Having had to eject from XM990 eighteen months before, Flight Lieutenant John Sims of 226 OCU had another Lightning moment on 13 April when flying in XM972. On this occasion he was in the right-hand seat opposite Flying Officer John Danning and after a successful sortie they returned to Coltishall for a precautionary or full-stop landing. The normal procedure was for the brakes to be released after the braking parachute had deployed but unfortunately this proved to be impossible as the brakes jammed fully on. This caused both tyres to explode, leaving the aircraft to run on the wheel rims. It eventually slid off the runway onto the grass where it came to a fairly rapid halt at a considerably lower level than was normal, the main undercarriage legs having sunk into the ground.

Another incident that could have had serious implications took place on 21 April. Two Lightnings of 56 Squadron, at 30,000 feet and

Mach 0.85, were being flown in line abreast battle formation 2 miles apart with the No.2 on the port side. The leader in XS934 called a 180 degree turnabout and selected full power assuming that the No.2, who appeared to be slightly above him, would remain high as they crossed. However, the No.2 descended and the leader did likewise, still expecting the No.2 to go above. The leader then over-banked and increased the 'g' to get below the No.2 but, as they still appeared to be on a collision course, he then rolled to the right maintaining the 'g' to pass above the No.2. His aircraft then yawed and flicked to the left, auto-rotated, and entered a spin to the left during which the main pitot tube was bent upwards, a fairly common occurrence with this type of incident. The pilot recovered from the spin and resumed level flight at 14,000 feet. After cross checking his standby ASI with his No.2 and carrying out a low speed handling check he landed safely at Akrotiri after a GCA.

After its take-off accident on 9 January 1968, XN728 of 92 Squadron had led a relatively quiet life but this all changed on 4 May when it was operating out of the Dutch Air Force base at Leeuwarden. It started to misbehave on its first sortie of the day when the starter control unit had to be changed when the No.2 engine failed to light. Following a successful trip the aircraft was turned round for a second sortie with Flying Officer David Moss in the cockpit, but during start-up there was an AVPIN explosion and it was damaged Cat.3. A flash fire had occurred in the fuselage just forward of frame 25 and the pressure created by the explosion was sufficient to cause a bulge in the external skin. The damage was repaired at Leeuwarden by a detachment from 431 MU at Bruggen and XN728 was returned for service with 92 Squadron two and-a-half months after the accident.

Not long after the incident related above 92 Squadron had another Lightning F.2A (XN793) that required repair work when a canopy was deposited on the Gutersloh runway on take-off on 29 June. The unfortunate pilot was Flying Officer Pete New but on this occasion at least the canopy managed to miss the leading edge of the fin so that the level of damage was rather less than normal. In mischievous fashion the Squadron Operations Record Book had an explanation for this as it claimed that Flying Officer New normally took off with crossed controls so that when the canopy broke away the aircraft would not have been heading in the same direction that it was pointing.

There were however mitigating circumstances to this incident as Pete New recalls:

I had been on leave for a couple of weeks and arrived back at base from the ferry at about 9am to find that the station was on a Mineval exercise [an evaluation exercise simulating wartime conditions]. I should have gone straight to bed as I had been travelling all night but being a keen young pilot I got changed and reported to the squadron. I was immediately told to go to the revetment and check in. I was not expected to be used but whilst strapping in, I was scrambled. In the resulting confusion and very short taxy to the runway, I can recall lowering the canopy on the hydraulics and thought I had pushed the handle fully down. I set off down the runway and as the nose came off the ground I realised the canopy was lifting. Reaching up I tried to hold onto the grab handle. Needless to say, it flew out of my hand and I was flying a GT Lightning. Luckily for me it missed the tail and did no further damage. I had a visual inspection and landed without further incident. The ground crew were magnificent and had a new canopy on the aircraft by the next morning. I was very, very embarrassed by the whole affair. Not only had I lost the canopy but it was from Alpha, the Boss's aircraft. He never lets me forget it, even to this day. Mind you he did give me a very stiff Squadron Commander's check in the T.4 about a week later.

This was, in fact, the second time that XN793 had lost its canopy on take-off as a similar incident had occurred on 24 September 1964 (see page 23).

Shortly before this accident an unusual mishap had taken place on 19 June when XP755 of 29 Squadron lost one of the Firestreak drill rounds that it was carrying during a training sortie. During a fighter combat exercise the pilot of XP755 began the pull-up for a high speed yo-yo manoeuvre at Mach 1.1 with wings level and a maximum pull of 4g. When he was flying at Mach 0.90 and 28,000 feet he felt vibration and noticed that the in-flight refuelling probe was oscillating from side-to-side. A visual check by the pilot of another aircraft brought the news that the port dummy missile was missing and that the left side of the fuselage was damaged. The sortie was aborted immediately and a return to base was made without further incident. A preliminary investigation revealed that a shear bolt had been incorrectly seated in the missile body at the time of issue and that, during some fifteen hours of subsequent flying, the threaded portion of the bolt had probably suffered fatigue. The end result was that the missile was able to slide backwards off the guide rails and ended up damaging the aircraft as it broke away.

Although most Lightning accidents occurred with the operational squadrons, occasionally the test pilots at maintenance units would be faced with a difficult situation when conducting air tests after servicing. This happened to XR724 of 11 Squadron which had been delivered to 60 MU at Leconfield on 3 May for a major service having accumulated 1,443 hours in the air. The servicing work was complete by the end of June but during its second test flight on the 28th the pilot received a Fire 1 warning. Returning to Leconfield for an emergency overweight landing he carried out an extended approach and touched down at 180 knots IAS, reducing power on No.2 engine to idle and operating the brake parachute handle. Since No.1 engine had been shut down during the fire drills carried out earlier in the sortie, the brake parachute did not deploy.

The pilot applied gentle wheel braking to retard his aircraft but on finding that this was not very effective he exerted rather more effort. After the aircraft had crossed the approach end RHAG he also lowered the arrestor hook with the intention of engaging the upwind hook wire. Shortly afterwards, however, the port tyre burst and the aircraft began to swing to port. Whilst the pilot was attempting to keep the Lightning on the runway the starboard tyre also blew out and directional control became extremely difficult. When it was obvious that the aircraft would end up on the grass No.2 engine was also shut down. Once onto the grass the brakes appeared to become a little more effective and the aircraft finally came to rest just off the runway and about 50 yards short of the upwind RHAG. The only damage to XR724 was caused by its excursion off the runway and this was assessed as Cat.2. The Fire 1 warning had been the result of a hydraulic flash fire in the No.1 engine bay, fluid having leaked from an outlet joint on a restrictor valve. This was because of a servicing fault as a tradesman had forgotten to fit a bonded seal to this particular joint.

The next barrier engagement took place at Wattisham on 12 July when XP694 of 29 Squadron was making a precautionary landing. Once on the runway the pilot found that the brakes were completely ineffective although the brake and services hydraulic pressure readings were normal. With both engines shut down directional control was maintained with rudder but the aircraft was still travelling at a speed of

30 knots when it went into the barrier, the result being Cat.2 damage. It was thought that the lack of braking action was caused by contamination of a Maxaret hydraulic line by foreign material, combined with a defective brake relay unit.

Over the years there had been some dramatic take-off accidents in Lightning aircraft and Wattisham contrived another on 7 August. Despite a number of previous incidents, stream rotation take-offs were still being flown and it was now proposed that five aircraft of 29 Squadron would perform rotation take offs in sequence during a forthcoming display. Although the lead aircraft had the benefit of a clear runway and clear air it was a different matter for the aircraft following as pilots had to contend with disturbed air that was created by jet efflux and wake turbulence. Another difficulty was that the airspeed indicator tended to fluctuate by quite large amounts so that the correct take-off speed often had to be estimated from experience, rather than from a direct instrument reading.

On the day of the accident five Lightnings entered the runway to practise the routine with Flight Lieutenant George Fenton in XP700 in the No.3 position. As per the briefing, all five aircraft were to line up on the runway in echelon before carrying out reheat take-offs, one after the other, with flaps selected up. Flight Lieutenant Fenton's take-off appeared to be normal but, having retracted his undercarriage, his aircraft began to sink and the ventral tank came into contact with the runway and remained so for a distance of around 500 yards. Unlike in previous cases the aircraft then became airborne again but the fuel that was streaming out of the damaged ventral tank was ignited by the No.1 jet pipe and produced a plume of flame the length of the aircraft itself.

Having made it into the air George Fenton's problems quickly multiplied and he was soon confronted with a Reheat 2 warning. However, after shutting down No.2 engine he felt the controls begin to stiffen and a few seconds later he had a controls hydraulic failure. This occurred some ninety seconds after take off and, having reached an altitude of around 2,000 feet he ejected, his aircraft crashing at Great Waldingfield, about 9 miles south-west of Wattisham. Although Fenton landed safely he sustained back injuries during the ejection. With the two aircraft lost as a result of the mid-air collision in February, this accident meant that 29 Squadron had written off three aircraft during the year to equal the number they had lost in 1971. It appears that there were some unexpected beneficiaries as a result of George Fenton's accident as the corn fire that his Lightning had started attracted a number of glider pilots who were taking part in a competition and were keen to take advantage of the thermal that had inadvertently been created.

On 16 August a characteristic of the Lightning that had been around virtually from its entry into service reappeared when XR771 of 56 Squadron was being flown on a simulated high speed interception. When descending to low level at a speed of Mach 0.90/620 knots IAS the pilot felt a vibration that lasted for about two seconds. The remainder of the sortie was uneventful until the aircraft was in the circuit when it felt sluggish. On landing there was a light-to-moderate crosswind from the port side and the pilot was unable to keep straight on the runway without the use of differential braking. On arrival back at dispersal it was noticed by ground personnel that the rudder was missing. Damage was assessed as Cat.3 and it appeared likely that the rudder may have broken away due to a fatigue failure of the top hinge bracket bolt. During the investigation into this incident it was noted that this was the fifth time that a Lightning had returned without its rudder since the aircraft's entry into service.

In the remaining few months of 1972 there was still time for another two Lightnings to end up at the bottom of the North Sea. The first was T.5 XS455 of 5 Squadron, which crashed on 6 September. This particular aircraft had already had an eventful life after its delivery to 226 OCU at Coltishall at the end of 1965, having suffered a landing accident, a lightning strike and a Cat.2 barrier engagement. On this occasion it was being flown by Squadron Leader Tim Gauvain and Lieutenant R. Verbist of the Belgian Air Force for a general handling and familiarisation exercise that included aerobatics at medium level. On completing a third consecutive slow roll at 7,000 feet the HYD 1 and 2 warnings illuminated, at which point Squadron Leader Gauvain took control and climbed to 11,000 feet. Having reached this height the controls went solid and there was just time to make a Mayday call before ejecting. Both pilots came down on land, Lieutenant Verbist injuring a leg on landing. Tim Gauvain's parachute descent was more straightforward, but he had already sustained back injuries on ejecting. Their aircraft came down in the sea just off Spurn Head. The most likely cause of the accident was aeration of the hydraulic control systems.

The other aircraft to be lost was also a two-seater. This was T.4 XM974 of 226 OCU, which went down on 14 December when it was being flown by Squadron Leader John Spencer with Flying Officer Geoff Evans in the right-hand seat. During the sortie XM974 acted as a high-speed low level target but problems began to appear when reheat was selected to accelerate to a speed of 600 knots IAS. At first the cockpit indications were normal but after a few seconds the No.2 reheat auto-cancelled. Both reheats were then disengaged and the throttles moved back to idle/fast idle, but almost immediately there was a series of loud bangs that gradually became worse. The bangs were accompanied by a severe vibration that could be felt through the airframe. The aircraft was put into a climb and shortly afterwards the Reheat 1 caption illuminated and at the same time it was noticed that rpm on No.1 engine was falling rapidly and jet pipe temperature was off the scale. No.1 engine was immediately shut down but the Reheat 2 warning came on and this was soon accompanied by a Fire 2 caption with a HYD 2 just for good measure.

By now the aircraft was at about 9,000 feet and Flying Officer Evans was the first to eject. He was followed by Squadron Leader Spencer who had noticed that the controls were beginning to stiffen before he ejected. Although both pilots came down in the sea they were quickly picked up by a SAR helicopter, their aircraft crashing in the sea off Happisburgh. The final moments of XM974 had been witnessed by the pilots of another aircraft who reported that as it was climbing they could see a severe fire in the rear of the aircraft and that 'incandescent blobs of matter' were being ejected from the nozzles. Although the fire appeared to go out around the time that Flying Officer Evans ejected, it then re-started at a lower intensity than before. John Spencer (later Air Commodore J. H. Spencer CBE AFC) recalls the events from his perspective:

> The sortie was to provide a high-speed low level-target for the QWI course. This meant flying at 570 knots and 250 feet whilst the hard-working student QWI tried to get into a position to simulate a successful missile attack. Initially I was going to use a single-seater but due to a programme change, I was allocated a T.4 (XM974). This meant that there was a spare seat going and Geoff Evans, who had just finished his course and was posted to 92 Squadron, expressed a wish to come along for the ride.
>
> Everything went fine until we were established on the first target run. I had increased power to 100 per cent but had not used reheat as it wasn't necessary, and the speed increased nicely. As

we approached 570 knots, I was about to start reducing power when there was a huge bang from just below my feet followed by what sounded like a 30mm cannon letting rip. This was extremely noisy and somewhat disconcerting, made more so by the large number of warning lights appearing on the two warning panels, together with the associated flashing lights and audio clangers. I automatically pulled back on the stick and reduced power and tried to make sense of what was rapidly becoming a confusing situation. According to the main warning panel, we had a fire in No.1 engine, a fire in No.2 engine and fires in both reheat bays. As well as this we also had a major electrical failure and had lost hydraulic power to the controls. I put out a Mayday call and was reassured to hear that the fighter had us in sight and that we seemed to be well on fire. That was it then, time to go. By now we were around 10,000 feet and 250 knots, which was just about ideal, and I don't think Geoff was too surprised to be told to eject. The canopy disappeared with a bang, and with another bang and a whoosh Geoff followed about a second later.

Now it was my turn. Even with the canopy gone, the cockpit was still a noisy place and I was quite glad to leave. I used the bottom handle and everything worked like it says on the tin and almost before I was fully aware of what had happened, there I was, suspended in a blessedly quiet and serene piece of sky. After the mad cacophony of the previous few minutes everything seemed amazingly peaceful and it felt good simply to relax and watch mother earth slowly coming up to meet me. As I descended I could hear a helicopter in the vicinity, which I hoped was for me but I was now nearing an unfriendly looking North Sea and everything speeded up as I splashed into the cold water. I had just about sufficient time to clamber aboard the dinghy and do those things that survival officers love to teach, before the most friendly-looking Sea King helicopter from Coltishall hove into sight and hauled me aboard. Almost the first face I saw was Geoff's and I was glad to see that he looked as fine as I felt.

We were taken to RAF Ely hospital where I was pronounced fit, but Geoff had unfortunately cracked a vertebra and his posting had to be delayed (never volunteer!). I don't think the cause of the accident was ever fully determined. My own view is that I probably hit a seagull or suchlike. At 570 knots a large bird would have an awfully large amount of kinetic energy to impart to the compressor blades of a jet engine. If there is such a thing as an ideal ejection, ours must have been close to it. A nice day, another aircraft in visual contact, time to set things up as regards height and speed and a helicopter base nearby. On my next sortie I had a Fire 1 indication but this time it was a false alarm.

Despite the most recent Lightning loss described above, the situation regarding in-flight fires appeared to be a lot better than it had been eighteen months before. Although the following account was written before the demise of XM974, it shows the progress that had been made with the Lightning's fire integrity:

About a year ago, the greatest single flight safety hazard in the Royal Air Force was, perhaps, that of airborne fires in Lightning aircraft. At that time statistics in the DFS Quarterly Report highlighted the serious situation that existed and mention was made of the tremendous efforts throughout the service to improve the fire integrity of the aircraft. In the DFS Report for the Fourth Quarter of 1971, a significant improvement was reported in the Lightning fire situation towards the end of 1971, and it was said that the improved trend would have to continue well into 1972 before it could be considered that success had been achieved.

It is now possible and wholly gratifying to report that those early signs of improvement have indeed continued. In the twelve month period from 1 October 1971 there have only been two accidents involving fires in Lightnings. One of these involved a starter explosion on start-up in May of this year [XN728], which resulted in Cat.3 damage to the aircraft. The other accident resulted in the loss of an aircraft in August this year [XP700] when the aircraft struck the runway on take-off. This latter accident arose from aircraft handling aspects and in no way threw further suspicion on the fire integrity of the Lightning. Thus, the end of the third quarter of 1972 marks a full twelve month period free from airborne fire accidents in the Lightning attributable to inadequate standards of fire integrity; a success achieved by all who have worked so hard in recent years to remedy an unhappy flight safety situation.

This improved trend was also apparent in the overall accident statistics for 1972, which showed that the Lightning's rate per 10,000 flying hours had fallen to 2.16 from 4.49 at the end of 1971. In comparison the accident rates for other aircraft in 1972 were as follows – Buccaneer 3.68, Harrier 9.11, Hunter 1.28 and Phantom 4.85.

Chapter 8
Still Supreme

At the beginning of 1973 the Lightning remained as the UK's premier interceptor with Nos. 29 and 111 Squadrons at Wattisham and Nos. 5 and 11 Squadrons at Binbrook. No.23 Squadron was based at Leuchars where it shared the air defence task with the Phantom FG.1s of 43 Squadron. In RAF Germany Nos. 19 and 92 Squadrons still operated the F.2A from Gutersloh and 56 Squadron remained at Akrotiri in the Mediterranean. Although the transfer of Phantom aircraft from ground attack duties to air defence was just around the corner, the Lightning would reign supreme for a little longer.

Unfortunately the sequence of accidents to two-seat Lightnings was set to continue as, on the last day of January 1973, T.5 XS420 went into the barrier at Coltishall after an aborted take off. The aircraft was crewed by Captain Gary Catren USAF and Flight Lieutenant George Smith and was lined up on the runway as the No.2 in a stream reheat take off. At first the take-off run appeared to be normal until, at a speed of 140 knots IAS, when the pilot was about to pull back on the control column to raise the nose-wheel, he noticed indications in the cockpit that his No.1 reheat had failed. Despite this he continued with the take-off and attempted to cancel reheat and select 100 per cent cold power on No.1 engine at the same time as endeavouring to raise the nose-wheel.

By the time the speed had increased to 155 knots IAS the nose-wheel was still refusing to lift and the pilot had the impression that the aircraft was not accelerating as it should. It was at this point that he decided to abort the take-off with about 1,500 yards of runway remaining. The No.2 reheat was cancelled and the braking parachute was operated, but this soon disintegrated due to the heat of the jet efflux. That, at least, is the official version of what happened. Another scenario has it that Captain Catren muttered an expletive that Flight Lieutenant Smith heard as 'chute George', at which point he popped the braking parachute which, not surprisingly, caught fire. Whichever version is true, the subsequent use of the brakes only reduced speed by approximately 50 knots so that the Lightning engaged the barrier still travelling at around 100 knots. With such a high entry speed it did not stop for a considerable distance and eventually came to rest in a field with its nose-wheel buried in the ground. Neither pilot was hurt but it would be nearly eight months before XS420 was returned to service.

This accident sparked a considerable debate on take-off technique and brought into question the validity of speeds quoted in Pilot's Notes for lifting of the nose-wheel and for the actual take off. A recommendation was put forward that a technique be adopted whereby progressive back pressure on the control column should be applied as speed approached the computed nose-wheel unstick speed, and that this backwards movement on the stick should be continued until the aircraft became airborne. A factor in the accident may have been the use of flap as this involved a lot of aft stick to raise the nose-wheel (early Lightning aircraft were taken off without the use of flap and did not need nearly as much back stick as a result). The use of flap was standard procedure for take offs in the F.6 although the F.2A took of flapless. Another contributory factor may have been the loss of reheat on No.1 engine as with reheat still operating on No.2 (upper) engine, this would have produced a slight nose-down pitch which might have been sufficient to prevent the nose-wheel from lifting.

There was another case of brake failure on a Lightning on 5 March when XP741 of 111 Squadron was being taxied back to its dispersal point at Wattisham. Although the hydraulic pressure indications were all normal, the brake lever was slack in the pilot's hand. On this occasion the incident occurred as the aircraft was still on the taxiway and so the pilot was able to bring it to a halt without endangering other aircraft. It transpired that the failure was caused by the complete severing of a brake cable and that there was evidence of a material defect or faulty manufacture.

Despite the improvements made regarding the Lightning's fire integrity this particular hazard was never very far away and a potentially serious incident occurred on 22 March. The aircraft involved was XS936 of 23 Squadron, which was flying at 20,000 feet and a speed of 350 knots IAS when the Fire 1 caption illuminated. The pilot carried out the emergency drills, including operating the fire extinguisher, and a few seconds later the light went out. The aircraft was safely recovered to Leuchars, where an engineering inspection revealed that there had been a leak from the fuel-draulic pressure relief valve and that fuel at a pressure of about 150 psi had escaped. The fuel had then atomised to become a fine mist that had ignited in the engine/exhaust area. Compared to what had happened in the past, however, this fuel leak was relatively minor and the fire was quickly put out by the extinguisher before any significant damage had been caused.

Another incident that took place six days later could have had serious consequences if the pilot had been forced to eject. F.1A XM171 of 226 OCU landed back at Coltishall after a gun-firing exercise but after stopping at its dispersal point the pilot was unable to raise his canopy due to a restriction. It was eventually opened by a combination of operating the canopy jack end release externally, banging the side of the aircraft near the canopy unlocking mechanism and operation of the canopy unlocking handle. It was subsequently found that the starboard shoot bolt had been jammed by a small alloy screw that had lodged behind the canopy-locking hook. It was thought that this might have occurred during aerobatics that had been flown after the gun-firing part of the exercise. A thorough check was made of the cockpit but the origin of the screw was not revealed. The point was made in comprehensive fashion that had the pilot been forced to abandon his aircraft the ejection would have failed as the canopy would not have released. Having been flown for the first time on 20 September 1960, XM171 was the first Lightning to exceed 2,000 hours in the air.

Having been successfully recovered from a spin the year before, XS934 of 56 Squadron was to meet its end when it had to be abandoned to the north-east of Akrotiri. On 3 April it was being flown by Flight Lieutenant Al Greer on a general handling sortie which included a practice diversion to Nicosia and circuits, both visual and instrument, at Akrotiri. On completion of one of these circuits, during which a failure of No.2 engine had been simulated, Flight Lieutenant Greer overshot into a climbing turn and increased speed to 350 knots IAS. There was an apparent lack of thrust during this manoeuvre but he considered that this was because No.2 engine was in cruise and the jet pipe temperature was lower than normal. At this time a slight flicker of No.2 engine rpm was also noticed. On passing 8,000 feet Greer began to ease the control column forwards as he intended to level off at 10,000 feet, but as he did so a severe vibration set in and, despite reducing power to idle/fast idle, it remained the same.

As Greer increased power on the No.1 engine, however, the Fire 1 caption came on so he turned towards land, put out a Mayday call and

Lightning T.5 XS423 is seen at the end of its service life having been stripped for spares. It was damaged Cat.3 on 17 January 1968 when the undercarriage collapsed on landing at Coltishall.

Lightning F.6 XS895 in the markings of 5 Squadron.

Seen with 11 Squadron at Alconbury in 1982, Lightning F.3 XP694 had two mishaps during its history, a hot gas leak on 21 July 1967 with 29 Squadron and a barrier engagement on 12 July 1972.

F.6 XR725 had one of the more unusual Lightning accidents when it sank into the taxiway at Sola in Norway on 26 October 1967 during service with 23 Squadron.

Lightning T.5 XS454 was yet another of the mark to suffer an undercarriage collapse on landing at Coltishall on 7 March 1967.

Lightning F.6 XR772 is seen during service with 11 Squadron. Having been transferred to 5 Squadron it crashed into the North Sea on 6 March 1985 after entering a spin. The pilot, Flying Officer Martin Ramsay, was killed.

Another view of Lightning F.6 XR761 which was lost over the North Sea on 8 November 1984.

Built initially as an F.3, XR726 was converted to F.6 standard and was the first aircraft to undergo the fire integrity programme.

F.6 XS928 of 11 Squadron is seen at Alconbury in 1983. It survived a fire on start-up with 74 Squadron on 6 April 1970 in which it was damaged Cat.4 and a titanium fire with 56 Squadron on 23 May 1974.

Lightning T.5 XS418 seen at Binbrook in 1975 at the end of its service life.

F.6 XS921 was the aircraft from which Flight Lieutenant Craig Penrice of 11 Squadron ejected on 19 September 1985 following a control restriction.

Unlike many of its contemporaries, F.3 XR718 had a relatively quiet life although it did lose its rudder on 21 August 1978.

Lightning F.6 XS933 is seen in the markings of 5 Squadron at Alconbury in 1986.

One of the last Lightning display aircraft, F.3 XP707 crashed on 19 March 1987 at Binbrook during an aerobatic routine when a slow-feeding ventral tank led to the CG moving beyond its aft limit.

Lightning F.3 XP764 in the markings of the Lightning Training Flight.

The only accident of any note that befell Lightning F.6 XR754 during its service life was an engine fire when returning to Binbrook from Akrotiri on 28 September 1984.

Lightning F.6 XP693 flying alongside Tornado F.3 ZE785. XP693 still survives in South Africa but ZE785 was scrapped in 2010.

carried out his emergency drills. By now he was flying at 12,000 feet and a speed of 300 knots IAS. At first it appeared that use of the fire extinguisher had been successful as the warning caption went out, but the vibration was still apparent and rpm on No.1 engine was only 20-30 per cent (the Fuel 1 and Oil 1 warning captions were also now on). Power was increased on No.2 engine but soon after the Fire 1 warning lit up again and Greer made his mind up to eject as soon as possible. After coasting out at Limassol Bay he ejected by using the face blind handle at a height of 11,000 feet and 300 knots IAS and was rescued by helicopter, having spent around fifteen minutes in his dinghy. Some wreckage was recovered but it was not enough to establish the cause of the accident with any certainty although, other evidence pointed to the fact that the aircraft had been subject to a fire as a result of a hot gas leak.

There was another close call for a Lightning pilot on 5 April when he very nearly flew into the ground in bad weather over Germany during the recovery from a high-level sortie. The incident involved XN791 of 92 Squadron, which had just returned from a major service at 60 MU Leconfield only two days before. The pilot separated from his leader at the top of the dive by completing an orbit, before descending after him. On being told that the weather at base was Amber he requested a GCA to land and, during a talkdown, he monitored his position by TACAN. At first he was unsure about the instructions he was being given, but his suspicions were allayed when heading instructions tallied with what TACAN led him to expect. He continued to obey the controller's instructions but not long after his doubts returned and he levelled at 400 feet. Although he was still in cloud he saw the ground briefly and observed a ground feature that proved he was not where he thought he was, i.e. on finals to land. He had in fact misheard a frequency change prior to letting down and had been following the instructions that were being given to another aircraft. Fortunately he had enough fuel to fly another GCA, which was completed successfully.

A further two-seat Lightning was lost on 5 June when T.4 XM988 of 226 OCU became the latest aircraft to crash into the North Sea. At the time it was being flown by Wing Commander Chris Bruce, who was on a solo conversion sortie that involved a supersonic speed run followed by an energy climb to high altitude. During a turn at around 38,000 feet the aircraft went into a spin that was maintained, despite repeated attempts at recovery action, right down to 10,000 feet, at which point Wing Commander Bruce ejected. The aircraft continued to spin until it hit the sea some 23 miles north-east of Great Yarmouth. Although his ejection and subsequent survival drills were completed in a relatively straightforward manner, Wing Commander Bruce's problems were not quite over, as he recalls:

> I don't remember much about the ejection except that it all went smoothly until I had been in the sea for some ten minutes or so. Then I noticed my dinghy was starting to sink under me as it was losing air. Not wishing to be dragged down by it should it eventually sink, I got back into the sea and held onto it with an arm. Luckily the helicopter appeared within a short time and all was well in the end. Later investigation showed that the CO2 bottle had frozen to the dinghy, and when activated it opened the dinghy by inflation but a part of the material remained attached to the bottle; hence the tear and the leak. The aircraft was never found so we never knew why it wouldn't do what I wanted, resulting in me parting company with it.

Despite the fact that there had been two Cat.5 write-offs in the last quarter, the accident statistics for the mid point of 1973 showed that the Lightning was heading in the right direction. For the twelve months ending on 30 June there had been a total of seven accidents giving a rate per 10,000 flying hours of 1.82. This was slightly down on the comparable figure for the previous year of 2.06. When a comparison is made with other aircraft the Lightning faired quite favourably. For the twelve months to 30 June 1973 the accident rates were as follows (figures for the twelve months to 30 June 1972 are in brackets) – Buccaneer 0.83 (5.30), Harrier 2.79 (13.30), Hunter 3.05 (4.21) and Phantom 3.19 (4.99). Even the venerable Shackleton airborne early warning aircraft had a higher accident rate during this period at 4.52.

A ground fire with a difference took place on 2 August during a detachment by Lightnings of 111 Squadron to the German Air Force base at Wittmund in which, for once, the aircraft was not responsible. During an operational turn-round with Squadron Leader Dennis Willison in the cockpit of XP738, a fault in the pressure refuelling apparatus meant that large quantities of fuel were sprayed over the wing. This soon came into contact with the hot wheel brake, which ignited the fuel and caused a major conflagration. Fortunately the fire crews were quickly at the scene, which saved a potential disaster as there was a possibility that the fuel bowser that was being used would have exploded as well as the aircraft. At the first sign of trouble Squadron Leader Willison vacated the cockpit and there were no injuries to any of the personnel involved. The damage to XP738 was assessed as Cat.3 with most of the work involving the replacement of electrical wiring. The work took three-and-a-half months to complete and the aircraft was returned to 111 Squadron on 17 November.

Since the Lightning had come into RAF service there had been numerous cases of barrier engagements but there was only one accident involving a Lightning hitting the barrier at the wrong end of the runway. This took place on 30 August during a period when 5 Squadron was operating from Leconfield due to runway repairs at its home base at Binbrook. The pilot was Flight Lieutenant Mal Gleave who was landing at night in F.6 XR751. While he had been in the air there had been a change of the runway in use but unfortunately the barrier had not been lowered so it was still in the upright position, but at the approach end. As the Lightning tended to land from a relatively shallow approach angle on short finals the main undercarriage of XR751 came into contact with the top cable of the barrier, which pitched the Lightning sharply forwards so that the nose-wheel hit the runway and immediately collapsed. The Lightning then continued down the runway on its nose before coming to a halt, the fact that it ended up still on the runway being a measure of Flight Lieutenant Gleave's skill in keeping it there. Despite the fact that the aircraft had hit the barrier at a speed of around 165 knots IAS, this dramatic arrival did not result in the level of damage that might have been expected and XR751 was soon in the air once more, having had a replacement nose-leg fitted.

As has already been mentioned, Lightning F.3 XP738 was returned to 111 Squadron on 17 November (after a prodigious number of man hours had been spent on its repair), but unfortunately a certain law then came into play as it was written off in an accident less than four weeks later. This was the result of as clear a case of finger trouble as it was possible to get as the pilot forgot to lower the undercarriage during a night landing on 10 December at Wattisham. The unfortunate individual was Flying Officer Keith Farnfield, who at least proved that it was possible to land a Lightning with the gear up whatever Pilot's Notes might have said. In fact the level of damage was assessed as Cat.4 (capable of repair) but as the F.3 was about to be taken out of squadron service with only the

F.6 remaining, it was later reassessed as Cat.5C as it would have been uneconomic to carry out the necessary repairs.

The first Lightning accident of 1974 took place at Gutersloh on 17 January when the weather, although still technically flyable, was about as bad as it could possibly be. To make matters worse it was at night, which was not the best time to receive a Fire 1 warning, especially as it occurred in the climb shortly after take off. The aircraft affected was XN788 of 92 Squadron, which was being flown by Flight Lieutenant Tim Miller. After dealing with the fire incident, Flight Lieutenant Miller returned to base for landing but unfortunately the aircraft swung off the left-hand side of the runway and the port undercarriage leg collapsed in soft ground. Although the level of damage was assessed as Cat.3 it was sufficient for the aircraft to be grounded for six months while repairs were carried out.

It was not long before the next Cat.5 write off and once again it was a 29 Squadron F.3 that was involved in an accident on 13 February (this brought to seven the number of F.3s that the squadron had accounted for in the last three years). The aircraft involved was XR715, which eventually crashed near Blyford Green in Suffolk having flown itself for around ten minutes after the pilot ejected. Not long before it had taken off from Wattisham with Flight Lieutenant Terry Butcher at the controls for a sortie that included low level practice interceptions. During one of these the Reheat 2 warning light illuminated and although it went out again it was then replaced by a Reheat 1 warning. This also went out after a few seconds but after the aircraft had been climbed to a safe altitude it came back on again and Flight Lieutenant Butcher became aware of a stiffening of the control column in the fore-and-aft sense. He therefore had no option but to eject, but his aircraft then continued to circle for some time before eventually crashing in open countryside, coming down perilously close to a house. XR715 was the aircraft that ended up in the barrier at Luqa on 2 September 1968 when Flying Officer Ted Girdler of 111 Squadron had brake parachute and then brake failure. By the time of its demise it had flown a total of 1,902 hours.

But for a superb piece of flying there would have been another to add to the long list of Lightning accidents on 18 February when a F.6 of 56 Squadron was taking part in a high-altitude practice interception exercise. The aircraft (XR759) was being flown by Flight Lieutenant John Ward, who was on the OCU staff and was at Akrotiri carrying out a standardisation check on the squadron. On attempting to recover after a diving attack, Flight Lieutenant Ward found that the control column could not be moved further aft than the neutral position, which meant that he was unable to pull out. Since the practice attack had been commenced at around 38,000 feet, by utilising maximum force on the stick the aircraft was eventually eased out of the dive at 22,000 feet. Having finally attained straight and level flight, Ward carried out a handling check in the landing configuration, but this led to another dive that required 10,000 feet to recover.

At the limiting speed with undercarriage down (flaps up) it was noted that the aircraft was in a gentle descent and a decision was made to attempt a landing, even though the fact remained that if the aircraft had pitched nose down at any time Ward would not have been in a position to do much about it. During the handling check it had been discovered that by moving No.1 (lower) engine into reheat a very slight nose-up pitch change occurred and this was all that was available to adjust the approach angle. The angle that the aircraft was descending had to be judged perfectly so that it coincided with the correct touch-down point and the Lightning was eventually landed at a speed of 240 knots IAS which was 70-80 knots higher than normal. Flight Lieutenant Ward was awarded an Air Force Cross for saving his aircraft and XR759 remained in service for another thirteen years until it eventually ran out of fatigue life in 1987.

Another 56 Squadron F.6 (XS928) was very nearly lost on 23 May when it was being flown by the unit's O.C., Wing Commander Martin Bee, on a low level practice interception exercise. During a high speed run at 2,500 feet the rpm on No.1 engine began to wind down rapidly with a corresponding increase in jet pipe temperature, although JPT then fell back again to a very low value. As there were no fire warnings in the cockpit Wing Commander Bee put out a PAN call instead of a Mayday and landed safely at Akrotiri. It was only when the aircraft was being examined on the ground that it was realised that there had been a titanium fire in No.1 engine, despite the fact that the required modifications as a result of previous incidents of this nature had been embodied. It was discovered that the source of the fire had been the tenth stage of the compressor and that the fire had not been contained within the engine as the compressor casing had been holed in three places. As the fire moved rearwards it had caused significant damage to the airframe between frames 31 and 39. By chance the fire detection system had been put out of action, which was the reason for the lack of fire warnings in the cockpit. Although the modifications had not prevented the fire, it was considered that the situation would have been considerably worse (and most likely the aircraft would have been lost) if they had not been incorporated.

On 24 June another Lightning F.3 had to be abandoned over the North Sea. This was XR748 of 111 Squadron, which was being flown on an air test by Flying Officer Kevin Mason after servicing work had been carried out. The following is a description of the flight and is taken from the official investigation into the accident:

The pilot was briefed to carry out an airborne check of the tailplane trim system and then, if the system was satisfactory, to carry out general handling, including aerobatics, to complete the sortie. He carried out a reheat take off and then fed into the ILS pattern for an auto-ILS, during which he checked the correct functioning of the tailplane trim system. As the system was serviceable, the pilot overshot and continued the sortie as briefed. At 7,000 feet he commenced his aerobatic practice and performed several manoeuvres involving the application of positive 'g' only. Still at 7,000 feet, he put the aircraft into a slow roll on an easterly heading and applied at least minus 1g. As the aircraft rolled out of the manoeuvre, the pilot noticed that the attention-getter was flashing, the HYD caption was illuminated on the SWP, and both HYD 1 and HYD 2 captions were illuminated on the AWP.

He transmitted a Mayday call on the Wattisham approach frequency and, keeping control movements to a minimum, allowed the aircraft to climb to 18,000 feet on an approximate heading of 080 degrees. He engaged the height and heading lock on the autopilot after levelling at 18,000 feet, and on checking the instruments found that, apart from the hydraulic warnings that were still illuminated, no other malfunctions were indicated. The Wattisham air traffic controller suggested that the pilot should turn his aircraft on to a north-westerly heading to fly parallel to the coastline and within range of the rescue services at Coltishall. Before the pilot started this turn, he realised that he had lost tailplane control, although he was able to maintain height by using differential engine power. However, on attempting to roll the aircraft out of the turn, he found that aileron control was lost and an ejection inevitable. After transmitting that he was ejecting, he lowered the ejection seat almost fully down and pulled the face blind handle. The ejection seat functioned correctly, but the pilot sustained back injuries during the ejection. The aircraft crashed into the sea and, despite an intensive salvage operation, only seven small pieces of wreckage were recovered.

The Lightning went into the sea 5 miles off Great Yarmouth and as far as Flight Lieutenant Mason was concerned it was fortunate that he also came down relatively close to the coast. Although his ejection was straightforward he had great difficulty in going through the necessary pre-landing drills as the parachute Quick Release Box was much higher than it should have been and he was unable to turn it to the unlocked position. As a result he hit the water still attached to his parachute and was dragged through the water until the parachute eventually collapsed. As he had not been able to release his harness, he had been prevented from inflating his Mae West, so instead he inflated his dinghy, but the drag from the parachute stopped him from climbing on board and eventually it turned over. He was therefore more than a little relieved to see a rescue helicopter heading his way and he was soon winched to safety.

The crash investigation was, of course, hampered by a lack of material evidence but from the evidence of Flight Lieutenant Mason and from previous experience of similar incidents, it was surmised that the hydraulic systems that powered the flying controls had been affected by aeration that had probably been introduced into the system during the service that had recently been carried out. This had then resulted in the control problems that had been experienced after the aircraft had been flown in negative 'g'.

The final Lightning accident of 1974 took place on 29 October when XR768 of 5 Squadron crashed in the North Sea approximately 13 miles east of Saltfleet in Lincolnshire following a reheat fire. The pilot, Flight Lieutenant Tex Jones, ejected safely and was picked up by SAR helicopter. XR768 had been the first F.6 built to full production standard, all previous machines having been produced to an interim standard before subsequently being upgraded to full F.6 specification. Apart from an AVPIN explosion on start-up on 4 November 1969 during service with 74 Squadron at Tengah, it had managed to stay out of repair hangars for much of its life and at the time that it was lost it had flown a total of 2,144 hours.

Chapter 9

Wind-Down

By the beginning of 1975 the Lightning force was undergoing radical change with a number of squadrons having already re-equipped with the McDonnell Douglas Phantom or were shortly to do so. The first to swap their Lightnings for Phantoms was 111 Squadron at Wattisham, which had disbanded as a Lightning unit on 30 September 1974. The changeover was followed three months later by 29 Squadron which also received Phantoms at the end of the year. Although 56 Squadron was to fly the Lightning for another eighteen months before it too converted to the Phantom, the British withdrawal of forces in the Mediterranean led to it becoming part of UK air defence once again from its new base at Wattisham. At Binbrook Nos. 5 and 11 Squadrons remained, as did (for the time being at least) Nos. 19 and 92 Squadrons at Gutersloh in RAF Germany.

With the gradual transfer of the air defence task to the Phantom there was no need for the continued existence of 226 OCU and the last Lightning course commenced at Coltishall in May 1974, the unit being formally disbanded four months later. Although there was still a need to train new Lightning pilots, the numbers needed were considerably reduced and the training task was initially taken on by C Flight of 11 Squadron before the formation of the Lightning Training Flight (LTF) at Binbrook in October 1975.

In one respect the year of 1975 showed a considerable improvement in the Lightning's safety record as only one aircraft was written off, but this accident unfortunately resulted in another fatality (the first for three years) when Squadron Leader David Hampton of 11 Squadron was killed in F.6 XR762 on 7 April. At the time the squadron was on detachment to Akrotiri from Binbrook and the aircraft came down in the sea off the coast of Cyprus. With a lack of material evidence and the death of the pilot the cause of the crash could not be established. Before serving with 11 Squadron, XR762 had flown with 5 and 23 Squadrons and had accumulated 2,273 hours in the air by the time it was lost.

As already related, Lightning aircraft had been involved in a number of mid-air collisions since entry into RAF service and there was another on the night of 15 January 1976, although on this occasion the contact was of a relatively minor nature and both aircraft were landed safely. It happened when three F.2As of 19 Squadron were engaged on a practice interception. Flight Lieutenant Dave Carden in XN777 was in the process of carrying out a visident on the Lightning flown by Flight Lieutenant Paul R. Cooper when the aerial on the top of his fin hit the port aileron of the target aircraft as he closed on it in the descent. The aerial was broken on Carden's aircraft and although the aileron on Cooper's machine was damaged, his aircraft was still controllable. This highlighted once again the difficulty of assessing the rate of closure of two aircraft at night, even when navigation lights were in use. Had Dave Carden's aircraft been six inches higher, then the outcome might have been rather different.

There is a saying that things happen in threes and for Flying Officer Clive Rowley of 19 Squadron this came true in the space of three months in 1976 when he had three separate Lightning incidents. The first took place on 5 May when he was flying XN776. He had just taken off from Gutersloh when his aircraft had a complete AC electrical failure, which meant that a number of his main instruments were inoperative. However his biggest concern was the fact that the main AC-powered fuel pumps had also failed leaving only the DC pumps to feed the engines. In this condition the F2A was limited to 85 per cent power on both engines (to avoid the possibility of flame out) and with his aircraft heavy with fuel, Rowley was thus left in an extremely difficult situation. However this particular emergency had been practised in the simulator and the landing procedure called for additional height to allow for that lost during turns and for speed to be maintained at 300 knots IAS until lined up on the approach. This was due to the fact that once height had been lost it could not be regained as there was insufficient power with the engines limited to 85 per cent rpm. This also meant that once the aircraft was on the approach it was committed to land and could not overshoot. In the event Clive Rowley judged his landing to perfection and his aircraft was completely undamaged.

His second Lightning moment occurred six days later on 11 May during a practice interception sortie in XN789, in which his playmate, was Flight Lieutenant Phil Owen. The exercise called for supersonic interceptions with Rowley acting as the fighter. Having climbed to

38,000 feet, and as he was accelerating through Mach 1.25 prior to intercepting the target aircraft of Flight Lieutenant Owen, he noticed a flicker in the engine instruments and then the No.2 Reheat auto-cancelled. Assuming that it was just a temporary malfunction Rowley re-selected the No.2 reheat but thirty seconds later the attention-getter operated and the Reheat 2 warning illuminated. He immediately carried out his emergency drills, which included shutting down No.2 engine, declared a Mayday and made for the Dummersee Lake, approximately 30 miles north of Gutersloh, which was the designated area in case he needed to eject. By now the Reheat 2 warning light had gone out leaving Rowley with no idea whether it had been real, or spurious like so many others had been. However, he had now been joined by Flight Lieutenant Owen who was able to report that he could see a hole that was about a foot in diameter in the rear fuselage just below the fin on the starboard side. From this it appeared as though some form of fluid was escaping.

The emergency procedures for a reheat fire in the Lightning now included the requirement to wait for five minutes before attempting a recovery to base. This was in view of the distinct possibility that tailplane control could be lost in a fire situation as had happened on many occasions in the past. It was assumed that if anything untoward was to happen it would occur within this five-minute period. As there was no apparent alteration in his aircraft's control responses, Rowley commenced his letdown into Gutersloh, although by now his fuel state was becoming a cause for concern. His approach and landing was without further incident, but the gravity of the situation soon became apparent after he had turned off the runway and had shut down the remaining engine. It was discovered that part of the structure in the jet pipe had broken away and had become jammed in the burner ring of the reheat, thereby deflecting part of the flame so that it damaged the airframe. The fluid that Flight Lieutenant Owen had commented upon turned out to be hydraulic oil that was leaking from the No.1 system (the other system was inoperative as No.2 engine had been shut down). It was later calculated that at the rate that it was escaping, Rowley would have only had another two minutes in the air before the flying controls seized up.

The aircraft that Rowley had been flying on 11 May had belonged to Squadron Leader John Spencer (O.C. B Flight) and on 4 August he had a similar situation in XN786, which was the personal aircraft of Squadron

Leader John May who was in charge of A Flight. He was the leader of a pair (the other aircraft was flown by 19 Squadron's commander Wing Commander Bob Barcilon), but shortly after take off at around 2,000 feet a loud bang reverberated through the aircraft and this was accompanied by a sudden deceleration. Not long afterwards the Reheat 1 caption lit up on the warning panel and once more Rowley was into the ritual of emergency procedures with which he was rather more familiar than most. There was an ominous development when fore-and-aft control column movements became extremely stiff, requiring a two-handed pull to obtain any response, although lateral control was unaffected. As well as being very difficult to move, control in pitch also became rather jerky so that it was not easy to maintain the correct attitude. Wing Commander Barcilon carried out a visual inspection of the aircraft but could see no real sign of damage except that the fin appeared to be bulged around its mid point when seen from behind.

At the time that the emergency started the cloud base was around 3,000 feet, but it was clearer to the south so Rowley headed in this direction, which at least allowed him to climb to 9,000 feet. At this relatively safe height he carried out an assessment of the aircraft's handling characteristics in the landing configuration. Although he had shut down No.1 engine it was still indicating 30 per cent rpm, which was unusually high, and this had the effect of creating considerable drag so that with undercarriage and flaps down it was impossible to maintain height even with full cold power selected on No.2 engine. Despite this it was decided to attempt a landing, but as the aircraft was still heavy with fuel the approach speed was higher than normal at 195 knots IAS. At least control in pitch did not get any worse and once again Rowley flew an immaculate approach and was able to land in one piece. As the braking parachute was operated by a system that worked from No.1 engine he was expecting it to fail so lowered his arrestor hook to engage the upwind RHAG. However, the parachute deployed satisfactorily, which was due mainly to the engine's high windmilling speed.

On inspection it was found that XN786 had suffered major internal damage, far worse than had occurred in Clive Rowley's previous incident with XN789. The emergency had begun when the intermediate jet pipe casing had fractured and split into two pieces. The general carnage in this area led to the burner assembly for the reheat being torn out and a huge hot gas leak that caused considerable damage to the rear section of the airframe. Part of the jet pipe had fallen away somewhere south of Osnabruck, but most of the remainder was blocking the airflow through No.1 engine at the rear which was the reason for the relatively high rpm reading. The stiffness in the elevator controls had been caused by part of the jet pipe material being forced up against the elevator control linkage and the bulge in the fin that had first been noticed by Wing Commander Barcilon had been caused by internal pressure build up. The damage to XN786 was considerable and although initially assessed as Cat.4, it was not flown again and was eventually used as a decoy aircraft at Gutersloh having flown a total of 2,659 hours from its first flight on 12 February 1963.

Clive Rowley's third, and last, incident occurred a week after another Lightning was lost. This was F.6 XS937 of 11 Squadron, which was abandoned over the North Sea off Spurn Head on 30 July. The aircraft was being flown by Flying Officer Simon Manning and a problem was apparent immediately after take off from Leconfield when undercarriage retraction produced two greens and a red (No.11 Squadron was operating from Leconfield at the time due to runway resurfacing at Binbrook). The red light signified that a main undercarriage leg had not retracted and so the usual repertoire of manoeuvres was flown in an attempt to assist the retraction process. This was unsuccessful, however, and several low level flypasts of the Tower at Leconfield confirmed that the leg was roughly in the halfway position. Indeed it appeared to be swinging as though it was not connected to its jack.

After a period of time it was decided that the only course of action was for Flying Officer Manning to eject over the sea and he did so from a height of 7,000 feet. In one sense he was fortunate as Leconfield was the home of B Flight of 202 (Search and Rescue) Squadron and so a Whirlwind HAR.10 helicopter was ready and waiting for him when he ejected. In fact his rescue was so swift that he had to endure jibes in the bar that he had ejected over the sea and had hardly got wet. A salvage operation was attempted but as a Phantom of 29 Squadron had crashed into the sea off Mablethorpe the week before, the RAF was more concerned to find the reason for this accident than to look for a Lightning that had apparently succumbed to an old problem. With no wreckage forthcoming the Board of Inquiry reasoned that the undercarriage malfunction had probably been caused by failure of the jack attachment lugs at the top of the main leg. The ejection had been watched closely by the operators of a local radar station who could clearly see the aircraft's blip split into two when Simon Manning ejected. As the first blip disappeared as the aircraft crashed into the sea, the remaining blip representing Manning was followed so that an accurate position fix could be given.

Before the imminent demise of the Lightning in RAF Germany there was still time for two more incidents. The first involved XM968 of 92 Squadron, which crashed near Gutersloh on 24 February 1977. The crew comprised Squadron Leader Mike Lawrance with Squadron Leader Granville-White (a Harrier pilot with No.4 Squadron) in the right-hand seat. The sortie was straightforward until the aircraft returned to base when Squadron Leader Lawrance realised that the airbrakes had not extended when they had been selected and he had also lost tailplane feel. Shortly afterwards he noticed that the port main undercarriage was showing red (although the aircraft was downwind in the circuit, the undercarriage had not been selected down at this stage) and that there had been a failure of the services hydraulic system.

Operation of the emergency system led to the nose-wheel coming down and locking, but the starboard undercarriage leg was now showing a red light as well as the port leg. A flypast of the Tower for a visual inspection brought the unwelcome news that although both main legs were visible, they were only partially lowered. Not long after the situation went from bad to worse when there was a HYD 1 warning so Squadron Leader Lawrance climbed to 2,500 feet in case he and Squadron Leader Granville-White needed to eject. Although lack of fuel was also becoming a worry he was still keen to find a way of recovering the aircraft if at all possible and was advised to apply positive 'g' to try to make the undercarriage lock down. He lowered the nose of the aircraft to pick up speed and then pulled into a climb, but as he did so the controls stiffened and so he ordered his passenger to eject, before ejecting himself. Although they landed safely, both men suffered back injuries. In the meantime the pilotless aircraft had caused a certain amount of consternation on the ground. As it had been abandoned in a climb it carried on upwards for a few more seconds before executing a stall turn and diving back towards the ground. However, instead of diving straight into the ground it pulled out and turned towards the airfield, eventually coming down in open countryside about half a mile from the airfield boundary and disintegrating on impact.

The other incident occurred shortly before 92 Squadron disbanded as a Lightning unit and it bore a number of similarities to the loss of

XM968. As part of the disbandment ceremonies a diamond-nine flypast was made over a number of airfields in Germany on 30 March but on return to Gutersloh Flight Lieutenant Phil Owen in XN793 was unable to get his starboard undercarriage leg to lower. His aircraft was checked from the air by Flight Lieutenant Roger McGowan and the leg was only just visible having come down about 10 degrees. At the time fuel was not a problem and Flight Lieutenant Owen shut down No.2 engine before making a concerted attempt to coax the leg into the down position. All his efforts were in vain, however, and permission was finally granted to use the emergency system. This also had no effect so Flight Lieutenant Owen headed for the Dummersee Lake and prepared himself for ejection. Shortly before he arrived in the area his aircraft shuddered violently and the red undercarriage light suddenly turned to green. By now fuel (or lack of it) was a big problem but he elected to return to Gutersloh and landed safely, although as he was on the runway the flying controls seized. It transpired that the undercarriage leg had been prevented from coming down by the D-door but eventually this had given way allowing the leg to extend. Unfortunately, as the D-door had broken away it had hit a hydraulic pipe from the No.1 system and this had led to a gradual loss of hydraulic oil and the eventual seizing of the flying controls. As the No.2 engine had already been shut down, only the No.1 system was operating.

No.92 Squadron was officially disbanded on 31 March and was re-formed the next day as a Phantom unit based at Wildenrath. With 19 Squadron having already disbanded at the end of 1975 (it also converted onto the Phantom at Wildenrath) the era of the Lightning in RAF Germany came to an end. From the safety aspect the F.2/F.2A had had the best record of any Lightning variant and of the three that had been written off since entry into squadron service in December 1962, only two (XN785 and XN786) had been the result of a technical defect and these two accidents were separated by twelve years. XN772 was lost as a result of a spin.

Over the next twenty-one months no further Lightnings were lost although there were several incidents. On 16 May 1977 XS899 of 5 Squadron was damaged Cat.2 when the nose-wheel leg collapsed on landing, but a potentially more serious incident occurred on 29 September involving XR752 (also of 5 Squadron), which was landed with the undercarriage up. At the time the aircraft was being flown by an extremely experienced pilot but having flown several circuits with the wheels down, on his final approach he inexplicably selected wheels up instead of flaps down. This was not quite a unique occurrence for the Lightning as one had been landed before with the gear up when the pilot also forgot to lower it. In addition, as has already been noted, a total of four aircraft had also been involved in failed take-offs that led to them sinking back onto the runway at high speed. On this occasion the aircraft slid for nearly the whole length of the runway at Binbrook before coming to a halt. Although there was the possibility that it could have cartwheeled if a wing tip had dug in, it remained upright and, as the ventral tank was empty, at least there was no fuel fire. The Cat.3 damage that was caused was subsequently repaired. In other incidents Lightning T.5 XS420 of the LTF was damaged Cat.3 as a result of a tail scrape on 20 March 1978 and XS459 (also LTF) had a Fire 2 warning on 4 April during an air test. On 18 July 1978 F.6 XS931 of 5 Squadron became the next Lightning to lose its rudder in flight and it was quickly followed by F.3 XR718, also of 5 Squadron, which also lost its rudder on 21 August.

Chapter 10

Lightning Lair

By now only Nos. 5 and 11 Squadrons remained as Lightning units at Binbrook together with the Lightning Training Flight; 23 Squadron had acquired Phantoms in November 1975 and 56 Squadron had done likewise in July 1976. The Lincolnshire base would now become a mecca for Lightning enthusiasts and would carry on for another ten years which was far longer than anyone at the time could have envisaged. Although at one time it appeared that another Lightning squadron would be formed to plug a perceived gap in the UK's air defences (No.74 Squadron was the strongest candidate), in the event this did not happen. By 1979 the aircraft that were retained for use at Binbrook all had well in excess of 2,000 flying hours apiece and some high-time machines were getting close to 3,000 hours. However, they were still flown hard, although perhaps not as hard as in the early years of Lightning operations, and with the accumulated knowledge that had been built up, the safety factor of the Lightning was significantly better than it had been in the early 1970s.

Despite this apparent improvement three more Lightnings were lost in 1979 and the first was XS931 of 5 Squadron on 25 May when Flying Officer Pete Coker was forced to abandon his aircraft over the North Sea after a control restriction. The aircraft came down off Flamborough Head and was later salvaged. The next Cat.5 accident was to XP737 of 11 Squadron, which was taking part in an Armament Practice Camp at RAF Valley. On 17 August, when it was being flown by Flying Officer Ray Knowles, it had an undercarriage malfunction that appeared to be very similar to the problem that had afflicted XS937 three years before. On this occasion it was the port main undercarriage leg that failed to lower and having exhausted all the possible courses of action, Flying Officer Knowles eventually ejected to allow his aircraft to crash into the Irish Sea. The final loss of the year was XR723 of 5 Squadron, which crashed on 17 August during a detachment to Akrotiri. The cause of the accident was an engine fire and the aircraft came down in the

Mediterranean 15 miles south of Akrotiri with Group Captain Peter Carter ejecting safely.

Lightning incidents around this time included the loss of another rudder on 15 August 1979, the unfortunate aircraft on this occasion being XR726 of 5 Squadron. Another familiar accident took place on 14 September when the nose-wheel failed to lower on XS903 during a test flight prior to delivery to the LTF. The aircraft landed at Coningsby with its nose-wheel still retracted and was assessed as Cat.3. F.6 XS899 (by now with 11 Squadron) had further trouble on 17 October 1980 when it had to divert to Leeming with a seized Air Turbine Gearbox and on 27 March 1981 another T.5 had its undercarriage collapse when XS459 of the LTF was landing at Binbrook.

The next complete loss of a Lightning took place on 23 July 1981 when XR765 of 5 Squadron flown by Flight Lieutenant Jim Wild crashed in the North Sea approximately 50 miles north-north-east of Binbrook. The exercise involved air defence training and called for a low level Combat Air Patrol (CAP) to be flown over the North Sea by two Lightnings. This was Flight Lieutenant Wild's second sortie of the day in the same aircraft, the first having been entirely uneventful and from which it had landed with no problems. After spending some time on CAP at 3,000 feet, the other Lightning departed to join up with a tanker aircraft to re-fuel but Flight Lieutenant Wild elected to continue his patrol. Having made this decision he shut down No.2 engine to conserve fuel, but after another fifteen minutes he informed Control that his fuel state now demanded that he either return to base or join up with a tanker to take on more fuel.

After a short period he was then informed that a tanker was available but his attempt to re-light No.2 engine failed and so he closed the No.2 HP cock. With full cold power set on the No.1 engine he was able to begin a slow climb, his intention at this stage being to make a single-engine recovery to Binbrook. Unfortunately, when he was still in the climb the audio warning sounded and a Reheat 1 fire warning lit up on the warning panel and this was followed almost immediately by a Reheat 2 warning. As his situation appeared to be rapidly deteriorating Flight Lieutenant Wild transmitted a Mayday call and requested a visual inspection of his aircraft to check for signs of fire. By now he had levelled at 10,000 feet and not long afterwards the arrestor hook warning light came on and there was a noticeable reduction in elevator effectiveness.

Flight Lieutenant Wild made another attempt to relight No.2 engine which had it been successful, would have allowed him to shut down No.1 engine. However, this attempt also failed and there was then a jolt, which was subsequently thought to have been the disengagement of the electrical air turbine and a progressive degradation of pitch control. This became so bad that the control column had to be moved fully forward to maintain level flight. If this was not enough the audio warning sounded again and several warning captions illuminated, although Wild did not have enough time to check what they were as his aircraft rolled uncontrollably to the left, at which point he ejected.

Despite his hurried departure his ejection was about as uneventful as an ejection can be. Jim Wild was meticulous with his strapping-in procedures and also made sure that his posture on ejection was correct. In the adrenalin rush of an ejection, events seemed to pass in slow motion and it was easy for a pilot to think that the seat was not working after he had pulled the ejection handle. If he then moved slightly in an effort to find out what had gone wrong it was likely that a back injury would be the result when the seat did operate after the canopy had departed. Having ejected, another hazard for the pilot was disorientation as the seat tumbled through the air and it was often best to keep the eyes closed or to keep the head buried in the face blind if this method of ejection had been used. After descending through cloud Wild eventually came down in the sea and although the parachute lines became entangled around his legs he was able to climb into his dinghy, from which he was rescued by a SAR helicopter. Although he was immediately taken back to Binbrook, he was flown to the RAF Hospital at Nocton Hall to be checked over by the doctors who were eventually happy that he had come through the experience unscathed and he was released the following day.

Pieces of wreckage were eventually found by a Dutch trawler three months after the crash and from these it was possible to confirm that the primary cause of the accident had been a major fire in the rear fuselage that had ultimately led to loss of control. Unfortunately the amount of debris that was recovered was limited and it was impossible to establish the source of the fire. The Board of Inquiry, acting on the expert advice of the Accidents Investigation Branch and experts from the aircraft industry, was of the opinion that a fuel leak had occurred in the No.2 engine fuel system and that this had prevented the attempts to re-light the engine.

It was also considered that the leaking fuel had drained from the engine bay and re-ingested into the rear fuselage via a ram air scoop and the No.1 engine reheat jet pipe cooling ducts. The temperature of the jet pipe had been sufficient for this fuel to be ignited and the resulting fire had ruptured the No.1 engine jet pipe which had allowed hot exhaust gases to impinge on the rear fuselage structure, which had distorted and burned. In doing so it had produced a white plume that had been seen by the pilot of another Lightning shortly before XR765 crashed into the sea. The Inquiry also found that the deliberate shutting down of No.2 engine and the subsequent re-light attempts had not been a factor in the events that followed and that it was therefore extremely unlikely that the pilot's actions had in any way contributed to the loss of the aircraft. By the time of the accident Jim Wild was an extremely experienced Lightning pilot with over 2,000 hours on type having passed through No.52 Lightning Conversion Course at 226 OCU in October 1969.

As a result of this accident it was thought that subsequent modifications may have invalidated earlier flight trials as regards the drainage of fuel, and so it was arranged that further trials would be carried out to determine whether any additional measures needed to be taken to prevent fuel being drawn into the aircraft in the hot areas at the rear of the fuselage. Although the Lightning was subject to comprehensive Fire Integrity checks, and had been since the spate of in-flight fires some ten years before, it was agreed that further checks would be introduced into the periodic servicing schedules.

There were no further Cat.5 losses for another two years, but in the meantime a number of incidents of varying degrees of seriousness afflicted the Lightning fleet. On 16 February 1982 T.5 XS452 of the LTF was damaged Cat.2 following a tailscrape on landing and F.6 XS919 of 5 Squadron went into the barrier on 26 August. There were similar accidents the following year and, on 2 August 1983, XS921 of 5 Squadron had a barrier engagement after it was unable to pull up on landing. Not to be outdone T.5 XS458 of 11 Squadron did a repeat performance just ten days later.

A rather more worrying incident had occurred earlier in 1983 when XS929 of 11 Squadron had suffered an engine fire during a night take-off on 20 January. Almost immediately after reheat had been selected, the No.1 reheat failed to light and auto-cancelled. On selecting reheat for a second time, there was a violent explosion and the Fire 1 caption came on, the pilot immediately becoming aware that a fire had occurred towards the rear of the aircraft and that the warning was not spurious. As the aircraft was travelling at a speed of only 100 knots IAS at the time the pilot decided to abort the take-off as there was sufficient runway distance remaining for it to be brought to a halt. During the time that the aircraft was decelerating the Fire 1 warning light went out and the Lightning was eventually stopped with about 800 yards of runway left.

As there appeared to be a fire raging on the left-hand side of the aircraft, the pilot vacated the cockpit over the starboard side and hurt both ankles as he jumped down and hit the ground. The subsequent investigation revealed that the accident had been caused by the disintegration of the 11th stage of the compressor disc of No.1 engine. This had resulted in the shearing of the casing through 360 degrees which had, in turn, led to the disconnection of a fuel pipe so that fuel under a pressure of 60 psi had been released and had subsequently caught fire. The level of damage was later assessed at Cat.3 and this took around 800 man hours to put right. As well as undergoing repair, XS929 went through the wing modification programme so that it did not fly again for another two-and-a-half years when it joined the Lightning Training Flight.

Another particularly tragic accident occurred on 26 August 1983, which resulted in the first Lightning fatality since the death of Squadron Leader David Hampton just over eight years before. The F.3 had been a favourite of Lightning display pilots over the years due to its excellent power-to-weight ratio and for the 1983 season the main display aircraft was XP753 of the LTF. The display pilot for that year was Flight Lieutenant Mike Thompson and on the 26th he was due to position the aircraft from Binbrook to Teesside Airport (formerly RAF Middleton St George) for an Air Show the following day. There is a certain amount of controversy regarding subsequent events as some details of the official accident report are contradicted by statements made by RAF personnel who were stationed at Binbrook at the time.

The official version of the flight was that Flight Lieutenant Thompson had planned a low level route to Teesside Airport in order to achieve some worthwhile training en route. Before taking off he had apparently been contacted to see if it would be possible for him to fly past an RAF recruiting exhibition that was being held at North Bay in Scarborough. According to the report Flight Lieutenant Thompson had agreed to what was being proposed, if it was at all possible, and that he would carry out two turns over the sea before continuing on to his destination.

Although he had not been formally tasked to carry out a display, Thompson arrived off Scarborough some ten minutes after he had taken off from Binbrook and began by making one low run over the sea parallel to the shoreline in a gentle right-hand turn. There were large numbers of people on the beach who then saw him turn through 180 degrees and make a second pass at low speed on a southerly heading, initially with undercarriage and flaps down. During this second pass both engines were put into reheat, the undercarriage and flaps were retracted, and the aircraft was put into a climbing turn to the left that took it out over the sea. Power was then reduced and at an estimated height of 1,500 feet, the aircraft began a tight descending right-hand turn back towards the coast.

At the southern end of North Bay was Castle Cliff, which was approximately 225 feet above sea level and was the site of a former castle and also a Roman signal station. Not only was it considerably higher than the bay area but it also projected some way out into the sea. As the Lightning approached Castle Cliff it appeared to be flying at low airspeed with a high angle of attack. It then crossed the road that ran along the base of the cliffs at a low altitude, still descending, in a noseup attitude and with a significant bank angle to starboard. On crossing the coastline again the angle of bank started to be reduced but the aircraft pitched up so that its nose was well above the horizon. After apparently hanging in mid air for a moment, the nose dropped and the aircraft rolled to the right, hitting the water about 200-300 yards from the shore. Sadly Flight Lieutenant Thompson was killed instantly when his aircraft came down.

As the aircraft had crashed in shallow water the wreckage was easily retrieved but, despite a thorough examination, no technical defect could be found as a possible cause of the accident. It was also established that the aircraft had not suffered a bird-strike, which might have led to a loss of power at a crucial moment. In fact the crash investigation had more than enough evidence to sift through as those on the beach who had watched the display were able to provide numerous witness statements, together with many photographs so that the flight profile could be worked out with a high degree of accuracy. It was concluded that Flight Lieutenant Thompson had misjudged his separation from Castle Cliff and that his speed and height during his final turn had not allowed for any margin of error. It was also considered that he probably did not realise his proximity to the cliff until the very last moment and that consequently he had stalled his aircraft in his efforts to avoid it.

Although the official report states that Mike Thompson was contacted by telephone to request a low level flypast at Scarborough, it appears that his display was, in fact, unauthorised. Although this form of impromptu display had taken place in the past it had been decided that it could now only take place with the permission of a senior officer and it seems that on this occasion the necessary authorisation was not given. It has been suggested that Thompson spent a considerable amount of time trying to get the decision overturned but was ultimately unsuccessful and therefore took off in a disturbed state of mind that may have affected his judgement at a critical part of the display. Mike Thompson was another graduate of RAF Cranwell and had been on the same course as Frank Whitehouse in 1963.

Over the coming months there were further landing incidents involving the Lightning T.5, which was still particularly prone to this type of accident. On 9 December 1983 XS457 of 5 Squadron suffered a tyre burst on landing that was severe enough for the aircraft to veer off the runway. Once on the grass the port undercarriage leg fractured and this resulted in Cat.3 damage. A similar accident occurred on 13 March 1984 when XS417 of the LTF also blew a tyre on landing. On this occasion the ventral fuel tank detached itself and the pilot decided to take off again. After assessing the damage the aircraft was landed again without further incident. However, the most spectacular accident involving a T.5 around this time took place on 19 July 1984 and involved XS416, which was being used by 5 Squadron as a replacement for XS457. After touch-down at Binbrook the undercarriage collapsed and the aircraft swung off the runway and ended up in a field on its belly. Once again Cat.3 damage had been caused and this accident resulted in a restriction that decreed that, until modifications had been carried out, all T.5s were to fly with their undercarriages down. By a twist of fate this aircraft was bringing an officer back from Germany where he had been taking part in a Board of Inquiry that had been set up to investigate a fatal Lightning accident that had occurred six days before.

The crash referred to above was that of a Lightning F.6 of 5 Squadron (XS920), which came down on 13 July. Lightning aircraft from Binbrook had been detached to Jever in Germany as they had been tasked with taking part in the NATO Tactical Leadership Programme, which had been formally set up in 1978 to give pilots the opportunity to fly combined air operations in a multi-national environment. Although the Lightning had been designed as a high-altitude interceptor, its role had changed dramatically as the threat was now largely at low level from strike aircraft that attempted to carry out attacks by flying under the radar cover. As a result the Lightning was now being operated in a role far removed from the original requirement but despite this (and its age) it was still an effective defensive fighter. In this new low level role it was also likely to come up against a wide variety of aircraft and on the 13th two Lightnings of 5 Squadron were required to carry out simulated attacks on a formation of four USAF A-10 'tankbusters'. This aircraft was an unusual and difficult target for a Lightning as it had been designed specifically for ground attack and could fly at relatively low speeds. It was also highly manoeuvrable. Because of this the A-10 pilots had been briefed as to the level of evasion that they could adopt when they were attacked.

The Lightnings were led by Flight Lieutenant Dave 'Jack' Frost and after take-off they were vectored by Ground Control towards the A-10s. The Americans were flying in low level battle formation consisting of two pairs, one behind the other, with each pair in a fairly wide line abreast. In fact there was roughly 10 nautical miles between the two pairs and the Lightnings became visual with the A-10s bringing up the rear. As they closed to around 1 nautical mile they were seen by the A-10 pilots who made two 90-degree turns to the right to try to spoil the attack. Although Flight Lieutenant Frost made an attempt to get on the tail of one of the A-10s, he was forced to break away and as he did so the Americans immediately turned to port to regain their original track. Having disengaged, Flight Lieutenant Frost then turned towards the A-10s once more and positioned his aircraft so that it was around 4,000 yards ahead of the left-hand aircraft on a collision course. As he was now above the A-10 he was seen by the American pilot who became increasingly concerned about the imminent proximity of the two aircraft and made two alterations in course to avoid a potential collision.

By the time the range had been reduced to 500 yards he assessed that there was still a distinct chance of the two aircraft colliding and made a sharp turn to starboard, at the same time as descending to ground level. The Lightning flown by Flight Lieutenant Frost passed the A-10 on its left-hand side and was seen to enter a steeply-banked turn to starboard at a relatively low speed, with the nose slightly low. Approximately three seconds later there was a bright blue flash as the aircraft flew through high-tension cables, and this was followed almost immediately by a fireball as it hit the ground. There was no time for Flight Lieutenant Frost to eject and he was killed instantly.

Although much of the Lightning had been destroyed in the post-crash fire, it was possible to conclude that there had been no structural or system failure before the crash. It was also established that at the time the aircraft came down the engines had been operating at a high power setting. An examination of the remains of the cockpit did, however, show that an engine fire warning had been lit when the aircraft hit the ground, but it was impossible to say whether this had been activated before contact was made with the power cables. No evidence of pre-impact fire could be found, and although it was concluded that fire was not the primary cause of the accident, it was conceded that a fire warning at a critical point in the low level breakaway manoeuvre could have distracted the pilot momentarily so that he failed to see the cables.

In examining this accident the Board of Inquiry also commented on the camouflage of the A-10, which was considered to be particularly effective. It was noted that when operating against this type of aircraft it was not easy to tell whether it was being viewed from head-on or tail-on. As the A-10 had been below XS920 in the early stages of Frost's second attack, he may have acquired it visually at quite a late stage, or if he had picked it up, his initial impression may have been that he was coming in from behind instead of approaching it head-on. Also, as the A-10 had made a sharp turn to the right from a position directly in front of the Lightning, it is likely that this manoeuvre would have generated considerable wake turbulence, which could well have been another factor in the accident if Frost had inadvertently flown through it.

By the end of September 5 Squadron was in the process of completing another armament practice camp at Akrotiri. All went well until returning to Binbrook on the 28th when XR754 suffered an engine fire in the air and was forced to land at the Greek Air Force base at Souda Bay in Crete. On this occasion repairs were quickly completed and '754 was back at its home base three weeks later complete with shark's mouth markings that had been applied during its unscheduled stopover.

Before 1984 was over another Lightning was lost when F.6 XR761 had to be abandoned over the sea approximately 10 miles off Spurn Head. At the time it was being flown by Flight Lieutenant Mike Hale of 11 Squadron, who was in the middle of a particularly interesting tour of duty at Binbrook that included interceptions of a Lockheed U-2 flying at an altitude of 66,000 feet and a British Airways Concorde that was cruising over the North Sea at Mach 2.0. If this was not enough he had also managed to join a select group of pilots in zoom climbing a Lightning to 85,000 feet plus. These flights were carried out in F.3 XR749 ,which was his regular aircraft and was generally regarded as being the best performing Lightning of them all.

One of his not so good moments on the Lightning took place on 8 November shortly after he had taken off from Binbrook on a regular training sortie. The first of a series of failures occurred almost immediately when the pitch trimmer ceased to operate. This meant that out-of-balance control forces could not be trimmed out, so that Flight Lieutenant Hale had to maintain a constant push force on the control column to ensure that the aircraft was in the correct attitude. As a result of this problem he elected to abort the sortie and flew over the sea to the east of Binbrook to use up fuel and reduce weight before landing.

After orbiting over the sea for approximately seven minutes he lined his aircraft up for a straight-in approach to Binbrook but when he was still 15 miles from touch-down he received a Fire 2 warning. This engine was immediately shut down and, after abandoning the landing, he flew to the east once more and out over the sea to assess the situation. Shortly afterwards the Reheat 1 warning illuminated and this was quickly joined on the warning panel by the Reheat 2 caption. Other failures were also apparent by this time as the aircraft generator and other electrical services had gone offline.

As was customary in such incidents another aircraft was flown alongside to check for signs of fire and to see if there was any sign of external damage. The pilot of this aircraft reported that he could see smoke coming from the No.2 engine jet pipe and that there also appeared to be a fire between the two jet pipe nozzles. However, by this time Flight Lieutenant Hale had been left in no doubt as to the gravity of the situation as his controls had begun to stiffen, a sure sign that control was about to be lost. The large number of warning lights that were glaring ominously back at him were then joined by indications that the two powered flying control systems had also failed and, as the controls finally seized, Hale ejected as his aircraft went into a spiral dive towards the sea.

Although his ejection and subsequent parachute descent were relatively straightforward Mike Hale's problems began as soon as he came down in the sea. He was dragged through the water for some distance by his parachute and his difficulties were made even worse by the lanyard that connected him to his dinghy becoming entangled in the parachute risers. As he was continuously being dragged underwater, he had great difficulty in breathing but eventually was able to separate himself from his parachute, although in the process of doing this he lost his dinghy. This meant that he only had his Mae West to help him stay afloat and in the event he had to endure twenty-five minutes in the water until he was rescued by helicopter. Only a small section of wreckage from XR761 was ever recovered from the sea and from this it proved to be impossible to determine the source of the fire that had occurred in the rear fuselage. At the time of the accident XR761 had flown a total of 3,049 hours.

What turned out to be the last fatal Lightning accident before the aircraft was retired from service took place during the morning of 6 March 1985 when two aircraft from 5 Squadron were carrying out air combat training over the North Sea. The exercise progressed as briefed until the second practice interception when XR772, flown by Flying Officer Martin Ramsay, was seen by his leader to enter a climbing turn to the left that was then reversed into a descending turn in the opposite direction. The wings were levelled while the aircraft was still in the right-hand turn at 11,000 feet but very soon afterwards it yawed sharply to the left and flicked into a spin. Flying Officer Ramsay made a R/T call to say that he was spinning, at which point he was advised by his leader to check his height for ejection. He then made another call that was heard as being 'I am going out', and the pairs leader then saw a bright flash from the cockpit area as Ramsay ejected. By this time the Lightning was descending at a high rate and it went into the sea about ten seconds after it had been abandoned. The location that the aircraft crashed was approximately 20 miles north-east of Skegness.

After transmitting an emergency call on the distress frequency, the pairs leader descended to low level where he was able to see the pilot floating in the water about 150 feet from some aircraft debris and an oil slick. After approximately thirty-five minutes in the water a rescue helicopter recovered Flying Officer Ramsay from the water but he was found to be dead with his parachute still in its pack. A large part of the aircraft was eventually salvaged (including the ejection seat) but this wreckage did not yield any clues as to why it had entered a spin. The most likely cause was mishandling at low IAS, although the possibility of structural failure or a malfunction within the flying controls could not be discounted. Of the Lightning aircraft that remained in service XR772 was a relatively high-time machine and when it was lost it had flown 3,842 hours. The fact that it had flown so many hours was partly due to its history, which was relatively problem-free compared with other aircraft with only a starter explosion on 7 October 1970 to trouble the engineers. One of the items recovered from the sea was the top part of the fin, which was presented to Binbrook Primary School on 19 June 1987 to commemorate the end of the Lightning era and to mark the close association between the station and the school. It was painted with 5 Squadron markings on one side with 11 Squadron colours on the other.

The Board of Inquiry into this accident was particularly concerned as to why Flying Officer Ramsay had died in a situation in which he should have been able to eject safely. Particular attention was paid to the ejection seat, the cockpit area and the pilot's flying equipment. Exhaustive investigations revealed that the ejection seat had functioned as it was supposed to, except that the parachute withdrawal line had been cut by the guillotine mechanism before releasing the parachute. This unit, which was used to separate the pilot from the ejection seat if the automatic sequence failed, normally only operated when the pilot was clear of the seat or if he operated the manual separation lever. In the case of Flying Officer Ramsay the reason for its operation could not be positively determined, although it was considered possible that the gyrations of the seat as it tumbled after ejection could have moved the parachute pack forwards and away from the container, which would in turn have activated the guillotine unit.

Later in the same year another Lightning was lost over the North Sea in rather different circumstances, although once again it happened during a one-versus-one combat training exercise in which each aircraft took it in turns to be the target. The accident happened in the late afternoon of 19 September and the unfortunate pilot was Flight Lieutenant Craig Penrice of 11 Squadron who was flying XS921. Following a series of successful practice interceptions that were carried out at 25-30,000 feet, one final PI was flown in which Flight Lieutenant Penrice performed the role of target. However, on completion of this, as he was in a left-hand turn back towards Binbrook, his aircraft continued in an un-demanded turn to port, which became increasingly violent as the control column moved, of its own accord, to full deflection. Despite his best efforts Penrice was unable to move the stick from the position that it had adopted and in a matter of seconds the nose began to drop as the aircraft became inverted. Very soon he was in a spiral dive as, unlike in a spin, the aircraft's indicated airspeed was increasing dramatically.

One possible reason for the loss of control was that there had been a glitch in the auto-stabilisation system. Although the Lightning was one of the few modern interceptors that could be flown without the auto-stabilisers in operation, these were usually used, especially in the transonic region, to alleviate the trim changes or cobblestones that were experienced as the aircraft accelerated or decelerated through the area just below Mach 1.0. Penrice switched off the auto-stabilisers but unfortunately this made absolutely no difference to the way the aircraft was behaving. Having eliminated this as a cause there was little time left to think of any other possibilities as by now the Lightning was nearing sonic speed in an increasingly steep dive. He eventually ejected at an altitude that was later thought to have been around 18,000 feet (having already lost around 9,000 feet) and, more importantly, a speed of Mach 0.95, or 450 knots IAS. Although he could remember initiating the ejection sequence by activating the seatpan handle, until the moment he came to in the cabin of a Wessex helicopter about fifty minutes later he had very little recollection of subsequent events and these could only be pieced together one-by-one as he began a slow recovery in hospital, although some were best left forgotten.

One interesting fact that emerged later was that Penrice was not wearing an immersion suit on this particular sortie, even though there was a possibility that he would have to eject into the sea. This was due to the fact that the sea temperature at that time of year was around 13 degrees C and it had been promulgated that suits did not need to be worn unless the sea temperature was lower than 10 degrees. Although this would appear to be an odd decision, the chances of survival without an immersion suit had been worked out in great detail taking into consideration sea temperature at various times of the year and the amount of time that a SAR helicopter would need to be able to come to the aid of a downed pilot (it was however assumed that the pilot would be able to climb aboard his dinghy). One thing was for sure, as the immersion suit was an extremely cumbersome piece of kit, pilots tended not to wear it if at all possible. So it was that on the day of the accident Penrice was only wearing a normal flying suit over light clothing.

Although he could remember nothing about his parachute descent, it appears that he went through most of the pre-landing drills, at least the ones that he was capable of. As he had ejected at an extremely high indicated airspeed, his limbs had been subject to flailing and he had severely damaged his right elbow and left knee so that he was unable to carry out all the tasks he was supposed to as he came down. As he descended, his playmate was busy circling the position that his aircraft had hit the sea in an attempt to see if there was any sign of him, unaware that he was still descending in his parachute several thousands of feet above him. Due to his injuries he was not able to utilise his dinghy so that his only aid in keeping him afloat was his Mae West. Even though the temperature of the North Sea was about the highest that it ever gets, Penrice was in for a difficult time before a helicopter arrived to pull him out, one in which his body temperature fell to dangerously low levels.

There were, however, two pieces of good fortune that probably saved his life. A recent modification to the Lightnings at Binbrook was the adoption of an automatic Personal Locator Beacon (PLB) instead of the previous item that had to be worked manually. This was obviously a significant improvement as it meant that a pilot who was incapacitated could be located as quickly as possible as the system operated from the lanyard that attached the dinghy pack to the Mae West. Unfortunately this new system had caused embarrassment for a number of pilots after returning to Binbrook. This was due to the fact that if the dinghy lanyard had not been disconnected, the PLB activated when the pilot stood up in the cockpit and a SAR helicopter was put on immediate standby. On this occasion, however, the location proved that the alarm was real and a helicopter was soon in the air.

Although he was not to find out about it until afterwards, the other item of good news for Flight Lieutenant Penrice was the fact that a Nimrod was on transit up the North Sea on its way back to Kinloss at the time that he ejected. This was able to react much more quickly than the Wessex helicopter that was making its laborious way to his position (XS921 had come down approximately 50 miles east of Flamborough Head), and it dropped a marker beacon in the water so that the Wessex could home straight to where he was, instead of having to carry out a search pattern to locate the signal once again from his PLB. Even so, by the time that he was picked up he was already suffering from the advanced stages of hypothermia and so the few minutes that had been saved were undoubtedly the difference between life and death.

After being admitted to hospital the immediate concern was his prolonged soaking in the North Sea and later in the day he was airlifted by a Sea King helicopter to the RAF Hospital at Ely where his condition was eventually stabilised. This was to take some time and during this period he lost 26 pounds in weight before his strength was gradually regained. The attention was then transferred to his elbow and knee and these were rebuilt during lengthy operations. Unfortunately, a nerve had also been severed in his arm so that his hand was severely limited in movement and, in another complex operation, this was repaired using nerve fibre from another part of his body. Against all expectations (except his own) he eventually returned to flying almost a year after his accident. After leaving the RAF Craig Penrice became a test pilot with British Aerospace on the Eurofighter Typhoon and in 2003 had to eject again, this time from a privately-owned Hawker Hunter over Wales, sustaining severe back injuries that required another lengthy stay in hospital.

Despite an extensive salvage operation very little wreckage was recovered from the sea and so it was impossible to determine the precise cause of the accident. However it appeared that the problem lay with the aileron PFCUs and here there were two possible explanations. The first was that there had been control runaway caused by an internal malfunction. However, the preferred reason was that a loose article from within the aircraft structure had jammed one of the PFCU input levers.

The remaining fleet of Lightning F.6s was still going through its fair share of incidents and on 5 December 1985 XS922 of 5 Squadron received Cat.3 damage to its nose leg during a landing accident at Gutersloh. On 26 February the following year XS927 of 11 Squadron had to carry out an emergency landing at Swinderby after an engine had flamed out and, just to prove that nothing ever really changed, XS898 (also of 11 Squadron) lost its canopy on take-off from Binbrook on 4 June resulting in a trip to ASF for Cat.2 repairs to the leading edge of the fin. This aircraft was soon followed into the repair hangar by XS923 of 11 Squadron, which suffered an explosion on start-up on 1 August 1986. The quantity of AVPIN that had been administered to the engine during several attempts at starting eventually reached critical levels and the resultant explosion was of sufficient violence as to blow the starter unit out of the aircraft via the nose radome.

No.11 Squadron was, in fact, having a particularly difficult time as, in addition to the incidents noted above, it had lost XR760 on 15 July. Although the fire problems of the Lightning had been given priority treatment for the last fifteen years, in-flight fires remained near the top of the list in terms of the number of technical defects reported for the aircraft. The next in line to have an engine fire was Flight Lieutenant Bob Bees, who was in the middle of an interception training sortie with another Lightning over the North Sea. After taking on fuel from a Victor tanker the Lightnings were directed towards a pair of aircraft but, during the subsequent engagement, Flight Lieutenant Bees was alerted by the sound of the attention-getters announcing that he had a reheat fire warning. After carrying out the appropriate emergency drills he flew his aircraft out over the sea and climbed to 10,000 feet. A visual inspection was carried out by the pilot of the other Lightning and this confirmed that there was a fire in the rear fuselage. The situation then developed rapidly and the control column began to move without any input from the pilot before it seized up altogether. Fortunately it jammed in a central position so that the aircraft at least was in an upright and stable attitude. On realising that he had lost complete control of the aircraft, Bees closed the throttles and ejected. He came down in the sea and was rescued after a short time by SAR helicopter. His aircraft crashed approximately 7 miles north of Whitby.

Even at this late stage in the service life of the Lightning an extensive salvage operation was carried out but only a small amount of wreckage was recovered. From the little evidence there was it was concluded that there had been a fuel leak and that this had caused a fire in the rear jet pipe areas which, in turn, had led to loss of control of the aircraft. The origin of the fuel leak could not be determined. During its life XR760 had had one particular moment of fame when it was the display aircraft at the Farnborough Air Show in 1970.

Chapter 11

Lightning Swansong

The fact that the Lightning had lasted so long was a compliment to its capabilities, although in recent times another more significant factor was a delay in bringing the new Tornado air defence variant into service. It finally arrived in late 1984 at RAF Coningsby in the shape of the F.2 for 229 OCU, although there were still serious problems with its Foxhunter AI system to the extent that early aircraft were forced to fly with ballast in place of the nose-mounted radar. This offered a further stay of execution for the Lightning, although it was becoming increasingly difficult to balance the operational requirements with a distinct lack of fatigue life in the remaining aircraft. Accidents only compounded the problem and over the remaining sixteen months of the Lightning's RAF service three more aircraft were lost, although in each case the pilot survived.

Before the first of these accidents another F.3 flew its last flight as an in-flight fire caused serious damage to the rear of the aircraft. This was XP751 of the LTF, which was being flown by Flying Officer Ian Black on 22 October 1986 on only his third solo flight in a Lightning. The sortie was a general handling exercise of maximum rate turns of up to 6g, which were to be carried out over the sea off Spurn Head at an altitude of 5,000 feet. The combination of the F.3's limited fuel and a high rate of consumption at low-level meant that Flying Officer Black was soon heading back towards Binbrook where he completed two circuits. With his fuel state at 800lbs per side he brought his aircraft in for a precautionary landing but, once on the runway, the braking parachute failed to deploy. By careful use of the brakes, however, he was able to stop before the end and pulled up on the ORP. It was immediately apparent that something had gone wrong as pieces of the parachute cable could be seen at the rear of the aircraft but, on closer examination, it was noticed that a hole had been burned in the No.1 jet pipe. It was later discovered that a fuel leak had led to a fire and that this had burned through the fire wire of the fire detection system so that there had been no warning in the cockpit. It was perhaps fortunate that this particular sortie had been of short duration. Any longer and Ian Black would probably have become the lowest-time pilot to eject from a Lightning. XP751 was not repaired after this incident and was withdrawn from use on 22 January 1987 having flown 3,101 hours.

Although the Lightning had always been popular at Air Shows, the fact that 1987 was to be its last display season brought increased interest, although the preparations got off to a bad start when XP707 of the LTF crashed at Binbrook during a practice display on 19 March. The aircraft was being flown by Flight Lieutenant Barry Lennon who had been authorised to carry out his routine at a minimum height of 5,000 feet above ground level. The first few manoeuvres were carried out without any difficulty but as he positioned his aircraft for a slow roll, Flight Lieutenant Lennon became aware that he had a slow-feeding ventral tank as the fuel flow to the wing tanks was less than normal. Having checked that he had enough fuel to complete the sortie, Lennon continued with his slow roll, which was to the left and was commenced at 5,000 feet and a speed of 330 knots IAS.

As he became inverted he realised that he was descending slightly so he increased the push force on the control column to hold the nose up. However, this control input generated considerably more pitch response (and consequently negative 'g') than he was expecting, so he eased back on the stick once more. Unfortunately this had no effect on the rate that the aircraft was now pitching and, as it was still inverted, the negative 'g' that was being experienced increased to a figure of around -3g. Events then happened extremely quickly and as it was still in a bunt manoeuvre the aircraft flicked sharply to the right with the nose well up. By now the Lightning was in heavy buffet with speed decreasing rapidly and on passing 160 knots IAS it entered an inverted spin, at which point Flight Lieutenant Lennon ejected. It was later estimated that the amount of time from the increase in negative 'g' to ejection was no more than six seconds. As Flight Lieutenant Lennon came down on his parachute his aircraft crashed about 500 yards from the airfield boundary.

The fact that the aircraft had gone out of control was due to the slow-feeding ventral tank, which eventually affected CG to the point where it was beyond the aft limit. The result was that stability in pitch had been reduced to a dangerous level and this had led to the aircraft over-responding to a forward movement of the control column. It had then g-stalled, pitched up (relative to the horizon), and had entered an inverted spin. With no further need for replacement Lightning pilots the LTF was disbanded four weeks after the accident and two of its F.3s were passed to 5 Squadron for use by Flight Lieutenant Jon Fynes, who took over as display pilot for the 1987 season.

The penultimate Lightning accident to result in a Cat.5 write-off took place during 5 Squadron's last Armament Practice Camp (APC) to Akrotiri. The squadron had flown out at the end of June and the accident took place on 1 July. These two-week detachments had always been popular with Lightning pilots as, in addition to excellent Mediterranean weather, the flying was interesting and varied and it made a pleasant change to be able to fire live ammunition, even if it was only at a target towed by a Canberra. The unfortunate incident that took place was a freak event that could not have been predicted as it had probably never happened before.

Flight Lieutenant Dave 'Charlie' Chan had been tasked with carrying out a live gunnery sortie against a banner target and had been allotted XR763. Apart from a barrier engagement shortly after being delivered to Binbrook in 1966, a detached canopy on take-off thirteen years later and a lost undercarriage D-door in 1986, this aircraft had not troubled the engineers greatly but it was about to go out with a bang. The first two firing passes at the target were made without difficulty but after breaking away from his third pass Flight Lieutenant Chan noticed a black circular object detach itself from the banner. Although he made an attempt to avoid it, the object struck the Lightning in the air intake (having somehow missed the radar bullet) and there was an ominous 'clang' as it was ingested by No.1 engine. On glancing at the engine instruments it was immediately obvious that the engine had seized as rpm fell to zero and jet pipe temperature rose above 900 degrees C (the maximum was normally 795 degrees C). Flight Lieutenant Chan immediately shut down No.1 engine, put out a Mayday call and set course for Akrotiri.

As he was on his way back Chan carried out a low-speed handling check, which did not reveal anything untoward but, shortly afterwards, he noticed that the No.2 engine JPT was now higher than normal. When he was on finals with about two-and-a-half miles still to go to the runway threshold there was a distinct loss of thrust from the remaining engine and he immediately selected full power in an attempt to maintain speed and height. Unfortunately this seemed to have little effect so he attempted to use reheat on No.2 engine but it would not light up. It was now obvious that he would not be able to make the runway so he made one last R/T call to say that he was losing power and would have to eject. He was soon faced with another problem as he was heading for the village at Akrotiri and so had to manoeuvre his aircraft to the right to avoid it. Having done so, he levelled the wings and ejected at a height of only 250 feet and a speed of 150 knots IAS. He landed safely a short distance away from his aircraft, which crashed and exploded in a vineyard. Although Chan was uninjured he was extremely fortunate in that his right leg had not been restrained as it should have been on ejection and so it was probably only the fact that he had ejected at a relatively low speed and at low altitude that had prevented a serious injury due to flailing.

When the target banner was inspected it was discovered that one of the rounds that Chan had fired had hit the upper wheel mounting and as it disintegrated, the wheel, and half of its mounting, was released into the air. During a subsequent investigation of the wreckage it was noted that there were marks on the engine air intake that corresponded to the dimensions of the wheel (this weighed approximately 1llb and was guaranteed to cause major damage to an engine if ingested). It was therefore concluded that the top wheel of the spreader bar had caused No.1 engine to seize almost instantaneously whilst it had been running at high power. In doing so, debris from the No.1 engine had then been ingested by No.2 engine. The level of damage that was seen on No.2 engine was consistent with a progressive disintegration that eventually led to the decreasing thrust that had been experienced, together with increasing JPT.

Back at Binbrook on 7 August XS899 of 5 Squadron became the last Lightning to land having lost its rudder in flight. On this occasion at least the pilot was aware of what had happened as he diverted to Coningsby, but it would be another six weeks before it was able to return home. As a result of its temporary exile, XS899 missed the Last Lightning Show on 22 August 1987, which was the final Open Day at Binbrook before it closed as well as being the last opportunity for enthusiasts to see large numbers of Lightnings in the air. As had become customary at the Lincolnshire base the weather did its best to spoil the event but the rain eventually relented in the late afternoon and this allowed a diamond-nine formation to be flown. The humidity that was still present in the air did, however, provide the opportunity for some spectacular passes from the solo aircraft that hurtled down the flight line wreathed in condensation from the shockwaves produced as they flew at near sonic speed.

Of the two Lightning squadrons at Binbrook the first to disband prior to re-equipping with the Tornado F.3 was 5 Squadron and this took place at the end of the year with the new unit being reformed at Coningsby on 1 May 1988. This just left 11 Squadron to soldier on a little longer with the Lightning until they too disbanded on 30 April 1988. The new squadron also flew the Tornado F.3 and reformed at Leeming in North Yorkshire the following November. Before the Lightning was finally retired, however, one more was to be lost in seemingly familiar circumstances.

On the morning of 11 April four Lightning aircraft took off from Binbrook for air combat training over the North Sea but only three were to return. The section was led by Flying Officer Ian Black with Flight Lieutenant Dick Coleman RAAF, a Mirage IIIO pilot who was on an exchange posting, as his No.2. The other pair comprised Flight Lieutenant Alan 'Porky' Page and Flying Officer Derek 'Grinner' Smith. The previous day it had been arranged that F-4J Phantoms of 74 Squadron would play the role of the bad guys and to complete the picture a Victor tanker was also available. After it had disbanded at Tengah 74 Squadron had remained inactive for some time but had reformed with the F-4J Phantom on 31 December 1985.

After departure from Binbrook the first priority was to rendezvous with the airborne tanker so that all four aircraft had a full load of fuel before the engagement with the Phantoms. This was accomplished without any difficulty and, after the arrival of the section from 74 Squadron, a CAP was set up as the Phantoms flew off to begin their attack. The first indication that an attack was imminent came when Ian Black was informed by Ground Control that four targets were heading towards his section at a range of 40 miles. The pulse-Doppler (PD) radar of the Phantom was much more sophisticated than the antiquated AI.23 system in the Lightning, but when operated in PD mode it could only pick up a target that was heading towards it so Black turned his section through 90 degrees so that they were side-on to the Phantoms.

Another trick was that window, or Chaff, had been stuffed into the airbrakes of the Lightnings so that when these were opened momentarily a cloud of aluminium strips was released into the air to further confuse the situation. In a matter of seconds visual contact was made and a number of individual combats ensued. As Ian Black was in the middle of a fight with one of the Phantoms he heard a Mayday call from Flight Lieutenant Dick Coleman (call-sign Schubert 2), who was also in combat with a Phantom several thousands of feet below him. Urgent calls were made for the fight to be called off and, having picked up Coleman's aircraft against a layer of cloud, Black descended to assist as best he could.

During his combat with the Phantom Flight Lieutenant Coleman had cancelled reheat at one point before easing back on the throttles in the cold power range. However, this produced a series of loud bangs so he moved the throttles slightly forwards once again and climbed in an attempt to clear the condition. Unfortunately the next thing to happen was that the Fire 1 caption illuminated on the warning panel. At the same time fumes and smoke entered the cockpit, although these did not last long and soon dissipated. It was at this stage that Coleman transmitted his Mayday call, after which he went through his emergency drills, which included shutting down No.1 engine.

From his position alongside, Ian Black could see that there was a streak of flame along the port side of XR769, the source of which appeared to be towards the rear of the No.1 engine compressor. There also appeared to be considerable structural damage to the external skin of the aircraft in the vicinity of the fire. By now the aircraft was heading back towards Binbrook at 10,000ft and the Fire 1 warning went out when it was still just over 50 miles north-east of the airfield. Although the warning light had gone out, the fire was still evident from Ian Black's position; indeed it continued to spread so that Coleman was forced to abandon any hopes that he might have had of saving his aircraft. He therefore turned his aircraft away from the coast once again, completed his pre-ejection drills and ejected at a speed of 300 knots IAS. Thankfully the last ever ejection from an RAF Lightning was successful and Coleman was rescued from the North Sea by Wessex helicopter after spending around fifteen minutes in the water. His aircraft came down about 5 miles off Spurn Head where it soon joined all the others that had been abandoned along the east coast.

With the end of the Lightning only three weeks away, it was perhaps not surprising that a salvage operation was not forthcoming. With a complete lack of material evidence and only the testimony of the pilot and photographs taken of the aircraft in its final moments to go on, the investigation had a difficult job in discovering exactly what had caused the accident. It was, however, concluded that the persistent fire and subsequent structural damage had been the result of an uncontrolled failure of No.1 engine following a severe surge. With the lack of any wreckage it was impossible to say exactly what had caused the surge. So it was that XR769, which had been the first F.6 to exceed 1,000 flying hours and at the end of its life had flown a total of 4,070 hours, became the seventy-sixth Lightning to be lost, either by an accident resulting in a complete loss, or by one that caused damage of such severity that it was deemed to be uneconomic to repair.

No.11 Squadron was declared non-operational on 30 April 1988 and to mark the occasion of the Lightning's retirement from active service the very last diamond-nine formation was flown. After a practice the day before, this took place on the 29th when the formation, led by Wing Commander Jake Jarron, the O.C. of 11 Squadron, performed a flypast over Binbrook. Even this was not quite the end of the Lightning in RAF service as aircraft continued to fly, albeit in ever decreasing numbers, over the next two months. One final detachment was made to Lossiemouth in May to work with the resident Buccaneers of 12 Squadron, but thereafter much of the flying that was carried out involved the delivery of aircraft for use elsewhere as decoys, or for static display in museums, and the last two aircraft were flown out of Binbrook at the end of June.

Although it was initially thought that the Lightning would remain in service for only ten years, in the event it had been a mainstay of the UK's air defences for a period of twenty-eight years. During this time for many it had become a symbol of national pride as it was the last wholly British-designed interceptor to see service with the RAF and its performance and earth-shattering noise made it the highlight of any air display. Although it suffered from a chronic shortage of fuel and was lacking in its range of weaponry its handling qualities brought a smile to any pilot's face that other aircraft, such as the F-4 Phantom, never could. As a single-seat aeroplane that utilised technology from the 1960s, the pilot's workload was extremely high, so that only the very best were allowed to fly it. The skills of its pilots were also tested to the full when things went wrong and from the events recorded in this book it will now be appreciated how often that happened. To put this into perspective the final chapter looks at the Lightning's safety record compared to other jet fighters of the period.

Chapter 12

The Final Reckoning

During research for a previous book on the Lightning, a former pilot happened to mention in a letter that English Electric's aircraft actually had a worse safety record than that of the Lockheed F-104 Starfighter. Over the years this view has also appeared in at least one book on the Lightning in which it was presented as a little known fact. Most of those with a sound knowledge of aviation will be aware of the problems that the F-104 had, particularly during service with the West German armed forces in the 1960s in which it acquired the nickname widow-maker. During this time the accident rate of the F-104 made headline news on a regular basis, but was the Lightning even worse?

With the introduction to service of a highly complex and advanced interceptor it is to be expected that the accident rate in the first few years will be relatively high, but normally it can be assumed that as experience is gained and the engineering problems are identified, the number of accidents will reduce to more acceptable levels. The layout of the Lightning showed little in the way of compromise as it had been designed from the outset to give maximum performance and certain aspects of its configuration, in particular the decision to employ two engines staggered one above the other, were to lead to serious safety problems. From the engineering point of view the arrival of the Lightning into the RAF was not straightforward as the service went from subsonic fighter types to one that was capable of Mach 2-plus performance in one jump. An additional, and related, point was the fact that the UK had opted out of the supersonic race in the immediate post-war years so that British aircraft manufacturers were playing catch- up with the USA and the Soviet Union and their learning curve was as steep as the RAF's.

It would also be fair to say, in one way at least, that the RAF was unprepared for the Lightning's entry into service. In typical British fashion the engineering organisation to support the Lightning was under-funded and the spares back-up was nowhere near what it should have been. This meant that the squadron's flying task was extremely difficult to achieve in the early days of operations due to aircraft being in various states of disrepair as they awaited spare parts. A further difficulty in this respect was an excessively high figure for maintenance man hours per flying hour as aircraft usually required a considerable amount of work after each flight.

As with any other new aircraft, considerable thought had been given to the likely accident rate of the Lightning, prior to its entry into service. The forecast figure for its introduction in 1960 was twelve major accidents (Cat.3 and above) per 10,000 flying hours, reducing to three majors by the time that it had been in service for five years. It was assumed that this figure of three major accidents per 10,000 flying hours would then continue for the rest of the aircraft's time in service. When looking at accident statistics for an aircraft over a period of time there is usually considerable variation. As an example the actual accident rate for the Lightning for 1963 was in excess of the projected figure, but this was an isolated spike as the years 1962 and 1964 were much better. Indeed for the first ten years of active service the Lightning was below the projected trend for accidents for approximately two thirds of the time.

By the end of 1969 the Lightning force had reached its strongest point with nine operational squadrons, the OCU and three Target Facilities Flights. Total flying time since the aircraft's entry into service amounted to 199,000 hours and during this time there had been eighty-one accidents and thirty losses (of these accidents six had been fatal). There was, therefore, a major accident every 2,457 hours on average, so that the accident rate per 10,000 flying hours was 4.07. As the rate for 1960/61 had been 11.7 and was still at 9.90 by 1963, it is evident that there had been a considerable improvement in safety in the second half of this period. This was highlighted by the figures for 1969, which showed only six major accidents (including one complete loss) in 36,000 hours and an overall accident rate of 1.70.

Another characteristic that is frequently found among accident statistics, however, is a hotspot in which, for a certain period of time, accidents are significantly above the norm for no apparent reason. This was the case with the Lightning in 1970/71 in which the number of in-flight fires reached crisis level. Over a seventeen-month period commencing in January 1970 there were twenty major accidents that resulted in twelve losses and four fatalities from a total of 56,000 hours flown. This meant that an aircraft was being written off on average every 4,667 hours. Although the overall accident rate for this period was 3.57, or just over double the previous year, it was still only just above the rate that was deemed to be an acceptable level. However, the most worrying aspect of Lightning accident statistics at this time was the high level of write-offs as a proportion of the total number of major accidents. This figure (60 per cent) was considerably higher than the average figure for the period up to the end of 1969, which stood at 35.8 per cent. After this difficult period the accident rate for the Lightning showed a return to previous levels so that by 1972 it was back down to 2.16.

In comparison with other RAF fighter types the overall accident rate of the Lightning up to 1970 was no worse, and, in some cases, it was actually better, although often there were wide discrepancies in the cause of accidents. In the early 1960s the nearest equivalent to the Lightning in RAF service was the Gloster Javelin, which was gradually replaced as the former appeared in ever increasing numbers. Although the Lightning had a higher accident rate in its first three years in RAF service (which was to be expected), it then showed a substantial improvement to the point where its accident rate was actually less than that of the Javelin during the period 1964-66, even though the Javelin had first entered squadron service back in 1956. During this same three-year period the Lightning's accident rate was closely comparable to that of the much simpler Hawker Hunter, which had first been delivered to 43 Squadron in 1954. In terms of cause, the Lightning had a relatively high number of accidents that were the result of technical defects (as did the Javelin), whereas the Hunter suffered a higher proportion of accidents that were put down to pilot error.

An examination of the safety record of the Lightning and the Lockheed F-104 Starfighter makes for an interesting comparison and some surprising conclusions. In some respects these two aircraft were similar in that they were both developed in the 1950s (although the Lightning took rather longer), and were both designed with high speed and a rapid climb rate as the principal aims. The similarities tended to end there as the Lightning emerged as a twin-engined design with 60-degree swept wings and a low-set tail, whereas the F-104 had a single engine, short straight wings with a thickness/chord ratio of only 3.36 per cent and a T-tail. The first XF-104 was flown for the first time on 4 March 1954, which was five months before the maiden flight of the English Electric P.1, the forerunner of the Lightning.

Much of the influence behind the design of the F-104 had been the experience of USAF pilots in the Korean War who longed for a more simple design of fighter that had an extremely high power-to-weight ratio and performance levels to match, so that it could dictate the terms of any fight. With the rapidly changing air scene in the late 1950s and 1960s, however, this somewhat simplistic view of air combat did not last long and although the F-104A entered service with the USAF on 26 January 1958, it did not find favour in the air defence role and had been withdrawn from first-line use by 1965. During its time with the USAF the F-104 developed something of a fearsome reputation, which was not helped by the fact that in an emergency the pilot was ejected downwards, as, with early US ejection seat design, it could not be guaranteed that the pilot would clear the T-tail if he was ejected upwards.

With a wing area of only 196 square feet, giving a wing loading in excess of 100lbs per square foot, some form of high-lift device together with lift augmentation were essential features if landing speeds were to be kept to a reasonable figure. These comprised leading-edge droop and flaps that were blown by air tapped from the engine compressor. The single General Electric J79 engine proved to be extremely unreliable at first so that a number of pilots were faced with the unenviable choice of a dead-stick landing at 230 knots or abandoning the aircraft via a relatively rudimentary ejection seat. The F-104A finally went past the 100,000 flying hour mark in April 1961, a little over seven years after the first flight of the XF-104, but the Starfighter's gestation had been so difficult that forty-nine aircraft had already been lost by this time and these accidents had resulted in the death of eighteen pilots. On average this meant that an F-104 was lost every 2,041 flying hours. The F-104 had the worst accident record of any Century-series fighter. In comparison the Lightning did not achieve a total of 100,000 flying hours in RAF service until March 1967, by which time twenty-three aircraft had been written off in accidents and four pilots had been killed. On average this represented an aircraft being lost every 4,348 hours.

Although the F-104 did not last long with the USAF, the basic design was developed by Lockheed as a multi-role strike/attack aircraft and it was eventually used widely by a number of air forces in Europe and elsewhere. The largest user of the F-104G was the West German *Luftwaffe* and *Marineflieger*, which eventually received a total of 916 aircraft. Unlike the Lightning, the F-104G was not a particularly easy aircraft to fly and in describing it one Lockheed test pilot commented that it would not forgive a single mistake. The combination of an unforgiving nature, a new low level role and the fact that it was to be flown by relatively inexperienced pilots, often in poor weather conditions, led to an extremely high accident rate. Although the F-104 had now been fitted with an upwards firing ejection seat, it was the Lockheed-designed C-2 that did not operate automatically like the Martin Baker seat as fitted to the Lightning. Although Martin Baker seats were fitted to the first batch of German Starfighters, the USAF was actively opposed to the British design at the time and refused to co-operate with its acceptance trials. Under pressure, the Germans agreed to accept the C-2 ejection seat and this undoubtedly was a key factor in the number of pilot fatalities in the early years, which as a percentage of the accident total was significantly higher than the Lightning. Eventually the inadequacies of the C-2 ejection seat were recognised and a contract was signed in 1967 for all aircraft to have their American seats removed and replaced by the Martin Baker Mk GQ-7A.

The West German Air Force began to fly the F-104G in 1961 and two aircraft were lost during the year. Thereafter the number of aircraft lost in accidents climbed steadily and in 1962 no fewer than seven aircraft were destroyed in crashes, including a formation of four F-104Gs that crashed when they flew into the ground near Knapsack on 19 June after the leader became disorientated. The greatest number of aircraft losses occurred in 1965 when twenty-seven Starfighters either crashed or had to be written off as a result of extensive damage. At this time the chances of a German pilot surviving an accident in an F-104G were only around 50 per cent and, during the accidents in 1965, a total of seventeen pilots were killed. On average this represented an F-104G loss nearly every two weeks. In comparison, just three Lightning aircraft were lost during the same year with no fatalities.

Throughout the period from the introduction of the Starfighter in 1961 to the end of 1969 a total of 117 aircraft were destroyed in accidents and sixty pilots were killed. Over the same timescale thirty Lightnings were lost with six pilots killed. Up to the end of 1969 the records showed that, on average, a Lightning pilot was killed every 33,166 flying hours. Assuming a four-year tour of duty in which a pilot flew twenty hours per month, the chances of him being killed during the course of his tour was 2.89 per cent. Figures for the complete life of the F-104G in West German service show that there was a fatality every 17,031 flying hours so that if the same length of tour is applied, there was a 5.64 per cent chance that a pilot would not survive a single tour.

Although the actual number of F-104G accidents in West German service was significantly greater than the total of Lightning accidents, this tends to be obscured by the fact that many more F-104Gs were delivered to the *Luftwaffe* and *Marineflieger*. Including the twenty development batch aircraft, Lightning production for the RAF amounted to only 280, whereas a total of 916 Starfighters were taken on by the German armed forces. It is only when an analysis is made of accidents per flying hour that the true picture begins to emerge.

During the first ten years of Lightning operations in the RAF (up to the end of 1969), a total of 199,000 hours was flown and in this time thirty-two aircraft were written off in accidents (this figure includes two Cat.4 accidents in which the damage level was subsequently upgraded to Cat.5). Thus, on average, a Lightning was destroyed for every 6,218 hours flown. During the complete life of the F-104G in West German service, total flying time amounted to 1,975,646 hours and there were 298 accidents that resulted in complete write-offs. A Starfighter was therefore lost for every 6,630 hours that were flown. If the seventeen-month period from the beginning of 1970 is included in this analysis of Lightning accidents the loss rate worsens to one in every 5,795 hours, and if this period is looked at in isolation an aircraft was being destroyed every 4,667 hours. These figures indicate that the accident rate per flight hour for the F-104G and Lightning, although not dissimilar, show that the latter did have an inferior safety record for at least some of its operational life. This was despite the fact that the F-104G was designed from the outset as a strike/attack aircraft so that it spent much of its time operating at low level, often in bad weather, and was therefore more vulnerable to terrain, bird-strikes and obstructions. In contrast the Lightning had begun its life at medium and high altitudes and it was only towards the end of the 1960s that it also took on a low level role in addition to its previous duties.

These differences in usage are reflected in the breakdown of accidents as 43 per cent of all F-104G crashes were attributed to pilot error, with 41 per cent being the result of a technical defect. In the case of the Lightning, the number of accidents put down to pilot error was generally around the 20 per cent mark, although write-offs as a result of technical defects were significantly higher at 65 per cent. Of all the Lightning accidents that were caused by technical defects, approximately two-thirds were due to fires both in the air and on the ground.

The F-104G was eventually phased out of West German service by the end of 1987, by which time 116 pilots had been killed. This compares with the fourteen pilots who lost their lives flying the Lightning. Although the number of aircraft that were written off overall were closely comparable in terms of accidents per flying hour, there can be no doubt that the chances of a German pilot surviving a crash in an F-104G were far less than his RAF equivalent in a Lightning. Of the accidents that occurred with the Starfighter involving complete loss of the aircraft, 39 per cent proved to be fatal whereas on the Lightning only 18 per cent of accidents resulted in the pilot losing his life.

Particularly in the 1960s the F-104G Starfighter was given a very bad press due to the large numbers of aircraft that were being lost in accidents. This became a highly charged political issue in West Germany but, compared to the number of Lightnings in RAF service, the Starfighter force of the *Luftwaffe* and *Marineflieger* was more than three times the size. With far fewer aircraft being lost, the Lightning did not come in for such close scrutiny from the wider community, even though the safety record of the two aircraft was quite closely matched when viewed over a long period of time. As with most aircraft types the accident statistics varied tremendously from year to year. The best year for the Lightning was in 1969 when only one aircraft was lost, but just two years later nine were rendered Cat.5 even though the numbers in service were no greater and the type of flying that was carried out and the number of hours flown were very similar. As already related, the low-point for the F-104G was 1965 with twenty-seven complete losses, and it was not until 1981 that the loss rate reached single figures when nine aircraft were written off.

It was not only West Germany that suffered a high loss rate in its Starfighter force as approximately 50 per cent of the aircraft delivered to the Royal Canadian Air Force were lost in flying accidents, but the air forces of some other European countries that also flew the F-104G, notably Spain, Norway and Denmark, had a much lower accident rate as a proportion of total flying time. This reflected the fact that the aircraft in service with these countries were used as interceptors, so their workload was quite different from the low level strike role as in West German service. In the case of Spain, although only eighteen F-104Gs and three two-seat TF-104Gs were delivered, none were lost in the seven years that they were flown.

It is fair to say that some air forces fly their aircraft much harder than others and usage was a factor in the high number of Lightning accidents. In the case of engine fires, the majority of these occurred when maximum power was being used or shortly afterwards. The greatest risk of an engine fire was thus in the climb after take-off, or during practice interceptions when pilots frequently used reheat. Over the years the fact that the Lightning had such a poor safety record has tended to be overlooked. Sadly in more recent times one of its principal weaknesses led to the death of Dave Stock who was flying Thunder City's Lightning T.5 ZU-BEX (formerly XS451) at an air display at Overberg in South Africa on 14 November 2009. Although at the time of writing the full accident report has not been published, it appears that the aircraft suffered a hydraulic failure and fire in the No.1 engine jet pipe. In another throwback to previous accidents, Stock attempted to eject but was prevented from doing so as the canopy failed to release.

In Memoriam

Flight Lieutenant Alan Garside – 111 Squadron
Flying Officer George Davie – 92 Squadron
Flight Lieutenant Glyn Owen – 74 Squadron
Flying Officer Derek Law – 56 Squadron
Flying Officer Alan Davey – 5 Squadron
Flying Officer Pete Thompson – 74 Squadron
Flight Lieutenant Tony Doidge – 11 Squadron
Flying Officer John Webster – 74 Squadron
Flight Lieutenant Frank Whitehouse – 74 Squadron
Captain Bill Schaffner USAF – 5 Squadron
Flying Officer Phil Mottershead – 29 Squadron
Flight Lieutenant Paul Cooper – 29 Squadron
Squadron Leader David Hampton – 11 Squadron
Flight Lieutenant Mike Thompson – Lightning Training Flight
Flying Officer Martin Ramsay – 5 Squadron

Glossary

A&AEE – Aeroplane and Armament Experimental Establishment
AC – Alternating Current
A/C – Air Commodore
ACM – Air Chief Marshal
AFDS – Air Fighting Development Squadron
AI – Airborne Interception
AIB – Accidents Investigation Branch
AOC-in-C – Air Officer Commanding in Chief
APC – Armament Practice Camp
ASF – Aircraft Servicing Flight
ASI – Air Speed Indicator
ATG – Air Turbine Gearbox
AWP – Auxiliary Warning Panel
AVTAG – Aviation Turbine Gasoline
AVPIN – Isopropyl Nitrate
BAC – British Aircraft Corporation
Cat – Category
CAP – Combat Air Patrol
CG – Centre of Gravity
DB – Development Batch
DC – Direct Current
DFS – Directorate of Flight Safety
FCTU – Fighter Command Trials Unit
FEAF – Far East Air Force
F/L – Flight Lieutenant
F/O – Flying Officer
FOD – Foreign Object Damage
Form 700 – A logbook containing the servicing and flying records for an aircraft.
G/C – Group Captain
GCA – Ground Controlled Approach

GCI – Ground Controlled Interception
GW – Guided Weapons
HE – High Explosive
HMS – Her Majesty's Ship
HP – High Pressure
HYD – Hydraulic
IAS – Indicated Airspeed
IFF – Identification Friend or Foe
ILS – Instrument Landing System
JPT – Jet Pipe Temperature
LCS – Lightning Conversion Squadron
LP – Low Pressure
LTF – Lightning Training Flight
M – Mach (number)
Mae West – Inflatable life preserver
Mayday – Radio distress call
Mineval – Station evaluation exercise
MU – Maintenance Unit
NATO – North Atlantic Treaty Organisation
OC – Officer Commanding
OCU – Operational Conversion Unit
ORP – Operational Readiness Platform
PAN – Radio call indicating a state of urgency
PFCU – Powered Flying Control Unit
PI – Practice Interception
PLB – Personal Locator Beacon
Precautionary landing – a full-stop landing that would be continued
    should the braking parachute fail to deploy
PSI – Pounds per square inch
QWI – Qualified Weapons Instructor
RAAF – Royal Australian Air Force
RFA – Royal Fleet Auxiliary
RHAG – Rotary Hydraulic Arrestor Gear
Rpm – Revolutions per minute
R/T – Radio Telephony
SAC – Senior Aircraftman
SAR – Search and Rescue
SARBE – Search and Rescue Beacon
SBAC – Society of British Aircraft Manufacturers

SEPECAT – Manufacturer of the Jaguar strike/attack aircraft
SOR – Special Occurrence Report
S/L – Squadron Leader
SWP – Standard Warning Panel
TACAN – Tactical Air Navigation System
TACEVAL – Tactical Evaluation
TFF – Target Facilities Flight
UFO – Unidentified Flying Object
UHF – Ultra High Frequency
UK – United Kingdom
USAF – United States Air Force
USMC – United States Marine Corps
VIP – Very Important Person
W/C – Wing Commander

Appendix 1

RAF Aircraft Damage Categories

An explanation of the category of damage to Lightning aircraft as recorded in the main text is as follows:

Cat.1 – The damage sustained by an aircraft was capable of repair on site by established first-line personnel.

Cat.2 – The damage sustained by an aircraft was capable of repair on site by established second-line personnel.

Cat.3 – The damage sustained by an aircraft was repairable on site but was beyond the technical resources of the unit. Assistance from a repair and salvage unit or civilian contractor was required.

Cat.4 – The damage sustained by an aircraft was not repairable on site. The aircraft therefore had to be removed to an established repair depot or civilian repair organisation.

Cat.5 – The aircraft was damaged beyond repair or was missing, or, in accordance with Ministry of Defence policy that was current at the time, was not worth repairing.

These definitions of categories referred to the damage to the aircraft as a whole.

A major accident was considered to be an aircraft that had sustained Cat.3, Cat.4 or Cat.5 damage.

Appendix 2

Lightning Write-Offs in RAF Service

Development batch aircraft and F.1 (total aircraft flying hours in brackets)

A/c	Date	Pilot	Remarks
XG334	05/03/60	S/L Ron Harding	Undercarriage malfunction (23.58)
XG335	1/01/65	S/L Andy Whittaker	Undercarriage malfunction (204.43)
XM134	11/09/64	F/L Terry Bond	Undercarriage malfunction – hydraulic failure (229.25)
XM136	13/09/67	F/L Jock Sneddon	In-flight fire and loss of control (742.00)
XM138	16/12/60	F/L Bruce Hopkins	Hot gas leak led to in-flight fire (74.50)
XM142	26/04/63	F/L Jim Burns	Hydraulic failure (418.00)

F.1A

XM174	29/11/68	F/L E. Rawcliffe	In-flight fire and loss of control (1,262.42)
XM179	06/06/63	F/L Mike Cooke	Mid-air collision (352.92)
XM184	17/04/67	F/L Gerry Crumbie	Landed with engine and reheat fire (1,013.67)
XM185	28/06/61	F/O Pete Ginger	Undercarriage malfunction – hydraulic failure (39.42)

A/c	Date	Pilot	Remarks
XM186	18/07/63	F/L Alan Garside	Loss of control after take-off and entered spin (420.67)
XM187	19/11/63	F/L Mike Smith	Landing accident (509.00)
XM188	21/06/68	S/L Arthur Tyldesley	Brakes failed when taxying and struck office (1,397.00)
XM190	15/03/66	Capt Al Petersen USAF	In-flight fire (854.00)
XM191	09/06/64	F/L Mike Smith	Engine failure and in-flight fire (554.58)
XM213	06/05/66	S/L Paul Hobley	Failed take-off (885.58)

F.2/F.2A

A/c	Date	Pilot	Remarks
XN772	28/01/71	F/O Pete Hitchcock	Failed to recover from spin (971.00)
XN785	27/04/64	F/O George Davie	Both engines flamed out due to lack of fuel (285.92)
XN786	04/08/76	F/O Clive Rowley	Damage to jet pipe and hot gas leak in the air (2,657.00)

F.3

A/c	Date	Pilot	Remarks
XP698	16/02/72	F/L Paul Reynolds	Mid-air collision (1,378.00)
XP699	03/03/67	F/O Stuart Pearse	In-flight fire (300.00)
XP700	07/08/72	F/L George Fenton	In-flight fire after sinking back on take-off (1,653.25)
XP704	25/07/64	F/L Glyn Owen	Entered spin during low level aerobatics (36.00)
XP705	08/07/71	F/L Graham Clarke	In-flight fire (1,520.00)
XP707	19/03/87	F/L Barry Lennon	Entered spin due to CG problem (2,392.00)
XP736	22/09/71	F/O Phil Mottershead	Control lost during high level PI (1,543.00)

A/c	Date	Pilot	Remarks
XP737	17/08/79	F/O Ray Knowles	Undercarriage malfunction (2,042.00)
XP738	10/12/73	F/O Keith Farnfield	Landed with the undercarriage retracted (1,978.00)
XP739	29/09/65	F/L Hedley Molland	Engines flamed out due to fuel starvation (180.00)
XP742	07/05/70	F/O Stu Tulloch	In-flight fire (1,258.00)
XP744	10/05/71	F/L Bob Cole	In-flight fire (1,300.00)
XP747	16/02/72	F/L Paul Cooper	Mid-air collision (1,336.00)
XP753	26/08/83	F/L Mike Thompson	Lost control during low level display (2,530.00)
XP756	25/01/71	Capt Bill Povilus USAF	In-flight fire (1,130.00)
XP760	24/08/66	F/L Al Turley	In-flight fire (428.00)
XR711	29/10/71	F/L Eric Steenson	Failed take-off (1,667.00)
XR712	26/06/65	F/L Tony Doyle	Engine failure and in-flight fire during display (145.00)
XR714	27/09/66	F/O Graham Prichard	Failed take-off (495.00)
XR715	13/02/74	F/L Terry Butcher	In-flight fire (1,902.00)
XR721	05/01/66	F/O Derek Law	Engine failure (220.83)
XR723	18/09/79	G/C Peter Carter	In-flight fire (2,,515.00)
XR748	24/06/74	F/O Kevin Mason	Hydraulic failure (1,499.00)

F.6

A/c	Date	Pilot	Remarks
XR760	15/07/86	F/L Bob Bees	In-flight fire (3,317.83)
XR761	08/11/81	F/L Mike Hale	In-flight fire and loss of control (3,049.00)
XR762	07/04/75	S/L David Hampton	Crashed into sea off Cyprus – cause unknown (2,273.00)

A/c	Date	Pilot	Remarks
XR763	01/07/87	F/L Dave Chan	Engines hit by debris from banner target (3,712.00)
XR764	30/09/71	F/L Richard Bealer	In-flight fire and loss of control (982.00)
XR765	23/07/81	F/L Jim Wild	In-flight fire (3,143.00)
XR766	07/09/67	S/L Ron Blackburn	Failed to recover from spin (213.00)
XR767	26/05/70	F/O John Webster	Flew into sea during night interception (680.00)
XR768	29/10/74	F/L Tex Jones	In-flight fire (2,144.00)
XR769	11/04/88	F/L Dick Coleman	In-flight fire (4,070.08)
XR772	06/03/85	F/O Martin Ramsay	Failed to recover from spin (3,842.00)
XS893	12/08/70	F/O Mike Rigg	Undercarriage malfunction (858.00)
XS894	08/09/70	Capt Bill Schaffner USAF	Flew into sea during night interception (650.00)
XS896	12/09/68	F/O Pete Thompson	In-flight fire and loss of control (400.00)
XS900	24/01/68	F/L Stuart Miller	In-flight fire (292.00)
XS902	26/05/71	F/L Alistair Mckay	In-flight fire (1,051.00)
XS918	04/03/70	F/L Tony Doidge	In-flight fire (866.00)
XS920	13/07/84	F/L Dave Frost	Hit HT cables during low level interception (3,645.00)
XS921	19/09/85	F/L Craig Penrice	Control restriction during high level PI sortie (3,061.00)
XS924	29/03/68	F/O Alan Davey	Control lost during air-to-air refuelling demo (407.00)
XS926	22/09/69	Major Charlie Neel USAF	Failed to recover from spin (709.00)

A/c	Date	Pilot	Remarks
XS930	27/07/70	F/L Frank Whitehouse	Lost control after rotation take off (799.00)
XS931	25/05/79	F/O Pete Coker	Control restriction (2,910.00)
XS934	03/04/73	F/L Al Greer	In-flight fire (1,816.00)
XS937	30/07/76	F/O Simon Manning	Undercarriage malfunction (2,317.00)
XS938	28/04/71	F/O Alistair McLean	In-flight fire (1,234.00)

T.4

XM968	24/02/77	S/L Mike Lawrance	Hydraulic failure and loss of control (1,908.00)
XM971	02/01/67	S/L Carlton – F/L Gross	Engine failure due to collapse of radar bullet (688.50)
XM974	14/12/72	S/L Spencer – F/O Evans	In-flight fire and loss of control (1,753.00)
XM988	05/06/73	W/C Chris Bruce	Failed to recover from spin (1,600.00)
XM990	19/09/70	F/L Sims – F/L Fuller	Aileron control failed at low level (1,282.00)
XM993	12/12/62	F/L Turley – W/C Gibbs	Undercarriage collapsed on landing (42.00)

T.5

XS453	01/07/66	F/O Geoff Fish	Undercarriage malfunction (31.00)
XS455	06/09/72	S/L Gauvain – Lt Verbist	Hydraulic failure and loss of control (1086.00)

Appendix 3

Lightning F.3 Selected Emergency Drills

Engine And Reheat Fires

1. **Engine Fire**

   a. Indications

      F1 or F2 on SWP and appropriate extinguisher button

   b. Immediate actions

      Close appropriate throttle / HP cock
      Select appropriate fuel cock switch off
      Reduce speed if practicable
      Press appropriate extinguisher button

   c. Subsequent actions

      1. If warnings persist:

         If F1 warning, jettison ventral tank
         Look for signs of fire; i.e. smoke, flame, control system malfunction or instrument indication
         If fire is confirmed, abandon aircraft

      2. If warnings go out or there are no signs of fire:

         Transfer fuel
         Land as soon as possible

Notes
1. A visual check by another aircraft will be of assistance
2. If the other fire warning appears, no extinguisher will be available
3. Do not attempt to re-light after a fire warning, the LP cock should not be re-opened
4. 350lbs gauged fuel cannot be transferred

2. **Reheat fire**

    a.   Indications

        RHT1 and/or RHT2 on SWP

    b.   Immediate actions

        Cancel reheat if selected and throttle back both engines
        If no warnings remain, use minimum practicable power and land as soon as possible
        If any warning persists, close appropriate HP cock(s) and select appropriate fuel cock switch(es) off

    c.   Subsequent actions

        1.   If both warnings still persist, abandon aircraft
        2.   If one warning still persists

            If RHT 1, jettison ventral tank
            Look for signs of fire: i.e. smoke, flame, control system malfunction or instrument indication
            If fire is confirmed, abandon aircraft

3. If no warnings remain or no signs of fire accompany a single persistent warning
Use minimum practicable power
Land as soon as possible

Notes
If at c3 above, both engines have been shut down, a re-light may be attempted on an engine that is not associated with a persistent warning

If the re-light attempt results in a renewed double warning, abandon the aircraft.

Hydraulic Failures

Services System Failure

a. Indications

> Services pressure gauge indicates persistent loss of pressure
> Services fail to operate when selected

b. Actions

> Select auto-pilot MASTER switch OFF
> Land as soon as practicable

c. Considerations

1. Leaking hydraulic fluid will create fire hazard
2. Aircraft should be landed on a long runway (minimum 7,500 feet) equipped with arrestor barrier
3. The following services will become inoperative:

> Undercarriage normal system
> Flaps
> Airbrakes
> Canopy operation *
> Nose-wheel centring *
> Feel simulator *
> Autostabilisers and autopilot *
> Wheelbrakes (accumulator gauge in cockpit) *
> (* indicates accumulator pressure should be available)

4. The effect on recovery of the aircraft will be –

> Only spring feel for tailplane and rudder after exhaustion of feel unit accumulator
> When preparing to land, select flaps down

Emergency system must be used to lower undercarriage: return fluid
  might lower flaps
If flaps still up, approach must be planned for flapless landing
HP cocks should be closed after landing
Brake parachute should be supplemented by a continuous, steady
application of wheel-brakes; maxaretting should be avoided, if possible

d. Partial failure

If services pressure fluctuates or slowly reduces (when no services are
operating)

1. Select GW arming switch SAFE, autopilot MASTER switch OFF and
    FEEL switch OFF
2. Land as soon as practicable. The considerations at c above will apply if
    all pressure is subsequently lost

Hydraulic Feel Failure

a. Indication

Marked lightening of tailplane and rudder forces

b. Actions

Reduce speed to below 400 kts
Gentle manoeuvres only

c. Considerations

1. Spring forces remaining are adequate at low speeds only
2. If a pitot system fault, flight instruments will be affected

Single Flying Controls System Failure

a. Indications

Either HYD1 or HYD 2 on AWP
Slight reduction in max operating rate of ailerons

b. Actions

Disengage autopilot, if selected
Do not exceed 2g
Return to base and land

c. Considerations

It is prudent to restrict speed and control movements to those necessary for
recovery to base
If HYD 1, emergency U/C lowering inoperative; brake parachute may be
available but should not be relied upon

Double Flying Controls System Failure

a. Indications

HYD on SWP
HYD 1 and HYD 2 on AWP
When accumulators exhausted, controls will stiffen and become inoperative

b. Actions

1. If failure due to double flame-out:

Establish and maintain 250 kts
Take action for double flame-out

2. If failure not due to double flame-out:

Prepare to abandon aircraft
Use minimum control movements to fly towards suitable rescue area
Abandon aircraft when controls stiffen

Index

Names (Ranks as contemporary)
Adams, F/O Paul 71
Aird, George 49
Alcock, F/L Tony 85
Aldridge, F/L Tony 40
Aylward, P/O Doug 23

Barcilon, W/C Bob 131-2
Barker, F/L Norman 102
Barr, Capt J. 41
Bealer, F/L Richard 103
Bee, W/C Martin 125
Bees, F/L Bob 151
Bendell, F/L Anthony 7-9
Bettell, F/L Mike 64
Black, S/L George 21
Black, F/O Ian 152-3, 156-7
Blackburn, S/L Ron 51-2
Bond, F/L Terry 22
Bramley, F/L Dave 56
Brooks, F/L Dennis 104-5
Bruce, W/C Chris 121-2
Bryan, F/O Al 103
Bryant, F/L John 100-1
Burns, F/L Jim 6, 14
Butcher, F/L Terry 124

Cameron, F/L C.M. 20
Carden, F/L Dave 129
Carlton, S/L Terry 42-4
Carter, F/L Peter 62, 137
Catren, Capt Gary 118
Chan, F/L Dave 154-5

Clarke, F/L Graham 69-70, 86, 97-8, 103
Clee, F/L Pete 25
Coker, F/O Pete 136
Cole, F/L Bob 85-6
Coleman, F/L Dick 156--7
Collins, F/L Peter 2
Cooke, F/L Mike 14-5
Cooper, F/L Paul 107-8
Cooper, F/L Paul R. 129
Cousins, F/L David 55
Coville, F/O Chris 65
Crumbie, F/L Gerry 50

Danning, F/O John 108
Davey, F/O Al 58-9
Davie, F/O George 19-20
Denny, F/O Jeff 21
Doidge, F/L Tony 69-70
Doyle, F/L Tony 25-31
Durham, F/L Ed 35

Ellender, F/O Tony 53
Evans, F/O Geoff 114-6

Farnfield, F/O Keith 123
Fenton, F/O George 97-8, 112-3
Fish, F/O Geoff 39
Fowler, F/L Merv 86
Frost, F/L Dave 143-4
Fuller, F/L Brian 77-8
Fynes, F/L Jon 154

Garside, F/O Alan 15-6
Gauvain, S/L Tim 113
Gibbs, W/C Charles 11

Ginger, F/O Peter 6-7
Girdler, F/O Ted 62, 124
Gleave, F/L Mal 123
Goodwin, S/L Ken 73
Granville-White, S/L 133
Graydon, F/L Mike 49
Greer, F/L Al 120-1
Gross, F/L Tony 42-4, 58
Gurney, F/L Dan 41

Hale, F/L Mike 144-5
Hampton, S/L David 128, 140
Harding, S/L Ron 1-2
Hargreaves, S/L Les 13, 36
Harries, F/O Geraint 108
Hawtin, S/L John 104-5
Hewitt, SAC D.J. 60
Hine, S/L Paddy 21
Hitchcock, F/O Pete 81-2
Hobley, S/L Paul 38
Hopkins, F/L Bruce 2-3
Hopkins, F/L Eric 77
Howe, S/L John 3

Jarron, W/C Jake 158
Jewell, F/L Jim 64
Johnson, F/O Mike 102
Jones, F/L Dave 17-8, 23
Jones, F/L Tex 127

Kingsley, F/L Terry 100-1
Knight, Don 24
Knowles, F/O Ray 136

Law, F/O Derek 36-7

Lawrance, S/L Mike 133

Lennon, F/L Barry 153

Lockwood, F/O Vic 58

Macfadyen, F/O Ian 23

Manning, F/O Simon 132

Mason, F/L Brian 19

Mason, F/O Kevin 126-7

May, S/L John 131

McDonald Bennett, F/O Trevor 57, 66

McGowan, F/L Roger 134

McKay, F/L Ali 86-7

McKnight, F/L Rick 39

McLean, F/O Alistair 83-4

McLeod, S/L John 25

Mermagen, F/O T. 5

Miller, G/C Mike 101

Miller, F/L Stuart 56

Miller, F/L Tim 124

Millington, A/C E.G.L. 11-2

Mitchell, S/L John 13, 32

Molland, F/L Hedley 32-4

Moore, F/L Malcolm 14-5

Morley, F/L Russ 80

Moss, F/O David 109

Mottershead, F/O Phil 101-2

Neel, Major Charlie 66-7

New, F/O Pete 109-10

O'Dowd, F/O Jack 18

Offord, F/L Bob 49

Owen, F/L Glyn 21-2

Owen, F/L Phil 129-30, 134

Page, F/L Alan 156

Pearse, F/O Stuart 38, 45-8

Penrice, F/L Craig 147-50

Petersen, Capt Al 37

Pieri, Capt Frank 54

Ploszek, F/L Henryk 59-61

Pope, F/O Roger 73

Povilus, Capt Bill 81

Prichard, F/O Graham 40-1

Ramsay, F/O Martin 146-7

Rawcliffe, F/L E. 64

Reynolds, F/O Paul 107

Rhodes, F/L Rich 81

Rigg, F/O Mike 74

Rogers, S/L John 4

Roome, F/O Dave 72

Rooum, F/O John 34

Rowe, F/L Chris 58

Rowley, F/O Clive 129-32

Schaffner, Capt Bill 75-7

Sims, F/L John 77-8, 108

Smith, F/O Derek 156

Smith, F/L George 118

Smith, F/L M.R. 18-20

Sneddon, F/L Jock 52-3

Spencer, S/L John 114-6, 130

Stanning, F/L P. 16

Steenson, F/L Eric 104-5

Stock, Dave 166

Stuart-Paul, S/L 45

Swiney, W/C Mike 39

Thompson, F/L Mike 140-2

Thompson, F/O Pete 62-4, 108

Tulloch, F/O Stu 71

Turley, F/L Al 11, 40, 49

Tyldesley, S/L Arthur 59

Verbist, Lt R. 113

Ward, F/L John 124-5

Watson, F/L Jim 81

Webster, F/O John 72

Whitehouse, F/L Frank 73, 96, 142

Whittaker, S/L Andy 24

Wild, F/L Jim 137-9

Wild, F/L P. 25

Willison, S/L Dennis 122-3

Wraight, F/L Mike 25

Wright, F/L Alan 6

Lightning Aircraft

XG311 24

XG332 49

XG334 1

XG335 24

XM134 22

XM136 52-3

XM138 2-4

XM139 79

XM140 13

XM141 6

XM142 14

XM144 23

XM145 16-7

XM147 67

XM163 2, 5

XM171 25, 120

XM172 83

XM174 64

XM175 22

XM176 4-5

XM179 14

XM180 77

XM181 5, 14

XM183 5, 10, 23

XM184 50

XM185 6

XM186 7

XM187 18-9

XM188 59

XM189 9

XM190 15, 37

XM191 9, 20

XM213 38

XM214 41-2

XM215 19
XM216 25
XM968 133-4
XM969 10
XM970 9-10
XM971 38, 42-5
XM973 13
XM974 114
XM988 121
XM989 25
XM990 77-8, 108
XM992 18, 21, 31
XM993 11, 13
XM994 34
XM996 83
XN726 108
XN727 100
XN728 55, 109, 116
XN730 15, 102-3
XN768 39
XN772 81-2, 134
XN774 17, 100
XN775 37
XN776 31, 129
XN777 11-2, 129
XN778 16
XN780 97
XN783 34
XN785 19, 134
XN786 31, 130, 134
XN787 108
XN788 124
XN789 21, 129, 131
XN791 121
XN792 99
XN793 23, 109-10, 134
XN794 79
XP694 50, 112
XP698 107
XP699 45-9
XP700 112, 116
XP704 21
XP705 97-8, 103
XP707 153
XP708 86
XP736 41, 101-2
XP737 64, 136
XP738 122-3

XP739 32
XP740 65
XP741 39, 53, 103, 119
XP742 71
XP743 37
XP744 85
XP745 72
XP747 38, 107
XP749 58
XP751 152-3
XP752 85
XP753 140
XP754 54
XP755 110
XP756 71, 81
XP760 24, 40, 49
XP762 34
XP765 56, 80
XR711 104-5
XR712 25
XR714 40-1
XR715 62, 64, 124
XR716 39, 51
XR718 135
XR719 25
XR721 36
XR723 95-6, 136
XR724 111
XR725 53
XR726 137
XR727 80
XR748 126
XR749 145
XR751 123
XR752 69, 134
XR754 144
XR758 66, 71
XR759 124-5
XR760 150-1
XR761 80, 144-6
XR763 41, 154
XR764 103
XR765 137-9
XR766 51
XR767 54, 72
XR768 127
XR769 157
XR771 113

XR772 146-7
XR773 57
XS416 142
XS417 38, 142
XS418 59-61
XS419 35
XS420 118-9, 135
XS423 56
XS450 64
XS452 139
XS453 39, 56
XS454 49-50
XS455 58, 95, 107, 113
XS457 58, 142
XS458 139
XS459 135, 137
XS893 74
XS896 62
XS897 72
XS898 150
XS899 134, 137, 155
XS900 56
XS902 86-7
XS903 137
XS918 69-70
XS919 139
XS920 142-4
XS921 64, 139, 147-9
XS922 150
XS923 65, 150
XS924 58
XS926 58, 66
XS927 64, 73, 150
XS928 71, 125
XS929 139-40
XS930 73, 96
XS931 135, 136
XS934 109, 120
XS936 119
XS937 132, 136
XS938 83-4, 87